Perspectives
on the
New Pentecostalism

Perspectives

on the

New Pentecostalism

Russell P. Spittler, Editor

Baker Book House
Grand Rapids, Michigan

Contributors

Richard A. Baer, Jr.

Stanley M. Burgess

Athanasios F. S. Emmert

Gordon D. Fee

J. Massyngberde Ford

R. Hollis Gause

Donald L. Gelpi, *S.J.*

Walter J. Hollenweger

Ray H. Hughes

Morton T. Kelsey

William G. MacDonald

Kilian McDonnell, *O.S.B.*

Clark H. Pinnock

William J. Samarin

Krister Stendahl

J. Rodman Williams

PREFACE

For some years it has been my hope to demonstrate the variety within the charismatic and Pentecostal movements. The opportunity came with the responsibility given me to arrange the program for the second annual meeting of the Society for Pentecostal Studies (SPS), which met in November, 1972, in Oklahoma City.

My design was to let representatives of various sectors of the movements speak for themselves. They did so, and their words are here preserved.

Represented are not only the classical Pentecostals but also the newer charismatics—including Protestant, Roman Catholic, and Eastern Orthodox representatives. In addition, there are reflections offered from highly diverse—but not unsympathetic—viewpoints from outside the Pentecostal tradition.

It is clear from these papers that not all that is charismatic is "evangelical," meaning by that term the sort of theology characteristic of the post-war conservative new evangelicalism which is now well known. But it should be equally apparent that the tendency of the charismatic renewal is to move in an evangelical direction—even within the Roman Catholic Church. It is just possible, in fact, that the Pentecostal-charismatic movement in the twentieth century will yield a renewal in piety as far-reaching in effect as the sixteenth century doctrinal renovation of the church.

One cannot avoid the ecumenical (or transdenominational) implications of the New Pentecostalism. If union efforts have aborted, shared brotherhood has widely characterized the transdenominational character of the newer charismatic thrust. Morton Kelsey in fact, in his essay here, argues that a courageous absorption of charismatic openness can produce a true spiritual unity—a unity not insensitive to doctrinal differences, but able to surpass them.

Somewhere in the early '70s it became clear that the classical Pentecostal churches and the charismatic movement are two different forces. Even though the new charismatics drew from the traditional classical Pentecostals, for the most part they did not join them. For the classical Pentecostal, whose heritage was that of a persecuted minority, the early puzzlement soon passed to a certain aloofness. The classical Pentecostals became an establishment in their own right within seventy years.

One point those of us who are classical Pentecostals will have to adjust to, surely not without some pain: our "distinctive testimony" is no longer ours alone. Not that all charismatics adopt the distinctive feature of (at least North American) Pentecostalism—the belief that speaking in tongues is the initial evidence of the Pentecostal baptism in the Holy Spirit. Some, as a matter of fact, do. But most teach rather that the likely, or available, or eventual, consequence of the Pentecostal experience will be glossolalia.

At any rate, it has been my hope in editing these papers to let varied shades of the charismatic and Pentecostal traditions get to know each other. And to place at public disposal some informed nuances of Pentecostal thought and history.

There is a good deal to be done in Pentecostal and charismatic research. We are at the point in historical research where individual biographic studies may be undertaken—persons like A. H. Argue, T. B. Barratt, Eudoras N. Bell, G. B. Cashwell, Glenn A. Cook, Florence Crawford, A. B. Crumpler, Alexander Dowie, Mary Woodworth Etter, Benjamin Irwin, Charles F. Parham, William J. Seymour (to name only a few).

With the maturity of the technique known as oral history, there is a particularly urgent need to record for subsequent analysis the memories of Pentecostal old-timers: there are but two known Azusa Street participants yet living.

In addition, regional histories of Pentecostalism are now in order. When Nils Bloch-Hoell translated from Norwegian his volume on *The Pentecostal Movement* (Oslo, 1964), he omitted over a hundred pages tracing the rise of Pentecostalism in Norway. Latin American Pentecostalism is not adequately known to North Americans. The same can be said for Pentecostal developments in South Africa, Eastern Europe, and the Far East.

Perhaps the suggestiveness of these essays may stimulate further research in Pentecostalism, its precedents and progeny.

The time required for the editing process allowed inclusion of several contributions not originally read at the SPS conference (even though some of these authors were present). For these contributions, I am specially thankful to Gordon Fee, Walter Hollenweger, Morton Kelsey, Kilian McDonnell, and William Samarin.

The extended time involved in editing, moreover, warranted advance publication of several of the essays. I am grateful to the editors who have allowed me to include here versions of the following articles earlier published: Richard A. Baer, Jr., "The Moods and Modes of Worship," *Theology Today*, 31 (October 1974), 220-27; Ray H. Hughes, "A Traditional Pentecostal Looks at the New Pentecostals," *Christianity Today* (June 7, 1974), 6-10; Clark H. Pinnock, "The New Pentecostalism: Reflections of a Well-Wisher," *Christianity Today* (September 14, 1973), 6-10; William J. Samarin, "Religious Motives in Religion Movements," *Internationales Jahrbuch für Religionssoziologie*, 8 (1973), 163-74.

Of course, I do not endorse all that is said herein—nor do any of the contributors, to my knowledge.

In editing, I have quite generally let the contributors speak for themselves. It would be difficult to formulate any uniform definitions of such terms as the New Pentecostalism or the charismatic movement: some authors here use the terms in ways that allow inclusion of the classical Pentecostal tradition. Readers unfamiliar with the Pentecostal and charismatic movements may first like to consult chapters 7 and 11, where some definitions of terms are offered.

That "Assemblies of God" appears regularly with a singular verb follows customary usage in that church, where the phrase abbreviates the longer but legal title "General Council of the Assemblies of God." I might also explain that a reference such as [3]1914 means "third edition, 1914."

I wish to thank Miss Laura Jarvis, my secretary, for her renewed patience in the typing of many drafts. I also owe thanks to student assistants, including Debbie Morris (nee Seaward), Jerry Hoggatt,

Gerry Shenk, and Jeanne Smith for additional help in typing and research. Finally, I owe gratitude to Southern California College, Costa Mesa, and to Fuller Theological Seminary for allowing editorial labors to be included among the demands of deaning.

Russell P. Spittler
Assistant Dean
Fuller Theological Seminary
Pasadena, California

CONTENTS

PART ONE
Historical Backgrounds

Stanley M. Burgess

Stanley M. Burgess came in 1959 to Evangel College, Springfield, Missouri, where he is professor of history and chairman of the department of social sciences. The son of a Pentecostal pastor, he holds the B.A. and M.A. degrees from the University of Michigan and the Ph.D. from the University of Missouri.

Dr. Burgess here reviews charismatic qualities attributed to various Roman Catholic saints throughout the medieval period. He cites several papal bulls (decrees officially issued by a pope) in which glossolalia figured as one of the bases for the elevation of certain devout Catholics to sainthood. Even though the credibility of such reports may be questionable at times and the language stylized, the essay provides specific documentation for medieval charismatic spirituality.

Medieval Examples
of Charismatic Piety
in the Roman Catholic
Church

1

Historians of Pentecostalism have devoted most of their attention to the period of apostolic outpourings and to the modern Pentecostal movement. In so doing, they have treated the intervening centuries as "the long drought,"[1] during which there were few evidences of the charismata, and these were hardly worth the trouble of further investigation.[2]

Neglect of Primary Sources

As a church historian, I have become increasingly interested in

1. Frank Stagg, E. Glenn Hinson, and Wayne E. Oates, *Glossolalia: Tongue Speaking in Biblical, Historical, and Psychological Perspective* (Nashville and New York: Abingdon, 1967), p. 56.
2. Morton T. Kelsey, *Tongue Speaking: An Experiment in Spiritual Experience* (Garden City, NY: Doubleday, 1968), p.61. Prudencio Damboriena, S.J., in *Tongues As of Fire: Pentecostalism in Contemporary Christianity* (Washington, DC: Corpus Books, 1969), p.4, suggests that modern Pentecostals consider the decline of charismatic gifts in the medieval church as a sure sign that the church had lost its original fervor and was being taken over by pagan influences in both theology and liturgy. While I would not suggest that Pentecostal scholars have purposefully avoided the study of medieval charismatics because the absence of information fits their thesis, it would seem a logical assumption that their interest in such a study would be reduced by their low opinion of the spiritual condition of the church during that period.

the study of my Pentecostal heritage. This concern has been amplified by my frustration over the indifference of Pentecostal scholars to their historical antecedents and over the total reliance of the few who have broached the subject of charismatic outpourings in the medieval and the early modern church on an account written by George B. Cutten in 1927, an account which is based on a lengthy study of Christian mysticism written about 1836 by J. J. Görres, a professor of history at the university in Munich.[3]

To make matters worse, Cutten, who was hostile to tongue-speaking, did not bother to search out the primary sources used by the erudite German scholar. Pentecostal historians have shown the same aversion to the primary records, with the result that the same stories are repeated again and again—usually without question—and mistakes once made are perpetuated and often compounded. For example, we read that both St. Augustine and Martin Luther spoke in tongues.[4] A careful study of their writings and of contemporary biographies, however, indicates that neither Augustine nor Luther had experiential knowledge of the subject and that Luther was thoroughly confused about Pentecostal phenomena.[5]

Difficulties also have arisen from ambiguities which Cutten copied from the Görres text. A good example of this is the tendency to confuse the charismatic experiences of St. Dominic and Angelus Clarenus as one, despite the fact that the primary records tell of two separate and unrelated outpourings of the Pentecostal experience on those men.[6] In addition, we are frustrated time and

3. George B. Cutten, *Speaking with Tongues* (New Haven, CT: Yale University Press, 1927), and J. J. Görres, *Die Christliche Mystik*, 5 vols. (Regensburg: G. J. Manz, 1836-42).

4. Carl Brumback, *What Meaneth This? A Pentecostal Answer to a Pentecostal Question* (Springfield, MO: Gospel Publishing House, 1947), pp. 91f. R. Leonard Carroll in *The Glossolalia Phenomenon*, ed. Wade H. Horton (Cleveland, TN: Pathway Press, 1966), p. 93, indicates that Luther was a charismatic. Other writers have made the same statement.

5. Augustine, "Homilies on the First Epistle of John," 6:10, *The Nicene and Post-Nicene Fathers*, ed. P. Schaff, First Series (Grand Rapids: Eerdmans, 1956), VII, 497f. Martin Luther, *Works*, ed. Jaroslav J. Pelikan and Helmut T. Lehmann (St. Louis: Concordia, 1955-), XL, 142.

6. For Dominic see *St. Dominic: Biographical Documents*, ed. Francis C. Lehner (Washington, DC: Thomist Press, 1964), pp. 52f. This translates an account by Gerardi de Fracheto found in *Monumenta ordinis Fratrum Praedicatorum historica*, ed. B. M. Reichert (Louvain: E. Charpentier and J. Schoonjans, 1896), pp. 74f. The story of Angelus Clarenus is found in the *Acta sanctorum quotquot toto orbe coluntur, vel a Catholicis scriptoribus celebrantur . . . notis illustravit Joannes Bollandus* (Antwerp: apud Ioannem Meursium, 1643-1931), June II, 1094. (Hereafter the *Acta sanctorum* will be referred to as *AASS*.)

again by teasing generalities, inadequate information, and unanswered questions. We read that certain medieval mendicants, Waldensians, and Albigensians spoke in tongues, but we are left with no identification of individual recipients and with few details about the exciting activity of the Holy Spirit among them. We read that St. Stephen, Jean of St. Francis, Martin Valentine, and Jean of the Cross spoke in tongues, but of these there is no additional identification. In fact, we are even left in doubt as to whether Jean of the Cross was male or female!

Finally, this total dependence on secondary sources has deprived us of any opportunity to make a reliable estimate of the authenticity of the primary evidence and of the credibility of what that evidence states. In short, the study of medieval charismatic phenomena through secondary sources is as futile and unrewarding as an attempt by a young man to make love to his sweetheart through the efforts of an interpreter!

Sources in Biographies of the Saints

Because of the obvious neglect of early records, it will be the purpose of this paper to focus on both the whereabouts and the nature of the primary evidence for the outpouring of the Holy Spirit on the medieval Roman Church, with a particular eye to the context of those events. Special attention will be given to the question of whether those elements which we in the twentieth century regard as basic to the Pentecostal experience were present in the medieval outpourings.

Those men and women whom Görres identified as medieval charismatics generally can be categorized as well-known members of leading religious orders, many of whom were canonized by the mother church after their deaths. His list is limited in this manner not because there were no other Pentecostals in the Middle Ages, but rather because we are favored with a vast store of primary literature which has been published in recent centuries for the purpose of perpetuating the memories of leaders in religious and monastic orders and of individuals singled out by the church for beatification and canonization.

The medieval church early realized the necessity of providing inspirational literature for the faithful. With the exception of purely devotional materials, the most important body of these writings was hagiographic. The hagiographer, or biographer of saints' lives, sought to impress his readers with accounts of holiness and of associated miracles, many of which defy the modern scholar's imag-

ination, and which even the modern charismatic would be hard-
pressed to believe. Such accounts frequently served as the basis for
the beatification and later for the canonization of stalwarts in the
faith. Because a certain number of miracles was required for each
step in this process, the miraculous was stressed in hagiography,
and it is in this context that much of our information on medieval
tongue-speaking is found.

Modern Editions of Hagiographic Texts

Later church historians who wrote on behalf of the Catholic
Reformation sought to enlist the support of historical evidence to
add credence to the Roman tradition. In the heat of their battle of
polemics it became apparent to many of them that this purpose
could only be achieved by employing the tools of historical
criticism on the primary materials.

Chief among these scholars were the Bollandists, an association
of Jesuits engaged in editing the *Acta sanctorum* (the "Deeds of
the Saints"), the most important of hagiographical collections.
Beginning at Antwerp in 1643, the Bollandists attempted to collect
all the information they could locate, from whatever sources, and
to preface each text with an evaluation of the author and his
credibility. In addition, explanatory notes were appended to each
chapter of the text. The work of the Bollandists on the *Acta sanctorum* now extends over three hundred years and is not yet completed. This monumental hagiographic series ranks, without question, as the most important single source for our knowledge of
medieval charismatic piety.

The Bollandists also have published a series of supplemental
volumes to the *Acta*, beginning with the *Analecta Bollandiana*, a
periodical review of recently discovered hagiographic materials
first appearing in 1882. Another valuable tool is the *Bibliotheca
hagiographica Latina*, which enumerates all documents written
before the sixteenth century that relate to the life of each saint,
together with an indication of where they can be found.

I have discovered additional primary evidence for the outpouring of the Holy Spirit during the Middle Ages in the publications of
certain leading religious orders. The Society of Jesus has contributed the *Monumenta historica Societatis Jesu*, which includes
the *Monumenta Xaveriana*, a collection of all the letters of the six-
teenth-century missionary charismatic, Francis Xavier, and an early
biography by Valignano. Some of the most important records of the
mendicant charismatics are to be found in the *Annales minorum,*

which is concerned with the Franciscans, and the *Monumenta ordinis Fratrum Praedicatorum historica*, produced by the Dominican order.

Finally, the historian of medieval Pentecostalism can gain considerable insight into the church's attitude toward heretical charismatics from the inquisitional records and the private letters of ecclesiastical leaders, many of which have been collected and published separately by church historians. The remainder that have been published are to be found in such general collections as Migne's *Patrologia Latina* and the *Monumenta Germaniae historica*.

Varieties of Medieval Tongue Speaking

A study of Cutten's account leaves one with the impression that all, or nearly all, tongue-speaking in the medieval church was limited to the ability to speak in a foreign language in the course of missionary activity. Morton T. Kelsey suggests that this was simply the result of a church ban on speaking in and interpreting an unknown language, a ban found in the *Rituale Romanorum* in a section describing characteristics of the demon-possessed.[7] John T. Nichol finds his answer to this curious problem in the teachings of Origen, who considered the miraculous knowledge of foreign languages to be a permanent endowment of gospel messengers since the Day of Pentecost.[8] Kelsey also insists that in our evidence of medieval tongue-speaking "... almost nothing is said about the religious emotions accompanying the utterance, or about ecstatic speech which could not be understood at all."[9]

The primary sources provide much more information on medieval tongue-speaking than is recorded in the secondary materials, especially with regard to the context in which the gift was exercised. For the purpose of analysis, I will distinguish among the reports of (1) xenolalia, speaking in a foreign language unknown to the speaker; (2) heteroglossolalia, a phenomenon in which each person hears his own language when the speaker is communicating in his native tongue; and (3) glossolalia, ecstatic utterance in an unknown tongue. Such a distinction may seem strange, and even unacceptable, to the modern Pentecostal. This form of analysis is necessary, however, not only to demonstrate the

---

7. Kelsey, *Tongue Speaking*, p.47; Philip T. Weller, *The Roman Ritual*, vol. II, *Christian Burial, Exorcism, Reserved Blessings, etc.* (Milwaukee: Bruce Publishing Co., 1952), pp.168f.

8. John Thomas Nichol, *Pentecostalism* (New York: Harper and Row, 1966) p. 21.

9. Kelsey, *Tongue Speaking*, p. 47.

doctrinal uncertainty of the medieval church concerning the tongues phenomenon, but also to gain a better understanding of the ecclesiastical attitude toward the exercise of charismatic gifts.

Xenolalia

Reports of xenolalia outnumber those of glossolalia and heteroglossolalia combined. St. Pachomius is reported to have miraculously spoken both Latin and Greek, although he never learned either language. The famous mendicant leader, St. Dominic, conversed in German. St. Colette spoke Latin and German. St. Clare of Monte Falcone conversed in French. Angelus Clarenus communicated in Greek. St. Stephen is reported to have spoken in Greek, Turkish, and Armenian. Jean of the Cross spoke with Mohammedans in Arabic, Francis Xavier spoke Tamil and the language of the Molucca Islands. And St. Louis Bertrand spoke in the language of the Moors under the inspiration of the Holy Spirit.[10] In what might be considered as a variation of this gift, we are told by two early biographers that St. Hildegarde wrote numerous books on music, the lives of saints, medicine, and devotional subjects—all in Latin, a language completely unknown to her![11] This must stand as the most unusual claim made on behalf of a medieval charismatic.

Heteroglossolalia

The phenomenon of heteroglossolalia is reported in the ministry of St. Vincent Ferrer, who is said to have been understood by Greeks, Germans, Sardinians, and Hungarians as he preached in the Spanish of late medieval Valencia. His biographer, Peter Ranzano, also asserted that the isolated Britons of France, who understood only their own dialect, fully comprehended his teachings.[12] It would seem that there were similar instances in the

10. For Pachomius see *AASS*, May III, 319-342; for Dominic see *St. Dominic*, pp. 52f.; for Colette see *AASS*, March I, 543, 568, and chapter 17, section 176; for Clare see *AASS*, August II, 687; for Angelus Clarenus see *AASS*, June II, 1094; for Stephen see Giuseppe Silos, *Historiarum Clericorum Regularium Congregatione condita* (Rome: Panormi, 1650-66), II, 13; for Jean of the Cross see Antonio Daca (Daza), *The Historie, Life, Miracles, Ecstasies, and Revelations of the Blessed Virgin Sister Ioane of the Cross, of the Third Order of St. Francis* . . . (St. Omer: Charles Bascard for John Heigham, 1625), p.15; for Francis Xavier see the *Monumenta Xaveriana et autographis vel ex antiquioribus exemplis collecta* . . . (Madrid: Typis Gabrielis Lopez del Horno, 1912), II, 224, 546f., 555, 689, 694, 698; for Louis Bertrand see *AASS*, October V, 322f., 382, 481, 483. I have been unable to trace the primary source for Jean of St. Francis, who—according to J. Görres *(Die Christliche Mystik*, II, 193)—conversed with the Mexicans.

11. *AASS*, September V, 699; *Analecta Bollandiana*, 2 (1883), 126f.

12. *AASS*, April I, 495.

life of St. Antony of Padua.[13] The Spanish of St. Louis Bertrand was understood by Indian natives in the Western Hemisphere.[14] And we are told that Francis Xavier's Portuguese was understood by both the Japanese and Chinese whom he encountered on his missionary journeys,[15] although this account has been challenged by modern Jesuit scholars.[16]

Glossolalia

Known cases of glossolalia—ecstatic utterance in an unknown language—are rare indeed. Our primary sources do give us several interesting examples, however. St. Hildegarde is said to have sung in unknown tongues to the extent that her biographer refers to these occasions as "concerts."[17] Apparently she had frequent ecstasies and visions, during which she also prophesied and wrote in languages unfamiliar to her.[18]

Cardinal Ludovisius, testifying on behalf of the canonization of Francis Xavier, related that the great missionary had been heard to speak the languages of angels.[19] In the bull canonizing him we read that his audiences were filled with amazement and ecstasy when they heard him speak in languages unknown to him.[20] According to the biographer Mosconio, an unbelieving physician, Philip, confessed that he had listened with envy as St. Clare of Monte Falcone

---

13. *Annales minorum seu trium ordinum ɔ S. Francisco institutorum* (1208-1540), ed. Luca Wadding (Florence: Tipografia Barbera, 1931), II, 191.

14. *AASS*, October V, 322f., 382, 483.

15. Benedictus XIV (1675-1758), *Opera omnia in unum corpus collecta et nunc primum in quindecim tomos distributa* (Venice: sumptibus J. Remondini, 1787-88), III, 250. In addition, this claim was made by the first biographer of Francis Xavier, Horatius Tursellini, in his *De vita Francisci Xaverii* (Rome, 1594), and later by Dominique Bouhours in *The Life of St. Francis Xavier, of the Society of Jesus, Apostle of the Indies and of Japan*, trans. James Dryden (Dublin: T. Haydock, 1812). While H. J. Coleridge in his *Life and Letters of St. Francis Xavier* (London: Burns and Oates, 1890), accepted Tursellini's report, the Jesuit editors of the *Monumenta Xaveriana* chose not to include the material on the Japanese expedition because of the unreliability of the witnesses involved.

16. *Analecta Bollandiana*, 16 (1897), 52-63; 48 (1930), 441-45.

17. *AASS*, September V, 683.

18. *AASS*, September V, 683f., 686, 699; *Analecta Bollandiana*, 2 (1883), 119. Before her death Hildegarde was denounced as a sorceress and a demoniac, and because of this her canonization was never achieved, although she is named as a saint in the Roman martyrology.

19. *Monumenta Xaveriana*, II, 698. The same claim has been made for St. Bridget, although I have been unable to locate the primary evidence.

20. *Monumenta Xaveriana*, II, 710.

uttered praise to God and engaged in holy conversation, speaking
heavenly words about heavenly things.[21]

There is no indication, however, that the Roman Church had
any real understanding of the significance of these ecstatic tongues,
nor do we have any record of these utterances being interpreted. It
would seem that there was no place for the gift of interpretation
when ecstatic speech in unknown languages was of an entirely
devotional nature, and when the sermons of missionaries were
understood in foreign lands without translation.

Medieval Charismata

Reports of tongue-speaking in the primary records do not stand
in isolation from the other charismatic gifts: discernment, prophecy, and the many miracles which were reported to have accompanied sermons, especially among epileptics and the demon-
possessed.[22] St. Colette enjoyed the gift of knowledge and the gift of
discernment, together with a reputation for ministering healing to
lepers and raising the dead.[23]

Vincent Ferrer was especially famous for his prophetic gift and
for the many miracles of healing which accompanied his
evangelistic ministry. So great was his reputation that in the
Netherlands an hour was set apart each day for the healing of the
sick.[24] While Francis Xavier himself claimed no charismatic gift
other than tongues, his disciples reported miracles at his hands
ranging from the healing of barrenness to the alleviation of pain in
childbirth.[25]

Antony of Padua was reported to have possessed the gift of
miracles, although some scholars have questioned this facet of his
ministry.[26] The bull of canonization for Louis Bertrand testified
that he laid hands on the sick in a hospital, with the results that
men regained their sanity and the dead were raised to life. Finally,
the bull assures us that Bertrand exercised the charismatic gifts of
the apostles.[27]

While the medieval church misunderstood the nature and the

21. *AASS*, August II, 687. The ecstasies of another saint, Pachomius, are mentioned in
AASS, May III, 314.

22. *Analecta Bollandiana*, 2 (1883), 120-24, 127f.; *AASS*, September V, 692f.

23. *AASS*, March I, 543, 568.

24. *AASS*, April I, 498f., 525.

25. *Monumenta Xaveriana*, II, 143f., 455, 512, 625f.

26. Hilarin Felder, *Die Antoniuswunder nach den alteren Quellen* (Paderborn: Schön-
ingh, 1933), p. 156.

27. *AASS*, October V, 481, 483.

significance of tongues, evidences of the charismata were often directly associated with the experiences of the first-century believers. The biographer of Antony of Padua identified his charismatic gift as the same one exercised on the Day of Pentecost when each man heard his own language.[28] Cardinal Veralli made the same association when he recommended Francis Xavier for canonization.[29] Similar references were made on behalf of Louis Bertrand and Vincent Ferrer in their respective bulls of canonization.[30] The latter specifically explained the miracles and gifts of Ferrer in the light of Mark 16:17f.

There are even reports of the medieval charismatics seeking the gift of tongues. St. Dominic is said to have "set himself to prayer and commenced immediately to speak German to the great astonishment of these [German] strangers. . . ."[31] Pachomius, an Eastern Christian ascetic, spoke Latin with a brother from Western Europe after praying earnestly for three hours.[32] Louis Bertrand is reported to have asked God to grant him the same gift as that of Vincent Ferrer, so that the natives of the Indies could understand his preaching.[33]

Non-normal Glossolalia

Despite the several parallels that have been drawn between the experiences of medieval and modern charismatics, the overwhelming impression that I have gained from a study of the primary sources is that tongue-speaking, while exercised on a very limited scale in the Roman Church, never was treated as a normal outgrowth of Christian living during the Middle Ages. Most of the great medieval theologians saw no immediate need for the gift of tongues at a time when the entire church could communicate in Latin. Typical of this doctrinal confusion was the suggestion by St. Thomas Aquinas that his contemporaries could have the same gift of tongues as that of the apostles, not through the inspiration of the Holy Spirit, but rather by a thorough study of each of the languages involved.[34]

28. *Annales minorum*, II, 191.

29. *Monumenta Xaveriana*, II, 694.

30. *AASS*, October V, 481 for Bertrand; *AASS*, April I, 525 for Ferrer.

31. *St. Dominic*, pp. 52f.

32. *AASS*, May III, 342.

33. *AASS*, October V, 382.

34. From *Summa Theologica*, Part I of Second Part, Q. 51, Art. IV, in *Basic Writings of St. Thomas Aquinas*, ed. Anton C. Pegis (New York: Random House, 1944), II, 392.

Part of the confusion over xenolalia, heteroglossolalia, and glossolalia certainly stemmed from the academic debate among medieval theologians over the precise nature of the miracle of Pentecost. The Venerable Bede contended that the miracle was in the ears of the hearers, while others—like Johann Eck, the sixteenth century antagonist of Martin Luther—insisted that the apostles on the Day of Pentecost actually spoke eloquently in the native languages of their audience.[35]

Perhaps the classic example of confusion in the church over the charismata is to be found in a report sent by Eckbert of Schönau to the archbishop of Cologne in 1163 concerning the Catharist heretics at Cologne. Eckbert attempted to describe the practice of *consolamentum*, i.e., baptizing the believer with the Holy Ghost and with fire. He reported that it was the custom of the heretics to meet together in secret for the purpose of rebaptizing their fellows because of their belief that water baptism was useless for salvation. The rite consisted of laying hands on the recipient. Eckbert concluded that it was called a baptism with fire because the believers were surrounded by a circle of lanterns, the fire of which was to dispel the darkness of their secret meeting-place![36]

Tongues as a Basis for Sainthood

Speaking in tongues, when practiced by believers in the mainstream of the Roman tradition, seems to have been accepted as an evidence of extreme piety and divine approbation, a miracle worthy of consideration in the processes of beatification and canonization.

In three bulls of canonization the gift of tongues was listed among the evidences of piety that were used in support of the elevation of the men concerned to the catalog of saints. The famous humanistic pope, Pius II, in 1455 declared that Vincent Ferrer had manifested all of the signs spoken of in Mark 16:17f., including

35. Johann Eck, *Homiliarum clarissimi viri . . . unici prope hoc seculo catholicae fidei assertoris, haeretico & qq. omnium impugnatoris* (Cologne: expensis M. Godefridi Hittorpii, typis Euchharii Cervicorni, 1538), III, EE4r.

36. *Facts and Documents Illustrative of the History, Doctrine, and Rites of the Ancient Albigenses and Waldenses*, trans. Peter Allix and Samuel Roffey Maitland (London: Rivington, 1832), pp. 344-50. Other sources for the *consolamentum* include *Patrologiae cursus completus: scriptores Latini*, ed. Jacques P. Migne (Paris, 1844-64), CLXXXII, cols. 676-80 (from Eberwin of Steinfeld against the heretics at Cologne), and CCIV, col. 777 (from Bonacursus, *Vita haereticorum*); Peter Allix, *Some Remarks upon the Ecclesiastical History of the Ancient Churches of Piedmont* (London: Printed for Richard Chiswell, at the Rose and Crown in St. Paul's Church-yard, 1690), pp. 142 (a report by Evervinus), 215 (an inquisitor reporting on the Waldensians).

that of tongues. He added, "And because of this we canonize him by the authority of the apostles. . . ."[37]

Pope Gregory XV in 1623 wrote that when Francis Xavier preached about the great works of God to an assembly of many nationalities, each one with astonishment and ecstasy heard the language of the country in which he was born. As a result of this miracle, the pope concluded, his audiences were greatly moved and received the Word of God.[38]

Finally, in a bull of canonization of 1671 Clement X declared that Louis Bertrand spoke only Spanish and normally had to use an interpreter in foreign lands. During his ministry, however, heaven conferred on him the gift of tongues, as well as of prophecy and of miracles. At another point in the bull, Clement asserted that Bertrand "had been granted all of the charismatic signs and the accompanying authority."[39]

Concluding Notes

I may offer the following observations in conclusion:

1. The medieval Roman Church developed a dual standard in the treatment of tongue-speaking. While condemning the ability to speak in an unknown language and to interpret that utterance as an evidence of demon possession, the church also honored a few of its more illustrious number for their tongue-speaking—even to the point of including the phenomenon among the miracles listed on their behalf in the canonization process. All of these occurrences—whether glossolalia, xenolalia, or heteroglossolalia—apparently were recognized as miraculous without distinction as to type. The orthodoxy of the individuals involved in tongue-speaking seems to have determined whether the phenomenon was viewed as a sign of sainthood or of demon possession.

2. Although the charismatic gifts were exercised by a few during this period, tongue-speaking was never considered to be a natural development in the life of the ordinary believer. This seems to have resulted from the doctrinal uncertainty or the mixture of doctrine in the church, and the tendency to associate the charismata with miracles that were somehow reserved for the ministries of only the most pious.

37. *AASS*, April I, 525.
38. *Monumenta Xaveriana*, II, 710.
39. *AASS*, October V, 481.

3. Our knowledge of medieval charismatics will continue to be severely limited by the inadequacy of the primary records. While our information on the Roman tradition can be enlarged by a careful examination of unpublished manuscripts, even this effort can not be expected to yield much data about the layman or the lesser clergy. An investigation of certain heretical groups and of Anabaptist sects might be more profitable.

4. Finally, I re-emphasize the need for a study of the primary materials in every period of the history of Pentecostalism, even when our evidence is limited and not entirely credible.

Athanasios F. S. Emmert

Father Athanasios Emmert was ordained in 1960 as a priest of the Greek Orthodox Patriarchate of Antioch, Archdiocese of New York and North America. After basic education at Muhlenberg College and Concordia Seminary, he studied graduate theology at Holy Cross Greek Orthodox Theological School (Brookline, Massachusetts), St. Vladimir's Orthodox Theological Seminary (Yonkers, New York), and the University of Athens. After serving congregations in West Virginia, Toronto, and Connecticut, Fr. Emmert organized and founded the Holy Spirit Orthodox Church in Huntington, West Virginia. Active and prominent in the leadership of the charismatic renewal in the Orthodox Church, he serves on the staff of *The Logos*—a magazine of Orthodox renewal (not to be confused with *Logos Journal*, which is published at Plainfield, New Jersey). He has participated in the Vatican-Pentecostal International Dialogue.

It may come as a surprise to some that Pentecostalism has reached the Orthodox Church. This chapter will introduce this lesser-known third major branch of Christendom—which originated nearly five hundred years before the Protestant exit from Roman Catholicism. Fr. Emmert also shows the historic openness of Orthodox theology to the person and work of the Holy Spirit.

Charismatic Developments in the Eastern Orthodox Church

2

The theology and spirituality of the Orthodox Church theoretically and practically is charismatic and Pentecostal, as the witness of its history and doctrine clearly indicates. St. Seraphim of Sarov, the "wonderworker" Russian saint of the last century, expresses this fact when he says, "The true aim of our Christian life consists in the acquisition of the Holy Spirit of God."[1] A contemporary theologian and spiritual authority, Archimandrite Lev Gillet, writes, "The Orthodox Church is inclined to consider charisms as the normal goal of the pneumatic life. . . . "[2] Professor Paul Evdokimov of St. Sergius Academy, Paris, writes as follows on the spiritual life, using a theme from one of Dostoevski's characters on the meaning of man's destiny in the context of time, the universe, and eternity:

> "All is in you Lord; I am yours; receive me." . . . His destiny finds
> the freshness of a passionately loved existence. It is only after this

1. *A Conversation of Saint Seraphim of Sarov with N. A. Motovilov: A Wonderful Revelation to the World* (Jordanville, NY: Holy Trinity Monastery, 1962), p. 2.

2. Lev Gillet, *Orthodox Spirituality. An Outline of the Orthodox Ascetical and Mystical Tradition. By a Monk of the Eastern Church* (London: SPCK, 1961), p.73.

"second birth," this personal Pentecost, that the spiritual life properly so-called begins.[3]

Both Protestant and Roman Catholic theologians recognize the charismatic spirituality of the Orthodox Church. A recent Presbyterian study describes us in this manner:

> Orthodoxy has often been spoken of as the Church of the Holy Spirit. . . . For the Orthodox there is nothing efficacious in the Church's life sacramentally nor in the Christian's life individually without the invocation of the Holy Spirit. . . . It is from this understanding of the Holy Spirit that the Orthodox view the world and the unfolding drama of the ecumenical movement before them.[4]

Charismatic developments in the Eastern Orthodox tradition are not new. They have flourished in the Church's history from Pentecost to the present, although they have not always been apparent to the non-Orthodox (nor, to some extent, even to some Orthodox), who are unfamiliar with her life, history, and tradition.

What is the Eastern Orthodox Church?

Many Christians do not know that there exists a tremendously large body of Christians outside of the Protestant and Roman Catholic churches and traditions. This has been most evident among those involved in the charismatic or Pentecostal movements, since there is little mention of the Orthodox in the ecumenical gatherings of these people or in their publications.

Throughout the world there are an estimated two hundred million Eastern Orthodox Christians, including some five million in the western hemisphere and nearly two million in the Western European countries and Scandinavia. The roots and background of these Christians lie in the areas first evangelized by the apostles and their followers, although today they include believers in all six continents of the civilized world. Orthodox people today arise from nearly every background: Greeks, Russians, Ethiopians, Romanians, Poles, Albanians, Finns, Bulgarians, Japanese, Koreans, Chinese, Armenians, Egyptians, Syrians, Lebanese, Georgians, Yugoslavians, Indians (American and East Indian), and Americans, as well as the many thousands in the rapidly growing and flourishing native African churches in Kenya, Uganda, and Tanzania. Only language,

---

3. Paul Evdokimov, *The Struggle with God*, trans. Sister Gertrude, S. P. (Glen Rock, NY: Paulist Press, 1966), p. 60.

4. Commission on Ecumenical Mission and Relations, *Toward A Protestant Understanding of Orthodoxy*. "Resources for Ecumenical Encounter, No. 2" (New York: The United Presbyterian Church in the USA, 1966), p.13.

ethnic tradition, and folk customs differ—since all Eastern or Greek
Orthodox confess, practice, and worship in one identical faith, life,
and tradition, sharing full communion with one another. Ad-
ministratively independent, the Eastern Orthodox churches comprise
one church through their common faith, rather than through a
carefully structured hierarchy such as is found in the Roman Catholic
Church.

It is doubtful whether there is any large group of Christians more
misunderstood by Protestant and Roman Catholic Christians than the
Orthodox. This failure to understand the Orthodox results mainly
from certain major factors in the history and present structure of the
church, which profoundly affect both its present spiritual state and its
place in today's world. In order to know what the Orthodox Church
is—and particularly to understand its charismatic and Pentecostal
nature—it is imperative that we consider these major factors, which
will provide the background for any comprehension of Orthodoxy
and the "Charismatic Developments in the Eastern Orthodox
Church."

Variation in Terminology

Until this century the Orthodox Church existed in almost complete
isolation from the rest of Christianity geographically, culturally,
historically, and linguistically.[5] There was little or no real communication with the currents of history and thought that produced
Roman Catholic theology and spirituality, especially from the ninth
century on. Likewise, Orthodox Christianity was isolated from the
events leading up to and following the Protestant Reformation.
Moreover, it had no connection with the development of that form of
Protestant spirituality which originated on the American frontier, the
peculiarly American form of piety that has had such an influence
upon the holiness and Pentecostal movements of the last hundred
years.

Out of this isolation there developed a terminology different from
that which is common to Western Christianity—both Roman Catholic
and Protestant—especially as applied to doctrine, spirituality, and
church order. The Orthodox Church uses terms common to all of
Christianity—doctrinal words such as faith, works, salvation, sin,

5. Some exceptions may be noted, viz. the Florentine Council of Rome, the Uniate
movement of Rome, the Crusades, the relations of Patriarch Cyril Lukaris with the
Reformed, the western-inspired "reforms" of Peter Moghila and of Peter the Great
among the Slavs, the Tübingen Lutheran theological correspondence with Patriarch
Jeremias II, and other limited contacts with the Lutheran pietists of the eighteenth century. None of these, however, really affects the basic point I make here.

sanctification, sacraments, and ecclesiological words such as hier-archy, priesthood, councils, infallibility. Yet there is often a vast dif-ference in content and meaning from what Protestants or Roman Catholics understand by the same terms.

This often results in confusion on the level of personal contact; Or-thodox are not even considered "Christian" or "saved" when they are encountered by zealous missionaries of Protestant or Roman Catholic churches. Similarly, when Orthodox use expressions such as "Theosis-de-ification," "uncreated light," "divine energies," or when they describe the Blessed Virgin Mary, the saints, the veneration of icons, such expressions cause bewilderment or horror in the western Christian's mind, particularly again in the case of missionary zealots.

Non-Orthodox must be especially careful not to draw incorrect conclusions from these differences. They should know from the begin-ning of any contact with the Orthodox that the gospel of our Lord Jesus Christ does not have to be expressed in Protestant or Roman Catholic terminology in order for it to be authentically Christian or "Pentecostal."

Time and space do not permit in this writing a full description of what all Christians, regardless of background, consider to be authen-tic gospel. However, I will try to make clear that when we call our-selves *Orthodox* Christians, we are exactly that—especially as the term applies to our understanding of the life in Christ and the Holy Spirit.

The Suffering Church

Without question no other church from its beginning to the present has ever experienced *over a sustained period of time* the suffering, per-secution, and tribulation undergone by the Holy Orthodox Church. The major part of Orthodoxy has not had a cessation of persecution or slavery until the present century, and even then only those Orthodox in the western hemisphere, Australia, Western Europe, and in missionary areas have experienced relative freedom. Most Christian churches have undergone persecution at one time or another, but the Orthodox have never had an intermission. Mark this well, for it is paramount in any understanding of our church.

This persecution and suffering are imposed basically from three directions.

Political Control and Interference by the Civil State

In the major areas of Orthodoxy the Church cannot function as a free church. History proves that regardless of the church or denomination, regardless of how benevolent or "Christian" the civil authorities may be, whenever the church is an organ of the state, willingly or unwillingly, there is an inevitable decline in spirituality. The rapid decline usually begins with the leaders in the church. Some Orthodox theologians tend to glorify this bond between church and state, particularly those who indulge in the romantic dreams of imperial Byzantium or of tsarist Russia. Careful historians of spiritual life will usually disagree with them, for the evidence suggests that in the long history of Orthodoxy great spiritual awakenings rarely occur when the Church is controlled by the state and the hierarchy function as civil servants. There are some exceptions, but candid examination will prove this to be generally true.

From the "age of Constantine" the Orthodox have continued to remain in political bondage. The political alliances of and persecution from the Byzantine-Roman empire, the Russian empire, the Arab and Turkish Moslem empires, the Austro-Hungarian empire, have kept the Church in bondage. The same control exists even today where the state is nominally benevolent or Christian, such as in Greece, Cyprus, Israel, or other Middle Eastern countries.

State-church relationships have tended to produce intrigue and political ambition within the leadership of the Church, often without regard for genuine Christian vocation on the part of the persons involved. In the more extreme forms of state-church relationships the entire Church is subordinate to the self-serving whims and political designs of the civil government, and the faithful cannot enjoy the freedom of life in Christ without interference.

Persecution from Non-Christian (or Non-Orthodox Christian) Regimes

˙ Orthodoxy is red with the blood of tribulation and persecution. A host of martyrs continues to fulfill the promise of our Lord, "In the world you have tribulation . . ." (John 16:33). The pagan Roman empire, the Tartars, the Arabs, the Turks, the Crusaders, the Polish and Lithuanian kingdoms, the Lutheran Swedes, and the Communists (the most evident persecution in the present century)—all have attempted to eradicate the Orthodox Church.

The Church has existed in a state of siege through all of these periods, and its main concern was mere survival at all costs. Coupled with the ecclesio-political unions and with the spiritually enfeebled state of the Church as described above, this persecution has rendered the Orthodox faith in these lands practically impotent. In the midst of struggling to survive, the Church suffered most from a lack of education, books, Bibles, a trained clergy, and an informed and evangelized laity. Only in this century has the Church begun to come alive to its heritage of Christian faith to the extent that illiteracy has been banished in these countries, Christian literature has been made available, and educational institutions have flourished to educate the Church leaders.

It is true that persecution of the Church usually results in a strong and healthy Christianity. This is no less true for the Orthodox. For in the midst of this persecution and suffering there are many glorious testimonies to the vibrant life in Christ through the power of the Holy Spirit. However, to the unceasing persecution must be added another trial. In some respects this threat is as vicious and debilitating to the Church as persecution itself.

Proselytism

No other church has suffered from proselytism of its faithful by other Christians as has the Orthodox Church. Christians of the West have persistently taken advantage of the weakened, persecuted Orthodox faithful down through the centuries to the present day in order to "save" or convert them. In the past, both Protestants and Roman Catholics have used every means to bring the Orthodox under their control or to outright conversion, either by political influence and intrigue with the conquerors of the Orthodox faithful or by outright force and occupation.

Even today, the Orthodox countries have a special attraction to non-Orthodox fellow Christians as territories for "conversion to Christ." Millions of dollars are spent by missionary groups and denominations in this country for the "spread of the gospel" to the descendants of those who were among the first to hear of the Lord Jesus from the lips of the apostles and who faithfully continued in that same faith for nearly twenty centuries, in spite of tremendous oppression from the hordes of the anti-Christ.

These same missionary groups and fellow Christians working in primarily Moslem countries, with Orthodox Christian minorities, do not concentrate their efforts on bringing the followers of Mohammed to the Lord Jesus Christ. Instead they center their efforts on converting the Orthodox! This continues today in Lebanon and Egypt in particular.

Monasticism as the Core of Orthodox Spirituality

Christian history reveals a very close relationship between the rise of monasticism in the East and the merger of the Church with the Roman Empire. Those who sought to live the Christian life in freedom chose to escape from the entanglements of the world in remote and deserted areas. It is no accident that spirituality developed in areas free from political interference either by the civil authorities or by the ecclesiastical hierarchy in conjunction with them.

Nearly all of the great lights of the charismatic life in the Spirit were monks. In solitude and freedom far from the "Christ-loving kings and emperors," in the wilderness and deserts of the Middle East and Russia, the Holy Spirit flowed through men and women in His fullness, manifesting Himself as in the New Testament times. This was possible because in those areas Christians were comparatively free from the ravages of persecution and the compromising spirit of the state churches and the civilized world. This call to the wilderness continued to the extent that wherever civilization advanced upon the monks, they would pick up and move even further away.

Consequently, the great spiritual writings and rich treasury of devotion of the Orthodox Church came from a monastic environment. Even those great charismatics who were called eventually to govern the Church as hierarchs still retained their monastic temperament and life. And many returned to the monastery after their services were no longer needed in the population centers.

The piety of the average layman or parish pastor throughout most Orthodox countries has also continued to be conditioned and inspired by the springs of spirituality emerging from the monasteries. There have always been charismatic figures such as St. John of Kronstadt (a parish priest all of his life, and a man of tremendous spiritual influence in the Russian Church at the turn of the last century), who, although not a monk, nevertheless reflected in his parochial duties and in his spiritual writings this same stream of faith and life. This remains true to this day in the average Orthodox parish, wherever priest and people endeavor to maintain more than a surface devotion to the faith.

Charismatic Aspects of Orthodox Theology and Spirituality

Time and space certainly do not permit a thorough exposition of the Orthodox faith. My purpose in the following is to present an overall view of Orthodoxy, which will attempt to indicate the decisive role of the Holy Spirit in all aspects of the faith and life of the Church. I present this with considerable dependence upon several Orthodox theologians, who have outlined this position in their writings.

Redemption and Salvation

Redemption and salvation involve the restoration of man to his true image—the image of God his Creator. Man's purpose is to know the truth:

> When man arrives at the reality of the Christian truth, whose essence is to abide in God, to know Him, to be bound by His communion—then he is really a free being, living in the human nature restored by Christ: "And ye shall know the truth, and the truth shall make you free" (John 8:32). . . . Man regains his freedom, not by choosing at one moment between two alternatives, but through the power of his transformation in Christ by the Spirit, and this is a continuous process beyond the power of human moral effort: it is God who accomplishes it and not man.[6]

Redemption and salvation are a *continuous* process of God working with man cooperating with God through the exercise of his free will, which has been made possible through the gift of the Holy Spirit given to man in his baptism. This must not be understood in either a Pelagian or semi-Pelagian sense, although to the Western theologian it may appear as such. Redemption and salvation are the work of God alone with man receiving the grace of redemption by his free act of the will: ". . . man is to be recreated in communion through the energies of the Holy Spirit, and *not by his own efforts.*"[7]

Orthodox theology does not view redemption and sanctification apart, but as one process. Certain forms of Protestant theology, on the other hand, consider salvation as a matter of stages, e.g., "being saved" or justified, followed by the work of sanctification, and (for some) the baptism in the Holy Spirit. Salvation and redemption begin with repentance, which "binds together all the creative faculties of sinful man, and allows God to perform His miracles in His Spirit: to create saints out of sinful men."[8] Repentance invites man "to receive the Spirit, realizing again and again in the grace of God this freedom as communion, based on the redemption given in Christ Jesus."[9] "A Christian is a person to whom something has happened, a person who by the power of the Holy Spirit acknowledges in joy his incorporation into the life of God. . . ."[10]

However, it is again important to stress that Orthodox remain faithful to the teaching of the ancient fathers of the Church in em-

---

6. Nikos A. Nissiotis, "The Importance of the Doctrine of the Trinity for Church Life and Theology," *The Orthodox Ethos. Essays in Honour of the Centenary of the Greek Orthodox Archdiocese of North and South America*, ed. Angelos J. Philippou (Oxford: Holywell Press, 1964), p.57.

7. Ibid., italics mine.

8. Ibid., pp. 57f.

9. Ibid., p. 58.

10. A. Philippou, "The Mystery of Pentecost," *The Orthodox Ethos*, p. 76.

phasizing that salvation is not by works, but by grace alone. "The Christian must be defined not in terms of what he himself does for his salvation, but of what *God* has done for him."[11] However, man must continue to appropriate this free gift of salvation to himself, through the means of grace in the Church. In keeping with the emphasis of St. John Chrysostom, Orthodox refuse to separate the two aspects of the Church's redemptive activity:

> . . . on the one hand there is the *finished* work of Christ which forms the essence of the Gospel; on the other, the divinely *continuous* work which, by the power of the Holy Spirit, "filleth all in all" (Eph. 1:23).[12]

"In the light of revelation, salvation has nothing juridical about it; it is not the sentence of a tribunal."[13] Both the Hebrew and Greek words for salvation have wide meaning, which involves deliverance from death as well as healing, curing, and restoring health. As Professor Evdokimov writes:

> Sinners are the sick who are threatened with spiritual death, more fearful than that of the body. We can then specify the therapeutic meaning of salvation: it is the cure of a being and the elimination of the germ of mortality. This is why the Savior called Himself the life, and the saved receive eternal life. The end joins the beginning when man, having received the breath of life, lives by participation in the Holy Spirit, creator of life.[14]

Receiving the Holy Spirit

The Orthodox Church believes with all Christians that the Holy Spirit is a gift of grace. He is active in the work of repentance as in all aspects of our life. Without Him we cannot live for He is the "lifegiver." The Holy Spirit is one. But He communicates Himself to believers in various ways, so that there is one Spirit but many "gifts" or, more properly, "manifestations."

The baptism in the Holy Spirit is *primarily* understood as taking place in the sacraments of water-baptism and "chrismation." Chrismation is a "sealing" of the gift of the Spirit in baptism, the imparting of the Spirit—who comes to dwell in the one baptized through the act of the anointing with the oil of chrism. One must be careful, however, not to confuse the rite of *chrismation* with the rite of *confirmation* in Western usage. Chrismation is understood and practiced

11. Ibid.
12. Ibid., p. 77.
13. Evdokimov, *The Struggle with God*, p. 157.
14. Ibid., p. 158.

in a much broader sense and is not exclusively a sacrament of initiation.

One of the monastic teachers of the Church, Theophan the Recluse, states what could be considered the principal view within Orthodoxy concerning the reception of the Holy Spirit: "All of us who have been baptised and chrismated, have received the gift of the Holy Spirit. He is in all of us, but He is not active in all of us."[15]

The fathers speak of the action of the Holy Spirit not only in connection with baptism and chrismation, but also in connection with experiencing both a "stirring up within," and a "coming down upon" those already baptized. Again, St. Theophan speaks of being "filled with the Spirit":

> . . . The commandment to "be filled with the Spirit" is simply an injunction to behave and act in such a manner as to cooperate with or allow free scope to the Holy Spirit to make it possible for the Holy Spirit to manifest Himself by perceptively touching the heart.[16]

St. John Chrysostom, St. Theophan recalls, answers the question, "Is it in our power to be filled with the Spirit?" with these words:

> Yes, it is in our power. When we purify our soul from lies, cruelty, fornication, impurity and cupidity, when we become kind-hearted, compassionate, self-disciplined, when there is no blasphemy or misplaced jesting in us—when we become worthy of it, then what will prevent the Holy Spirit from drawing near and alighting within us? And He will not only draw near, but will fill our heart.[17]

Once again, in spite of what the Orthodox Church expresses formally in its theological writings, it is careful to emphasize that the Holy Spirit cannot be absolutized or contained within a set form. One of the foremost contemporary theologians, Father Lev Gillet, is careful to make this distinction when he writes:

> But just as baptismal grace extends beyond the sacrament of Baptism in the strict sense, the gift of the Holy Ghost cannot be exclusively identified with Chrisma. . . . In many modern cases we should not dare to deny the reality of a "Baptism of the Spirit" conferred upon men who had not received it sacramentally. "The wind bloweth where it listeth" (John 3:8), and "God giveth not the Spirit by measure" (John 3:4).

> The grace of the Spirit, of course, is already active in the baptism with water, as well as the grace of the Father and the grace of the

---

15. *The Art of Prayer. An Orthodox Anthology*, compiled by Igumen Charitou, trans. E. Kadloubovsky and E. M. Palmer, ed. Timothy Ware (London: Faber and Faber, 1966), p. 172.

16. Ibid., p. 174.

17. Ibid.

Son. But there is a special sending of the Spirit to man; and a Baptism with water not completed by the Baptism with the Holy Ghost would manifest a deficient Christian life. . . . The question of Paul to the Ephesian disciples "Did ye receive the Holy Ghost?" (Acts 19:2) is asked of every one of us. It would not be enough to answer: I have received the mystery or sacrament of the Spirit after my Baptism, when I was anointed with the holy Chrism. The question is whether and how this seed of the Spirit has been afterwards developed within the soul.[18]

"Pentecostal grace cannot, anymore than Baptismal and Eucharistic grace, be fixed, as it were, crystallized around the outward ministration of the Holy Mysteries."[19] The charismatic and Pentecostal life, which is the very essence of the life in Christ, in all of its aspects for the Orthodox, as described here, takes for granted that every believer will strive to let the Holy Spirit both dwell in him and renew him in every area of his life.

Prayer in the Charismatic Life

Throughout the history of the Orthodox Church, prayer has often been placed in a position that supersedes all other ways toward union with the Holy Trinity. In the monastic tradition the chief aim is spiritual growth through prayer. Father Gillet states:

. . . we always can and must practice what St. Jude (20) calls "praying in the Holy Ghost." This means either a prayer in which the words and intentions are not our own, but are given by the Spirit, or a praying silence in which the soul unites herself to the unknown and continuous prayer of the Spirit.[20]

The state of true prayer is a charism of the Holy Spirit. St. Seraphim counsels: "We ought to pray until the Holy Spirit descends upon us. . . . When He has come to visit us, we cease praying."[21]

The Orthodox life of prayer has elevated the form of prayer known as the "prayer of Jesus" to a position above all others. The great power connected with the repetition of the name of Jesus in contemplation is attested to by many of the fathers. Prof. Evdokimov writes:

The "prayer of the heart" frees and enlarges it, and attracts Jesus to it by the incessant invocation: "Lord Jesus Christ, Son of God, have pity upon me a sinner!"

18. Gillet, *Orthodox Spirituality*, p. 63.
19. Ibid., p. 66.
20. Ibid., p. 78.
21. *Conversation of Saint Seraphim*, p. 6.

In this prayer, which is that of the publican in the Gospel, the whole Bible with its entire message is reduced to its essential simplicity: confession of the Lordship of Jesus, of His divine filiation, therefore, of the trinity; then the fall that called for the abyss of divine mercy. The beginning and the end are gathered here in a single word charged with the sacramental presence of Christ in his name. This prayer ceaselessly resounds in the depths of a man's soul, even outside his will and consciousness. Finally, the name of Jesus resounds of itself, taking on the rhythm of the man's respiration, in some way "attached" to his breath; even during sleep. . . .[22]

St. Barsanuphius confesses: "There are powerful beings like St. Michael, but for us, the weak, there remains nothing but to take refuge in the name of Jesus."[23] St. Climacus adds: "Strike your adversary with the name of Jesus; there is no more powerful weapon on the earth or in the skies."[24]

Within the Orthodox tradition of prayer, great stress is laid upon the use of few words, and especially upon silence. All of the fathers emphasize that the highest form of prayer "in the Spirit" is not to be found in the use of many words. St. Macarius says: "It is not necessary to use many words; it is sufficient to keep one's hands elevated."[25]

Orthodoxy and the Present Charismatic Renewal

Reviewing only the barest examples of the significance of the life of the Holy Spirit in the theology and spirituality of the Church, as presented above, one could reasonably conclude that "charismatic renewal" has always been a primary goal in the Orthodox Church. However, with the exception of some comparatively recent developments in some parishes or groups, the thrust of the world-wide awakening of our present generation has yet to be experienced and lived in Orthodoxy. In most of the exceptions, the awareness of Neo-Pentecostalism has come about largely through influence from without the confines of the Orthodox Church. As for those Orthodox who have experienced this new encounter in religious experience, it has caused them to discover nothing really new but rather to re-examine within the Orthodox tradition and spirituality that which has always been there.

The spiritual gifts of 1 Corinthians 12, with the possible exception of glossolalia, have always been considered normative by nearly all of the Orthodox within the life of the Church. The supernatural gifts of

---

22. Evdokimov, *The Struggle with God*, p. 182.
23. Quoted by Evdokimov, *The Struggle with God*, p. 183.
24. Ibid.
25. Ibid., p. 178.

faith, the word of knowledge, and the word of wisdom through the Holy Spirit have been continuously manifested in the lives not only of the monastics but of the laymen as well. Almost every Orthodox lay person knows of a saint (or even a member of his family in many instances) who in his religious experience has manifested one or more of these gifts.

The working of miracles is no exceptional activity within the lives of Orthodox Christians. It is understood to be related to the degree of faith and personal holiness of those concerned.

The discerning of spirits, whether angelic or demonic, is very real to the average Orthodox, especially to those in the Mediterranean countries. The ministry of deliverance through the prayers of the faithful and the clergy is practiced as a normal part of religious life. The great "Efchologion," or prayer book of the Church, abounds in prayers and forms for this ministry of loosing those who are captive to unclean spirits.

Healing by supernatural means is actively prayed for and anticipated either through the laying on of hands accompanied by anointing with oil or through material objects believed to be endowed with the grace of the Holy Spirit, such as were the "handkerchiefs" of St. Paul in Ephesus (Acts 19:12).

Prophecy—particularly understood as encouragement, edification, and supernatural insight into the future—has nearly always accompanied the lives of persons who have received extraordinary endowments of the power of the Holy Spirit in their lives.

It can safely be understood that the average Orthodox sees nothing exceptional in any of these seven gifts. However, they are nearly always associated with those persons in whom or places in which holiness and devotion are most evident.

The gifts of glossolalia and the interpretation of tongues are not in evidence as extensively as the other seven gifts in the life of the Church. There are many reasons for this, and to include them all would require a special study. Briefly, however, it might be noted that speaking in tongues (as history records) appeared to die out rather rapidly. Most of the later fathers of the Church did not appear to understand the phenomenon, at least in so far as it was exercised in Corinth. The supernatural tongues at Pentecost were easily understood, but any connection with the tongues as exercised in the early assembly at Corinth was not comprehensible to the later fathers in their exegetical attempts. A superficial survey of the writings of these fathers reveals that their general consensus of opinion that the phenomenon was beyond their comprehension was quite honest. As a result, the significance of glossolalia was minimized by the later fathers or limited only to local situations for the apostolic period. And, of course, when a gift is not anticipated or expected, however much it may be of the Holy Spirit, it is not received.

Serious Orthodox theologians have yet to enter into a complete study of speaking in tongues, and it is hoped that the presence of this phenomenon today both in Orthodoxy as well as in other denominations will cause them to do so. In the light of the understanding of the dynamic role of the Holy Spirit in the life of the Church and throughout the Orthodox tradition, Orthodox theologians may well serve to formulate within their theology a very positive contribution to the charismatic renewal of Christendom.

In my own opinion, the undeniable awakening within all of the spheres of Christendom and the accompanying resurgence of the gifts of the Spirit (with the resulting fruits in the lives of so many people throughout the world) demand from the Orthodox a clear study and a positive examination. Orthodoxy itself desperately needs renewal and an awakening in the lives of its faithful if it is to survive in this age. For the faithful to ignore the need of awakening within Orthodoxy may well result in the eventual decline of the great Church of Eastern Christendom into a facsimile of the apostolic church it claims to be, while the rest of Christianity passes it by. Its own faithful then will be denied the apostolic life in Christ experienced by so many outside its bounds.

The words of the great tenth century saint of the Orthodox Church, Simeon the Theologian, admonish every Christian believer and denomination today, especially the Orthodox:

> In the same way, a man who imagines that he has the Holy Spirit in him, yet in reality has nothing, when he hears that the actions of the Holy Spirit are clearly recognizable in those who possess Him, refuses to believe it; neither does he believe that there can be in our generation men who are equal to the Apostles of Christ and to the saints of all ages, and are, like them, moved and influenced by the Divine Spirit, or consciously see and apprehend Him.[26]

---

26. Simeon the New Theologian, *Practical and Theological Precepts*, p. 57. This translation from E. Kadloubovsky and G. E. H. Palmer, *Writings from the Philokalia on Prayer of the Heart* (London: Faber and Faber, 1961), p. 109.

Walter J. Hollenweger

As the thesis for his doctorate in theology taken at the University of Zurich, Walter J. Hollenweger—who left the ministry of the Swiss Pentecostal Mission for the Swiss Reformed Church—presented a ten volume handbook on Pentecostalism *(Handbuch der Pfingstbewegung)*. For several years, as secretary for evangelism, he served on the staff of the World Council of Churches in Geneva—a post which gave him unique opportunity to observe Pentecostalism around the world. The benefits of his background, travel, and study appear in his major work *The Pentecostals* (Minneapolis: Augsburg, 1972), a nearly encyclopedic survey of international Pentecostalism. Currently professor of mission at the University of Birmingham, Prof. Hollenweger has produced many writings (partial listing in *The Pentecostals*, pp. 538f.) which seek to introduce the Pentecostal and ecumenical movements to each other.

In this article, Prof. Hollenweger sketches charismatic movements in France and Germany which, although they arose in the first decades of the twentieth century, did not identify with the classical Pentecostal churches. On the contrary, they remained within traditional Protestantism and did not take on all the social, doctrinal, and ecclesiastical features of classical Pentecostalism. Prof. Hollenweger also makes a brief analysis of British Catholic Pentecostalism, particularly as represented by the Dominican Simon Tugwell.

"Touching" and "Thinking" the Spirit: Some Aspects of European Charismatics

3

Since the early 1910s there has existed in Europe a charismatic movement within the traditional churches. In many cases it was the starting point of what are now termed "classical Pentecostal churches" but in all cases referred to below (perhaps with the exception of Great Britain) it existed and exists alongside classical Pentecostal churches.

Obviously I have to be highly selective and want therefore to present only a few of the more outstanding of the charismatic theologians. One of the most sympathetic was

Jonathan A. A. B. Paul (1853-1931)[1]

He was a Lutheran pastor in Germany. His father was diaconus at the church of St. Stephen in Gartz an der Oder. His mother came from a doctor's family. He was baptized "Jonathan" by his father "because he pledged little Jonathan to become at some time a

---

1. Ernst Giese has written a scholarly and reliable biography, *Pastor Jonathan Paul, ein Knecht Jesu Christi. Leben und Werk* (Altdorf/Nbg.: Missionsbuchhandlung und Verlag, 1964). Further literature in my *Handbuch der Pfingstbewegung* (available from ATLA Board of Microtexts, Divinity School, Yale University, New Haven, CT 06510), 08.097, and in my *The Pentecostals* (Minneapolis: Augsburg, 1972).

preacher of the Gospel." Jonathan Paul wrote later about his (infant) baptism:

> My father had five sons. It is only me whom he had pledged by God's providence to become a pastor. And I am the only one that in fact became a pastor of all the five sons. I can therefore not deny that the words uttered at my baptism were of prophetic significance.[2]

That might be one of the reasons why all his life Paul defended infant baptism[3]—while not denying the possibility of believer's baptism—and why the Mülheim Association of Christian Fellowship,[4] a federation of Pentecostal communities (partly of a free-church character, partly within the existing established Lutheran and Reformed churches), practices both infant *and* believer's baptism up to the present day. It is a fact that these churches, although the oldest and strongest Pentecostal organization in Germany, have been consistently ignored by most Pentecostal authors writing in English.[5] Michael Harper even called this organization "a very small group and barely Pentecostal."[6]

It is all the more important to bring to light the leader and pioneer of this oldest and strongest Pentecostal group in Germany. Paul became a conscious Christian through the sermons of his father.[7] In Stettin's gymnasium he discovered the richness of German literature. In 1872 he passed his matriculation examination and went to the university. He would have preferred to study medicine, but in obedience to his father's pledge, he took up the study of theology at Greifswald and Leipzig. He passed his second theological examination with a thesis on "The Doctrine of the Holy Spirit" (written in Latin!). Although a successful pastor and youth worker he was

---

2. J. Paul, "*Um eine unvergängliche Krone,*" *Heilszeugnisse 23* (June 15, 1931), 165.

3. Jonathan Paul, *Taufe und Geistestaufe: Ein Beitrag zur Lösung einer ungemein wichtigen Frage, besonders auch für solche, welche in Gewissensbedenken sich befinden* (Berlin: Deutsche Ev. Buch- und Tractat-Gesellschaft, 1894, 1896, 1898), and *Die Taufe in ihrem Vollsinn* (Mülheim: Verlag der Gesellschaft fur Mission, Diakonie und Kolportage m.b.H., 1930).

4. On this see W. Hollenweger, *The Pentecostals*, pp. 218-43.

5. Christine Carmichael, "Pentecost in Germany," *The Pentecostal Evangel*, Aug. 20, 1961, pp. 25f.; Nicholas Nikoloff, "New Awakening in Germany," *The Pentecostal Evangel*, April 24, 1960, pp. 4f.; but *not* Donald Gee in *The Pentecostal Movement: A Short History and an Interpretation for British Readers* (1939; second and enlarged edition 1941; third edition under the title *Wind and Flame*, incorporating the former book *The Pentecostal Movement* with additional chapters [London: Assemblies of God Publishing House, 1967]).

6. Michael Harper, *Renewal*, 41 (Oct.-Nov., 1972), 10.

7. Christian Krust, *Fünfzig Jahre deutsche Pfingstbewegung Mülheimer Richtung* (Altdorf/Nbg.: Missionsbuchhandlung und Verlag, 1963), p. 204.

constantly searching for a deeper spiritual life. When burying little children he read from the Lutheran liturgy, "Like as a father pitieth his children, so the Lord pitieth them that fear him." When he came to the passage, ". . . unto such as keep his covenant and his testimonies," his conscience awoke and asked him: "You, pastor, when will you begin to keep his covenants?"[8]

On June 17, 1890, Paul underwent an experience of sanctification which was associated with a vision, and which led him among other things to abstain from smoking. He did not regard smoking as a sin in itself, but he wanted to devote the money saved to the church's mission. His biographer, the Lutheran pastor Ernst Giese, says that Paul's experience of sanctification

> . . . is by no means of a mystical or ecstatic nature. If the account is read closely, it can clearly be seen that it is dictated not by an extraordinary mental impulse, or any exalted emotion, but by a perfectly sober self-criticism, which was the basis of this decisive crisis experience. Therefore Paul never regarded himself as a mystic or ecstatic.[9]

According to Scripture, Paul thought, this experience of sanctification—also known as the baptism of the Spirit—ought to occur suddenly. But Paul was unwilling to assert that those who have not experienced this sudden baptism of the Spirit do not possess the gift of the Holy Spirit.[10] On various occasions Paul testified about this experience, and he laid particular stress on one point: "I would like to express the wish that . . .what I have said should not be understood as a doctrine but as what it is, a *testimony* of what the death and resurrection of Jesus have brought *me*."[11] But for him one thing was certain: "One who is reborn not only desires to do the will of God, but is also able to do it."[12]

In accordance with that part of the early Pentecostal movement which had strong ties with the holiness movement, Paul's understanding of regeneration and Spirit-baptism (sometimes the two terms are identical) had a strong connotation of sanctification. Yet Paul's teaching of sanctification has not been properly understood,

---

8. J. Paul, "Um . . . Krone," p. 165.

9. Giese, *Pastor Jonathan Paul*, p. 27.

10. Jonathan Paul, *Ihr werdet die Kraft des Heiligen Geistes empfangen* (Altdorf/Nbg.: Pranz, 1896, ³1956), p. 17.

11. Quoted in Paul Fleisch, *Geschichte der deutschen Gemeinschaftsbewegung bis zum Auftreten des Zungenredens (1875-1907)*, vol. I of *Die moderne Gemeinschaftsbewegung in Deutschland* (Leipzig: H. G. Wallmann, ³1912-14), p. 127.

12. Jonathan Paul, *Ihr werdet die Kraft*, p. 41, quoted by Giese, *Pastor Jonathan Paul*, p. 51 (I could not find this passage in the third edition of Paul's book).

either by his opponents[13] or by his friends. Admittedly the responsibility for this to some extent lies with the obscure and contradictory nature of his accounts, which is the result of the different pastoral situations in which they were made.

Paul's doctrine of sanctification is expressed in a laborious and inflated style in his voluminous writings. If one attempts to reduce it to a clear formula, however, it turns out to be a doctrine of perfection such as had already been taught by Wesley.[14] This can be seen clearly from his concept of sin:

> Only culpable failings are sin, not blameless ones. . . . Where there is disobedience, there is sin; and where there is obedience, there is no sin, but human short-sightedness and limitation. . . . Consequently, a pure heart is a heart purified of disobedience (Heb. 8:10). We see from this that what matters is not the extent of the knowledge one possesses, but obedience. . . . Thus what matters is that *according to one's knowledge* one is obedient to the Spirit of God and allows oneself to be led by him.[15]

This is confirmed by his comments in his translation of the New Testament, the so-called Mülheim Testament.[16]

From the very beginning Jonathan Paul and his colleagues[17] rejected the doctrine of the "initial evidence." Already in the first issue of his magazine *Pfingstgrüsse* he wrote: "It is not our view that only those who have spoken in tongues have received the Holy Spirit."[18] Speaking in tongues is to be desired as a gift of the Spirit (and in fact Paul himself practiced speaking in tongues frequently), but—in contrast with the teaching of many other Pentecostals—it is not the sign

13. Pastor Thimme, *Auf der Warte* (1920-21); Paul Fleisch, *Die Pfingstbewegung in Deutschland*, vol. II, part 2, of *Die moderne Gemeinschaftsbewegung* (Hanover: Heinr. Feesche Verlag, 1957); cf. J. Paul, "Antwort an Pastor Thimme," *Pfingstgrüsse*, 6 (March 1, 1914), 168ff.

14. "In the view I hold I am in the fullest sense a follower of John Wesley; I have also been conscious of being in full agreement with the substance of Stockmayer's doctrine in his tract *Gnade und Sünde* ('Grace and Sin'), even though I have used other expressions, in accordance with my own understanding of Scripture" (J. Paul, *Lied des Lammes*, Oct. 1919, quoted in Giese, *Pastor Jonathan Paul*, p. 223).

15. J. Paul, "Das reine Herz," *Die Heiligung*, 139 (April, 1910), 19f.

16. *Das Neue Testament in der Sprache der Gegenwart. Neue Mülheimer Ausgabe mit Anmerkungen und Wörterverzeichnis* (Mülheim/Ruhr: Verlag der Gesellschaft für Mission, Diakonie und Kolportage m.b.H., 1914; Altdorf/Nbg., Missionsbuchhandlung und Verlag, ⁷1968).

17. E.g., the Reformed pastor C. A. Voget (Hollenweger, *Handbuch der Pfingstbewegung*, 08.543), the Lutheran pastor R. Lettau (ibid., 07.843), and Karl Ecke (see note 23).

18. J. Paul, "Was sollen und wollen die Pfingstgrüsse?" *Pfingstgrüsse*, 1 (Feb., 1909), 2. Cf. also Christian Krust, "Geistesbewegung oder Zungenbewegung," *Heilszeugnisse*, 52 (Feb., 1967), 24ff.; 52 (March, 1967), 38ff.

that the baptism of the Spirit has been received.[19] The fact is also recognized that speaking in tongues is a natural human gift which the Holy Spirit can use if He wishes.[20]

This has been the doctrine of the Mülheim Association until today.[21] Recently ecumenical contacts have been established between the Mülheim Association, the World Council of Churches and the other (Catholic and Protestant) churches in Germany.[22]

In summary, the pioneering ministry of Paul and his colleagues is important for the following reasons: They practiced spiritual gifts, including speaking in tongues, within a loose federation which contained "Pentecostal free churches" *and* communities within the established churches.[23] They did not teach a baptism of the Spirit with

19. J. Paul, "Beantwortung von Fragen," *Pfingstgrüsse*, 2 (Oct., 1909), 8; 2 (July 24, 1910), 151; cf. *Der Kampf um die Pfingstbewegung. Sonderabdruck aus den Pfingstgrüssen* (Mülheim/Ruhr: Verlag der Gesellschaft für Mission, Diakonie und Kolportage, n.d. [1916-18?]), pp. 2f. and 6f.

20. Quoted in Fleisch. *Pfingtsbewegung*, pp. 79f.; cf. R. L[ettau?]., "Aus meiner Briefmappe," *Pfingstgrüsse*, 2 (Jan. 23, 1910), 7; J. Paul, "Das Verhältnis von natürlicher Begabung und Geistesgaben," *Pfingstgrüsse*, 8 (March 26, 1916), 201-03; 8 (April 2, 1916), 209-11.

21. Christian Krust, *Was wir glauben, lehren, und bekennen* (Altdorf/Nbg.: Missionsbuchhandlung und Verlag, 1963).

22. Christian Krust, "Pentecostal Churches and the Ecumenical Movement," *The Uppsala Report 1968. Official Report of the Fourth Assembly of the WCC Uppsala, July 4-20, 1968*, ed. N. Goodall (Geneva: WCC, 1968), pp. 340ff.; idem, "Bericht vom Mülheimer Hauptbrüdertag (3.-6. April 1967)," *Heilszeugnisse*, 52 (July 1, 1967), 98-102; idem, "Wie sich die Pfingstbewegung im Lichte des Neuen Testamentes als Kirche versteht," *Heilszeugnisse*, 52 (Sept. 1, 1967), 131-36; idem, "Bericht vom Hauptbrüdertag in Mülheim-Ruhr (April 23-25, 1968)," *Heilszeugnisse*, 53 (Aug. 1, 1968), 114f.; idem, "Die Ökumenische Bewegung," *Heilszeugnisse*, 53 (Aug. 1, 1968), 116-18; idem, "Die Vierte Vollversammlung des OeRK in Uppsala," *Heilszeugnisse*, 53 (Oct. 1, 1968), 146-59; 53 (Nov. 1, 1968), 163-66, 171-74; idem, "Der Heilige Geist und die Katholizität der Kirche. Bericht der Sektion I an die vierte Vollversammlung des OeRK in Uppsala, Juli 1968," *Heilszeugnisse*, 53 (Dec. 1, 1968), 180-85; H. Rottmann, "Bericht vom Hauptbrüdertag in Mülheim-Ruhr vom 8.-10.10.1968," *Heilszeugnisse*, 53 (Dec. 1, 1968), 179f.; L. Steiner, "Oekumenische Konsultation in Gunten," *Heilszeugnisse*, 52 (Jan. 1, 1967), 3f.; Ch. Lemke, "Ein Tag der Begegnung," *Der Leuchter*, 21 (Feb. 1970), 5f.

23. Already in 1911 (!) Karl Ecke, a Lutheran charismatic pastor, began publishing the results of his research on Schwenckfeld. K. Ecke, *Schwenckfeld, Luther und der Gedanke einer apostolischen Reformation* (Berlin: Martin Warneck, 1911; abridged second edition, *Kaspar Schwenckfeld, Ungelöste Geistesfragen der Reformationszeit* [Gütersloh: Bertelsmann, 1952]; revised third edition, *Fortsetzung der Reformation. Kaspar von Schwenckfeld's Schau einer apostolischen Reformation*, ed. H. D. Gruschka in connection with the Schwenkfeld Library, Pennsylvania [Memmingen: Missionsverlag für urchristliche Botschaft, 1965]); cf. too the following titles by K. Ecke: *Der Durchbruch des Urchristentum seit Luthers Reformation. Lesestücke aus einem vergessenen Kapitel der Kirchengeschichte* (Altdorf/Nbg.: Süddeutscher Missionsverlag Fritz Pranz, 1950; second edition, n.d.); *Die Pfingstbewegung. Ein Gutachten von kirch-*

speaking in tongues as the initial sign, but believed in growing into deeper experiences of the Spirit. They did not discard theological scholarship. In fact they rejected the doctrine of the verbal inspiration of the Bible as unchristian.[24] On the other hand they saw clearly that theological learning is only of relative importance.

France

A very old and highly indigenous charismatic movement exists in France (after all, the tradition of the Camisards has never been completely forgotten[25]) and in French-speaking Switzerland.[26] Already in the thirties the Swiss Reformed ministers Jean and Fritz de Rougement had opened their churches to Pentecostal preachers like Douglas Scott and Donald Gee. Pentecostalism has always had friends and even supporters within the French Reformed Church.

One of the most interesting leaders of these charismatic pastors within the Reformed Church is Louis Dallière.[27] In the middle of the 1920s he invited a number of pastors and their wives to a retreat. The participants signed a "commitment card" which contained twelve points. These points included:

> In the morning of every day I will give my first thought to God in speaking a short prayer, in reciting a Bible verse or a stanza from a hymn.
>
> Every day I will have my quiet time. . . .

licher Seite (Mülheim/Ruhr; Christlicher Gemeinschaftsverband GmbH, 1950); Sektierer oder wertvolle Brüder? Randglossen zu einem Sektenbuch (Mülheim/Ruhr: E. Humburg, Verlagsbuchhandlung, 1951); Der reformierende Protestantismus. Streiflichter auf die Entwicklung lebendiger Gemeinde von Luther bis heute (Gütersloh: Bertelsmann, 1952); Ecke and O. S. von Bibra, Die Reformation in neuer Sicht (Altdorf/Nbg.: Süddeutscher Missionsverlag Fritz Pranz, 1952).

24. Krust, Was wir glauben, pp. 117, 120; C. O. Voget, Pfingstbotschaft (1921), pp. 201ff., quoted in Krust, Fünfzig Jahre, pp. 237ff.; P. Gericke, Christliche Vollkommenheit und Geisteserlebnisse (Rietenau/Württ.: Gericke, 1950), p. 16.

25. Robert P. Gagg, Kirche im Feuer. Das Leben der südfranzösischen Hugenottenkirche nach dem Todesurteil durch Ludwig XIV (Zürich: Zwingli Verlag, 1961); Pierre Poujol, La Cévenne protestante, 5 vols. (Paris: Published by the author, 29 rue Bonaparte, 1963-67).

26. On this see the forthcoming French version of W. Hollenweger, The Pentecostals. The two periodicals of the newer charismatic movement in French-speaking Europe are Ichthus and Actes (both published in Geneva). George R. Stotts has prepared a thesis on the Assemblées de Dieu in France which also contains some material on the charismatic movement in France: "The History of the Modern Pentecostal Movement in France" (unpublished Ph.D. dissertation, Texas Tech University [Lubbock, TX 79409], 1973).

27. Louis Dallière, D'aplomb sur la parole de Dieu. Courte étude sur le réveil de Pentecôte (Valence: Imprimerie Chaprin et Reyne, 1932).

In remembrance of Jesus I will take part in the Lord's Supper whenever there is an opportunity.

I will give ten per cent of my income for the work of the Lord.

Every day I will pray for the revival of my church and for the coming of the Kingdom of God. . . . [28]

It was not expected that all participants would fulfill all the requirements. On the back of the card was written: "In order to use this card properly, one chooses at the beginning only one or two resolutions which one wants to carry out. One writes the number of the resolution and the date on the back of the card, signs and carries out this commitment faithfully."

This did not lead, as one might think, to the formation of a new sect. On the contrary ecumenical relations very soon were taken up with other Protestant churches, with Orthodox churches[29] (very rare in Pentecostal circles!), and as of late also with the Catholic churches.

The movement was called Prayer Union. In the thirties this Prayer Union invited Pentecostals like Douglas R. Scott, George Jeffreys and Donald Gee to their conferences. In the region of the Ardèche (where the Prayer Union was strongest) Pentecostalism has not created any divisions, writes Henri Schaerer.[30] This is probably exaggerated for one can find in the yearbook of the French Assemblées de Dieu some assemblies in this very region. Nevertheless they came much later and were not split away from the Prayer Union. The relation between the Prayer Union and the classical Pentecostals is described by Jean Paul Lienhard as follows: In spite of the obvious similarity of the Prayer Union to the classical Pentecostal churches (which came into being ten years later!) the Prayer Union has little contact with those

28. Henri Schaerer and René de Richemond, *Retour historique sur les origines de l'Union de Prière*. Speeches given August 24, 1969, in the Reformed Church of Charmes, p. 4 (mimeographed).

29. In his report to the Reformed Regional Synod of Tournon of November 10, 1958, L. Dallière said: "I was in complete concordance with the Greek fathers, and above all with Gregory from Nyssa, for whom the whole mystical life is inspired and undissolvably tied to the sacramental life. . ." (L. Dallière, "L'Eglise devant les réveils, en particulier les mouvements de Pentecôte, rapport du pasteur Dallière présenté au Synode régional de Tournon le 10 novembre 1958," quoted by Jean Paul Lienhard, "Un aspect de l'oecuménisme: le dialogue entre églises de multitude issues de la réforme et communautés de professants dites 'évangéliques' nées du réveil. Recherche sociologique sur quelques tentatives de rapprochement à différents niveaux entre 'oecuméniques' et 'évangéliques' dits 'conservateurs' dans la France actuelle. La quête difficile de l'unité du Protestantisme" [unpublished thesis, University of Strasbourg, 1967], p. 77).

30. Schaerer, *Retour*, p. 8.

churches and in fact with other evangelical circles.[31] Louis Dallière confirms this, writing:

> My ministry and my thinking have been certainly enriched by the Pentecostal movement. The Prayer Union is open to certain teachings of the Pentecostals. In this respect there is rapprochement. But there is no real dialogue. For these brethren I am more of a "black sheep." In their opinion I should have left the Reformed Church and joined them. Because I have not done this, I am a compromiser, an unfaithful, I am wrong.[32]

Yet the Prayer Union has built up a charismatic movement within the Reformed churches of France which is resolutely determined to serve the whole church and rejects all attempts at sectarian isolation. One does not exclude the possibility that the Prayer Union, having fulfilled its purpose, might be dissolved.[33]

The "Charta" of the Prayer Union is one of the most interesting theological documents which one can find in the Pentecostal and charismatic movement. It tries to combine a kind of non-monastic "Pentecostal religious order" with the breadth and generosity of the Reformation-based concept of faith. Here is an example:

> It is well possible that the number of the saved ones at the last judgment is greater than the number of the people who have been converted and have consecrated their lives to Christ. And the reverse is possible also: that amongst those who consider themselves to be converted there might be hypocrites who will be rejected at the last judgment. Despite these provisos we believe that the church is normally composed of "living stones," i.e. of those people who have met Jesus, who have been gripped by him (that being the reality of baptism) and who serve him with all their heart within the church (that being the meaning of the eucharist) (1 Peter 2:5).[34]

In a most instructive chapter on the Jewish people the Charta describes "the conversion of the Jewish people, prophetically foretold in the Scriptures" as "a general subject for the intercession of the Prayer Union,"[35] an insight which the authors of this document gained when studying again Romans 9—11 during the persecution of the Jews under the German occupation.[36] This has had far-reaching consequences—obviously under the influence of Karl Barth, who

---

31. Lienhard, *Un aspect*, p. 78.
32. Letter of L. Dallière to J. P. Lienhard (quoted in Lienhard, *Un aspect*, p. 78).
33. Schaerer, *Retour*, p. 17.
34. *Charte de l'Union de prière* (Charmes, ²1966, mimeographed), paragraphs 5-7.
35. Ibid., par. 25.
36. Schaerer, *Retour*, p. 12; *Charte de l'Union de prière*, par. 45.

seems to have influenced also their understanding of baptism.[37] But a mission to the Jews is radically rejected, "because the goal assigned here to prayer is not that some Jews might be converted (which has always happened), but that all that which is from God in Judaism might be integrated at once into the body of Christ."[38] "One can expect that God will raise among the Jews themselves apostles who will speak of Christ to their brothers."[39]

On the "visible unity of the body of Christ" the Charta has this to say:

> The Prayer Union prays that within the Catholic church more and more people might become faithful disciples of Christ, a fact which will overcome the tremendous difficulties between Rome and the other two branches of Christianity.[40]

The Prayer Union is not against culture and education.[41] Yet on the subject of money they are rather critical: "This idol has to be struck down in order that Christ might reign,"[42] a program which is carried out by means of generous financial giving (about which every member decides individually). The spiritual gifts which are known in the Pentecostal movement are practiced but "these experiences are in no case a condition for becoming a member of the Prayer Union. The members who do not feel called to exercise these gifts are fully free in this respect."[43]

It is clear that these French charismatic Protestants have made an original theological, ecumenical, and political[44] contribution, which combines ecumenical breadth and biblical discipline within the framework of a Pentecostal spirituality. Without exaggerating one can say that the charismatic movement in France not only came thirty years before American Neo-Pentecostalism, but it pioneered a "theology on living and thinking charismata" which in my opinion

37. Schaerer, *Retour*, p. 12.
38. *Charte*, pars. 25-29.
39. Ibid., par. 30.
40. Ibid., par. 37.
41. Ibid., par. 111, and Dallière's report to the Synod of Tournon (see note 29), quoted in Lienhard, *Un aspect*, p. 77.
42. *Charte*, par. 110.
43. Ibid., par. 104.
44. The fact that they reject a mission to the Jews means that they accept them as equal partners, and this acceptance is in itself a highly political testimony. It means of course that they were part and parcel of that company of Christians in France who risked their lives in hiding the Jews from the Germans.

has overcome some of the weaknesses of classical and Neo-Pente-costalism.[45]

Catholic Pentecostals

I want to mention only in passing the older[46] and newer[47] charismatic movement in Great Britain, the newer charismatic movement in Germany,[48] in Holland,[49] and Scandinavia,[50] and to present in this last part some aspects of the Catholic Pentecostals in Europe. Groups are known to exist in almost all the European countries. Some of the literature of the American Catholic Pentecostals has been translated into European languages, but European Catholic Pentecostals have also produced their own theological evaluation.

One of the most articulate of these charismatic Catholic theologians is the Dominican Simon Tugwell from Oxford. He has presented several meditations for the British Broadcasting Corporation, one of them containing a piece of singing in tongues by three Catholic sisters—which elicited several hundred letters of thanks to the BBC. It was prayerfully and meditatively prepared in the studio, of course to the dismay of the technicians who did not appreciate the purpose of this "waste" of valuable studio time and technical facilities "just for meditation." The actual meditation was then done extempore.

In several publications Tugwell has defended the use of speaking in tongues, which appears to him "to mean the production of genuinely linguistic phenomena, which may or may not be identified by some one present as some definite language, but which do not convey any ordinary semantic significance to the speaker himself."[51] It is not simply identical with "praying in the Spirit," nor is it simply "God's kin-

45. A similar ecumenical charismatic center is "La Porte Ouverte" (Chalon-sur-Saône).

46. Here particularly important are Alexander A. Boddy (Anglican minister) and Cecil Polhill.

47. See the many books by Michael Harper (London: Fountain Trust) and his periodical, *Renewal*.

48. See the literature in W. Hollenweger, *The Pentecostals*, particularly the writings by A. Bittlinger and E. Käsemann, and the article by Wolf-Eckart Failing, "Neue charismatische Bewegung in den Landeskirchen," *Die Pfingstkirchen: Selbstdarstellungen, Dokumente, Kommentare*, ed. W. Hollenweger (Stuttgart: Ev. Verlagswerk, 1971), pp. 131-45.

49. Here particularly important is the periodical *Vuur* and the pastoral letter by the Reformed Church, *De Kerk en de Pinkstergroepen* (Herderlijk Schrijven van de Generale Synode der Nederlandse Hervormde Kerk, 1960, [3]1961).

50. Ivar Lundgren, *Ny pingst. Rapport från nutida väckelse i gamla kyrkor* (Stockholm [?]: Den Kristna Bokringen, 1970).

51. Simon Tugwell, OP, "The Gift of Tongues in the New Testament," *Expository Times*, 84 (Feb. 1973), 137.

dergarten." "Prayer that we cannot ourselves fully understand is an essential part of Christian praying: tongues is a particularly straightforward embodiment of this principle."[52] But it is—from a phenomenological point of view—ambiguous. That applies, says Tugwell, to all pneumatic activities. He concludes that the New Testament does not put pressure on anyone to seek the gift of tongues, but it encourages those who receive it to use it to grow into fuller and richer experience of the Christian life as a whole. Thus Tugwell suggests that this gift does have a part in the wholeness of the Christian life. "This does not in any way commit us to accepting the Pentecostal understanding of it, nor to their kind of religion."[53]

And in fact, Tugwell goes on to state that "the Pentecostal doctrine is scripturally and theologically unwarrantable"[54] and is for the theologian "cause for alarm." Yet he maintains that

> Pentecostalism does represent a genuine eagerness for the original, undiluted message of the Gospel which is "not in words of persuasive wisdom, but in demonstration of Spirit and power" (1 Cor. 2:4); this too makes a legitimate demand on the theologian's interest and sympathy.[55]

He rejects the notion that the baptism of the Spirit adds anything more to Christian faith. "Anything *more* than fundamental Christianity is actually *less* than the Gospel."[56] Thus the "supernatural" can be seen within an old Catholic tradition as "being precisely the fulfillment of our nature."[57]

Tugwell uses categories of medieval mysticism in order to interpret his and his fellow Catholics' spiritual experiences. Mysticism, he says, "is not intrinsically Christian, but it can be *made* Christian."[58] He differentiates between oracles and prophecy, between idols and icons. "An idol is a god, or a manifestation of god, or an experience of god, or a doctrine of god, that one has 'made a thing of.' " Those using oracles and idols always try to get power over God, showing thereby how right they are. But "Christ is larger than his media of communication."[59] Prophecy and icon "strip us down before God, peeling

---

52. Ibid., p. 139.
53. Ibid., p. 137.
54. S. Tugwell, "Reflections on the Pentecostal Doctrine of 'Baptism in the Holy Spirit,' " *Heythrop Journal*, 13 (July 1972), 268. This and similar statements have evoked the pointed protest of Michael Harper. See his review on S. Tugwell (*Renewal*, 39 [June-July 1972], 8).
55. Tugwell, "Reflections," p. 269.
56. Ibid., p. 280.
57. S. Tugwell, *Did You Receive the Spirit?* (London: Darton, Longman, and Todd, 1972), p. 18.
58. Ibid., p. 94.
59. Ibid., p. 95.

off our masks and pretences, our false selves."[60]

Tugwell knows of course that definitions and names (also a kind of idol) are sometimes necessary for our sanity, but they never capture God adequately. Only "when we have overcome" (Rev. 2:17) shall we find our full identity, will there be full correspondence between the reality of the experience of God and its definition. That is why Tugwell sees *no phenomenological difference* between Christian and non-Christian mysticism, between oracle and prophecy, between idol and icon. The difference does not lie on the level of phenomenology, but on that of signification. From outside both these mysticisms look exactly alike. Only by its function, when it creates room for freedom, does mysticism become Christian. From this Tugwell draws the conclusion that in a charismatic community there must be freedom to speak in tongues and extempore prayer, and also freedom to abstain from such kinds of spirituality without losing one's face.

So one comes to the somewhat astonishing conclusion that to this date the Dominican Tugwell has developed the "most evangelical" understanding of charisma, i.e., an understanding which rests on the plurality and freedom of the Spirit, a thought which has been expressed by Protestant and Catholic[61] theologians alike. One of them, G. Hasenhüttl,[62] a student of Hans Küng, describes "charisma" as "the ordering principle of the church." On the basis of a very careful exegesis and with knowledge of the World Council of Churches' study *The Church for Others*, Hasenhüttl, who dedicates his book "to those who have left the church or are about to leave it," works towards a remarkable reordering of the structures of the church which, according to him, should be defined by the charism (and not, as is usually the case, the other way around)! Yet in his book he never mentions the Catholic Pentecostals although they would perhaps be prime examples for his scholarly work.

The dialogue between those who "think" the Holy Spirit and those who "hear" and "touch" the Holy Spirit in their charismatic meetings is probably still missing!

60. Ibid., p. 98.
61. Josef Sudbrack, SJ, "Streiflichter des nordamerikanischen Christentums," *Geist und Leben* 43 (Nov. 1970), 369-87. There are two important books by Hans Küng: *The Church* (London: Burns and Oates, 1968) and *Structures of the Church* (London: Burns and Oates, 1965).
62. Gotthold Hasenhüttl, *Charisma. Ordnungsprinzip der Kirche* (Basel and Vienna: Herder, 1968). See also Heribert Mühlen, *Die Erneuerung des christlichen Glaubens. Charisma-Geist-Befreiung* (Munich: Don Bosco Verlag, 1974). An exhaustive bibliography and a concise interpretation of Catholic Pentecostalism can be found in W. J. Hollenweger, *Pentecost Between Black and White. Five Case Studies on Pentecost and Politics.* (Belfast: Christian Journals Ltd., 1975).

PART TWO
Theological Viewpoints

William G. MacDonald

An ordained minister of the Assemblies of God, William G. MacDonald serves as professor of biblical and theological studies at Gordon College in Wenham, Massachusetts, on Boston's north shore. He holds degrees from Florida Southern College (B.A.), Wheaton Graduate School (M.A.), Gordon-Conwell Theological Seminary (B.D.), Concordia Seminary (S.T.M.), and Southern Baptist Theological Seminary, Louisville, Kentucky (Th.D). For over a decade, his booklet *Glossolalia in the New Testament* (Springfield, MO: Gospel Publishing House, 1964) has provided the exegetical basis for a larger theology of the Holy Spirit on which he is currently at work.

Here, Dr. MacDonald provides some sketches of an approach to a theology of the Holy Spirit from the perspective of a traditional Pentecostal.

Pentecostal Theology:
A Classical Viewpoint

4

The limits within which I conceive of my topic deserve mention at the outset. By "Pentecostal" our minds are directed biblically to the immersion of the New Testament church in the Holy Spirit on the Pentecost feast day occurring seven weeks after our Lord's resurrection. But the adjective "Pentecostal" has a twentieth-century denotation as well. It signifies that segment of the body of Christ that ardently proclaims that Pentecost is *repeatable*, that there were repetitions of Pentecost *mutatis mutandis* within the post-Pentecost biblical history itself, and that a remarkable number of believers in the twentieth century have undergone a similar experience of being clothed with the same robe of heavenly power that mantled the human spirit of Jesus as He carried out His mission in this world.

A second limitation derives from the fact that Pentecostal theology consists of *oral tradition* rather than of extensive creeds and theological tomes. Not the least of the aims of contemporary Pentecostal scholars is to reduce to writing for scholarly inspection the basic beliefs of third-generation sons of the Pentecostal revival and to bring all our theologizing under the continuous judgment of Holy Scripture.

Certainly it is no discredit to our spiritual forefathers in this century

if they confined themselves primarily to the vehicles of popular written communication (e.g., tracts, magazines and sermon books). These
were the generations of change and revival, and the literature was appropriate to the cause. Now the success of the Pentecostal revival calls
for consolidation and advance, for continuous searching of the Scripture, careful scholarship, competent sifting of the oral tradition, and
comparative study with other Christian traditions.

Traditionally Pentecostals have feared the word "tradition,"
although it is a good biblical word.[1] Ostracized from their denominational homes, they were often denominated as radicals, because they
had departed from their respective traditions. Since in their eyes the
traditions of men thwarted the free movement of God's Holy Spirit,
they determined not to let tradition gain the ascendancy and cir-
cumscribe divine activity in their lives and churches. This was commendable as an ideal. But the belief that a movement can endure
without the evolution of a tradition is humanly naive, as F. F. Bruce
has hammered down so cogently in a recent work:

> One does from time to time meet churches or individual Christians
> who profess a pure biblicism and deny that they have any tradition
> or traditions apart from what is written. But a pure biblicism is rare-
> ly so pure as it is thought to be. Let these friends be confronted with
> an interpretation of Scripture which is new to them, held (it may be)
> by others but unknown in their own circle, and they will suddenly
> realize that what they had always taken to be the plain sense of
> Scripture is really their traditional interpretation.[2]

Rare is the person who can look through an old family picture
album without some irreverent laughter. So, too, do we remember the
anti-tradition statement of one Pentecostal body in their formative
council affirming that they would not codify their beliefs into creeds.
So what did they do? Two years later under the pressure of theological
faction they spelled out what they considered to be the essentials of
their doctrine.[3] Very quickly did tradition develop—and inevitably
so. Without tradition there can be no theology. Theology, then, is
tradition, although it be a tradition with biblical underpinnings
throughout.

Where, then, is Pentecostal theology to be found? The confessions

---

1. " . . . Hold to the traditions *[paradōseis]* which you were taught by us, either by
word of mouth or by letter" (2 Thess. 2:15).

2. *Tradition Old and New* (Grand Rapids: Zondervan, 1970), p. 20.

3. William W. Menzies, *Anointed to Serve: The Story of the Assemblies of God* (Springfield, MO: Gospel Publishing House, 1971), p. 118.

of faith of the Pentecostal denominations afford outlines, but the more substantive matters by and large must be traced to the oral traditions that implement them. At the same time it must be acknowledged that Pentecostals have always rested the authority of their doctrines with the Holy Spirit and not with their own ability to theologize and establish tradition. With our classical prototype, Tertullian, we are quick to confess: " . . . we . . . are followers of the Paraclete, not of human teachers."[4]

My remarks have already taken us to the third key word in my topic: "classical" is subject to the same kind of ambiguity noted in the use of the word "Pentecostal." As used here it has reference not to the biblical period of the New Testament nor to the century thereafter, but rather to the twentieth century from its beginning up to the sixties when the transdenominational character of Pentecostal experience became widespread. My task is to expose the contribution of the classical Pentecostal theology as it has fed the Neo-Pentecostal theology indirectly and as it continues on its own course in the seventies.

Linguistically, the alternative to "Neo-Pentecostal" would be "Paleo-Pentecostal." Apart from the pleasing alliteration of the p's, however, little can be said in advocacy of the term, for it connotes a notion that whatever it describes ought to be encased in a museum somewhere. "Classical," therefore, if understood as meaning "old-line," "standard," will serve our purpose as a compatible designator. One of the questions that we will keep simmering on the back burner is this: Are the differences between the old and new sufficient to warrant the ascription of separate designations, whether they be "classical," "neo-" or what have you?

Now let us inquire again as to the source of classical Pentecostal theology. When we contend that it is found primarily in the oral tradition, this does not mean that there are not any written sources of value for the earnest inquirer. But it does point up the fact that predominantly, in both past and present, Pentecostal theology has had the character of a "witness" experience. This witness tends to have at its deepest level an oral-aural rather than an optic-literary transmission. It is well suited for preaching, testifying, and one-to-one contacts. That the one addressed is "there" and in some sense accountable to God is the dynamic of the "witness." The witness-event, then, transmits itself via a divine ark from one believer to another. It works

---

4. "Against Praxeas," 13, *The Ante-Nicene Fathers*, ed. A. Roberts and J. Donaldson (Grand Rapids: Eerdmans, 1951), III, 608.

on the not unbiblical principle that belief in a person's integrity justifies belief in his witness, especially if that witness is a testimony of what God has done for him and is willing to do for anyone. Purity of doctrine is preserved by checking to see that the new witness has experienced all that was experienced by the first witness and that both conform to the primary "witness," the Holy Scriptures.

Finally, the limitation implied in my title by the word "Viewpoint" must be recognized. I write—should I rather say, "speak"?—as a classical Pentecostal by experience and conviction, but without the onus of speaking officially for any ecclesiastical body. My attempt to delineate and assess classical Pentecostal theology must therefore be regarded as partaking of the same "witness" character of which I have spoken, and invites the critical scrutiny of those who hear the oral tradition differently from my analysis.

Experience-certified Theology

One of the chief contributions that Pentecostal theology has to make to the church at large stems from its championing of a dynamic experience of God. Belief in the availability of God's preternatural power and presence is foundational. It means a theology of a God-near-at-hand, who gives abundant evidence of His powerful presence in the church. This theology concerns itself with a deep and on-going experience in God.

"Full gospel" has been one of the catchwords of classical Pentecostal theology. This ready-made sermon outline for conventions, camp meetings, and large gatherings has been what well may be called *the* characteristic Pentecostal sermon. In this "full gospel" four facets of Christ's ascended activity are featured, viz., (1) Christ, the Savior; (2) Christ, the Healer; (3) Christ, the Spirit-baptizer; (4) Christ, the coming King.

Such an understanding is not the full gospel of the New Testament, contends J. M. Davies, a polemist against Pentecostal teaching. His full gospel is "the death, resurrection, ascension and reign of Christ."[5] Now both schemes are fourfold and Christ-centered, but the difference lies in the apprehension of the extent of the work of Christ in terms of what He is now prepared to do in our lives as a continuing work. Of course, there is no gospel until the *kerygma* proclaims the *pro me* character of the objective events in Jesus' mission. Pentecostal theology builds upon the kerygmatic data, emphasizing in the oral

5. *Pentecost and Today: Tongues and Healing* (Kansas City, KS: Walterick, n.d.), p. 51.

tradition that Jesus Christ, our Lord, may be *experienced* as Savior, Healer, Spirit-filler, and proleptically in some sense as the imminently arriving King. "Full gospel," then, means the full experiencing of all the possible ways in which Christ can minister to us on the basis of His earthly mission and heavenly session.

The objective gospel must be clarified subjectively as a package of God's provisions "for us." What happened to Jesus in His mediatorial activities forms the objective basis of the gospel, but one does not really hear the gospel as "good news" until the results of His objective acts are certified to us as to their meaning for us. This good news as subjective gospel explains to us that the purpose of His passion-glorification is to regenerate us, heal us, fill us with holy love and Spirit, and finally to return for us to share His glory. It is not a question of either/or, objective gospel or subjective gospel, for all evangelicals would agree that there is a subjective dimension in the gospel.

The real question remains as to how much Christ is willing to do for us, or to put it subjectively again, "How much can one expect to experience of the reality of Christ?" Do we content ourselves to believe that justification of the sinner through Christ exhausts the provision of God? On the contrary, the Pentecostal has been quick to ask with Elisha for the "double portion," in short, for the full reception and experiencing of all that the mediatorial work of Jesus has made possible for us to receive. He readily acknowledges that healing of the spirit by the grace of God is primary; yet if Jesus is willing to heal bodies today also, he, too, desires to be healed in the whole man.

The "full gospel" epigraph is even more applicable in conserving the idea of a *full* experiencing of the Spirit in contrast to an initial work of the Spirit in one's life. Moreover, the constant anticipation of the *parousia* with all its concrete fulfillment of one's faith and hope tends to heighten all present experience of God with the eschatological overtones of a future breaking forth in the present. The full gospel, therefore, has been both present- and future-oriented, and on the whole has favored the dispensational vision of the future. Now when one reduces the fourfoldness of the full gospel to a one-dimensional verity, he finds that the biblical epigram in Hebrews 13:8 has said it best: "Jesus Christ is the same yesterday and today and for ever."

Full gospel means "fully experienced gospel," and the content of those experiences is Jesus Himself in His multi-dimensions. This conserving of the value of experience does not deny that Pentecostal theology is a theology of the Word. We do not begin with Schleiermacher's man of religious feelings. Nor do we begin with philosophical man's ideas about God. We begin and end with Jesus our Lord as certified to us in the divinely breathed *graphé*. The written Word has both shown us the way and also stood as the absolute criterion for testing all our professed experiences of God. Francis A. Schaeffer, a leading evangelical apologist today, has lauded the "old Pentecostals" for their building upon biblical content as one of their "strong, positive" features and as being "a dynamic source of evangelism."[6]

Classical Pentecostals insist that it is not enough for truths—even biblical truths—to be precipitated in the mind and viewed philosophically. There must be submission to the truth in faith and reverential adoration in worship. This is worship of truth that is not merely imprisoned *in* the mind but is personified transcendently *over* the mind in the glorious person of Christ. And when this kind of worship touches Christ, we have "experience." It is decidedly an experience of Christ as subject and not just object that constitutes genuine "experience" as we are using the term here.

Does this holy experience result in an experience-centered theology? Hardly. The better way to label it is this: Christ-centered, experience-certified theology. Please note that we do not equate theology as used here with "the truth." Christ Himself is the truth. To know the truth is to experience Christ, and the greater the experience the greater the knowledge (Phil. 3:10-15). Theology will always be words about God and His relations to man and must never become the terminal point of a believer's knowledge. We believe in good Hebrew fashion that there is no dichotomy between knowledge and experience in biblical revelation, that to "know" God for a believer means to have direct contact with Him as Spirit meets spirit.

One can hardly conclude a discussion of the important place of experience in classical Pentecostalism without alluding to the possibility of overemphasis on experience in the form of emotionalism. By emotionalism I do not mean the experiencing of strong emotions. Jesus' experience in this world contained "prayers and supplications, with loud cries and tears" (Heb. 5:7). When Pentecostals are faulted for their being emotional, Jesus, by implication, is being condemned, too. But the real test of whether we have emotionalism is not the degree or intensity of emotions as measured by a psychometer. Rather emotionalism consists of the seeking and stimulation of emotions as ends in themselves, and not as the by-products of real experience in truth

6. *The New Super-Spirituality* (Downers Grove, IL: Inter-Varsity, 1972), p. 15.

and in God. Emotionalism in this pejorative sense is of the flesh, and
we do not claim that there have not been those among us who were
culpable of mistaking effects for causes in this manner. However, we
would assert unequivocally that any genuine experience with the living God will leave an emotional wake in a man's psyche. This is not
emotionalism but man's being humanized again by the liberating
Spirit of God.

The Distinctive Pentecostal Experience

From this point forward our consideration will pivot on one aspect
of the fourfold classical Pentecostal understanding of the gospel.
When one speaks of "*the* Pentecostal experience," it is not usually
necessary to designate that he means the experience of being filled by
the Lord with the Spirit to the point that the Spirit can articulate
through him in another language—unlearned—the praise and glory of
God. This is not the place to trace the full defense of the Pentecostal
dogma that the initial indication of one's having been filled with the
Spirit is invariably speaking in other languages under the Spirit's control. Such a doctrine is abstracted from the biblical precedents in the
inspired history of the early church. That is, whenever it was Luke's
purpose to tell in his narrative what happened when believers were
filled with the Holy Spirit, the constant factor in the varied situations
was the Spirit's speaking through them in languages other than their
own.

On this score we constantly infuriate our evangelical brothers by
our *ex post facto* approach. They contend that we dogmatize as
follows: "Everyone must speak in tongues in order to receive the
fullness of the Spirit." And we merrily agree with them that such a
precept is not to be found in the New Testament! However—and there
was hardly ever a "however" with greater amplitude—we assert
forthrightly on the basis of biblical precedents and our own experiences, that all believers *in fact do speak in tongues subsequent* to
their being submerged completely in the Spirit. This they do, and their
glossolalia is *evidence* of what has taken place in them, not the
epitome or embodiment of the experience itself.

It is much easier to demarcate the glossolalic evidence than to ex-
patiate on the experience itself. For what one experiences is the work
of Jesus as He fills one with Himself, not corporeally in His resurrected body of flesh and bones, but in and with His Holy Spirit whom
He and the Father have jointly sent. There is no meaningful experience of glossolalia without this intense overshadowing of the
human spirit by Jesus in His glory. Pragmatically, one might say that

tongues are necessary as a consequent of this experience in order to radiate and release the praise pent up in one's heart for the Lord lest the human spirit disintegrate in the blaze of His glorious presence.

Even as I present this I can hear chairs, as it were, scraping across the floor as some straight people will move back from such a declaration of mystical experience. But did not the great Baptist say of Jesus: "He shall immerse you in the Holy Spirit"? How can we conceive of that act in any way less than mystical experience? Let us sanctify the language of sarcasm with love and say very humbly, "Either you know what I am talking about [by experience] or you do not. If you do not, you would not know if I told you."

Now quite succinctly I would like to list what classical Pentecostals teach relative to the *effects* of a filling with Christ's Spirit as distinguished from the *evidence* of the Spirit's full control of the psyche in glossolalia. The first four are internal and the last two are external in terms of visible results. They are:

1. Pre-eminently, there is the effect of a heightened sense of the reality of Jesus in and over one's life.

2. One's spiritual sensitivity is revitalized so as to facilitate the whole process of being constantly led by the Spirit.

3. The written Word of God glows within one's heart with a new intensity of illumination as the Teacher opens it to us.

4. Prayer may now be made "in the Spirit" as well as in the ordinary manner. This new edifying manner is not limited by the constrictions of the believer's knowledge and oral competence.

5. The whole process of sanctification is intensified in one's life in the world. It is neither initiated nor consummated by the experience, but is reinforced by it. Even those classical Pentecostal brethren who teach sanctification as a prerequisite to Pentecostal filling do not deny the intensifying character of this experience on the one so filled.

6. Finally, one so clothed by the Lord in the power of the Holy Spirit is enabled to give a dynamic testimony in the world to the central truth of Christianity, namely, that Jesus is alive and is drawing all men to Himself.

Gifts as Signs of the Lord in the Church

As glorious as is the outpouring of the Spirit in fullness for the individual, the very success of that experience creates the potential for the even greater experience of corporate worship "in the Spirit." The deep, deep love of Jesus unifies worshipers as nothing else can. And nothing is more precious in the Pentecostal heritage than the ability of Spirit-filled worshipers to recognize, celebrate, and respond to "the Lord in the midst" of His gathered worshiping church.

According to the oral tradition, the problem in the non-Pentecostal churches is "formalism." Yet this word does not adequately express the difficulty. For Pentecostals are not against structure per se; in fact, they recognize that the first work attributed to the Spirit in Genesis is that of bringing order to the creation as it came into being. The real difficulty lying behind the charge of formalism is the question whether the Lord in the midst of His people will be accorded His proper "form"—that is, as the object of adoration and head of His church.

Here it would seem that we are leaving theology for liturgics. Not at all. For in Pentecostal thinking theology that is not practical is valueless, and right theology is believed to culminate always in worship.

Nowhere is the priesthood of all believers celebrated more gloriously than in our corporate worship. Never would a Pentecostal pastor turn his back on the people and bow in prayer to a God "behind the curtain" in Old Testament fashion. Instead he faces the group of assembled believers, because the Lord is not outside but stationed among the saints. There are those times when the leader of worship will stand in God's presence, and times when he too will sit when the people are sitting. In these seemingly leaderless moments, there is always leadership by the One whose divine presence is being recognized.

How do we account for this priestly character of the congregation? Surely all Christians, no matter what their denomination, are priests by virtue of their regeneration. But it is peculiarly the gifts distributed by the Lord, who moves about where He is accorded the freedom, that enable the church to minister in the "holy place." These spiritual gifts facilitate an awareness of the Lord's presence. They are by definition "manifestations of the Spirit" (1 Cor. 12:7)—in which "Spirit" is construed to be an objective genitive. They glorify God's wisdom and knowledge, His faithfulness and power, His holiness and healing hand upon men, and His revelations as the communicative God. Moreover, there is one gift peculiarly suited to preserve this direct lordship of Christ over His people. If another spirit, whether it be carnal or diabolical, seizes the freedom of the meeting for manifesting itself, it is recognized and halted through "the ability to distinguish between spirits" (1 Cor. 12:10).

Where the gifts of the Spirit are bestowed the Lord is recognized in the midst; and conversely the more the Lord's presence is valued and given place, the more He will manifest Himself (in accordance with His Word in John 14:21). For in the final analysis a gift of the Spirit is supremely a revelation of God, and only secondarily do the gifts reveal states and conditions of men. Their edifying property derives from their pointing, like the hand of John the Baptist, to the Lord among His people.

The Frontiers of Classical Pentecostal Theology

It would be a mistake to assume that in the last seven decades Pentecostal theology has been developed to its limits. On the contrary only certain basics have taken theological form. Foremost among these stands the doctrine that the filling with the Spirit is invariably accompanied by speaking in other languages under the Spirit's control. Though two influential European Pentecostal pioneers, T. B. Barratt and George Jeffreys, did not hold to this tenet, it has maintained a general preponderance of acceptance over the years by classical Pentecostals, and it appears to be no less entrenched in Neo-Pentecostal theology.[7] This central belief remains open for further clarification and certification as does any doctrine. When in this section we speak of "frontiers," therefore, it is to direct our attention to areas not articulated in the firm tradition, to areas where there is a measure of confusion among the strands of the tradition, or to areas where theology and experience are at odds.

My plan will be to state the problems as I see them in order of their priority. No attempt at comprehensiveness is envisioned here. Only hints at answers can be sketched, but it is hoped that Pentecostal scholarship will provide answers with deep footings under them in the years that lie ahead.

Problem one. "When does one receive the Holy Spirit?" Are we to equate the receiving of the Spirit with such expressions as "baptized in the Holy Spirit," "filled with the Spirit," being "clothed with the Spirit" and similar terms? One might arrive at such a conclusion

---

7. Don W. Basham, *A Handbook on Holy Spirit Baptism* (Monroeville, PA: Whitaker Books, 1969), pp. 62-68; Dennis and Rita Bennett, *The Holy Spirit and You* (Plainfield, NJ: Logos International, 1971), p. 64f.; Larry Christenson, *Speaking in Tongues* (Minneapolis: Bethany Fellowship, 1968), p. 54; Howard M. Ervin, *"These Are Not Drunken, As Ye Suppose"* (Plainfield, NJ: Logos International, 1968), p. 54; Jerry Jensen, *Baptists [Lutherans, Methodists, Presbyterians] and the Baptism of the Holy Spirit* (Los Angeles: Full Gospel Businessmen's Fellowship International, 1963), p. 5 (in each of the four books).

from a superficial reading of Acts 2:38 and Acts 8:15, 17, 19; 19:2.
One aberrant strand of the tradition has it this way: In regeneration
we receive Christ; in the baptism in the Spirit we receive the Spirit.
But believing as we do in the ascension of Jesus, we must confess that
it is the Spirit of Christ that we actually receive at regeneration as
Romans 8:9 indicates. Indeed, no man can be a Christian without
having received the Holy Spirit. Jesus taught in John 14 that one cannot have Him come without also receiving the Father and the Spirit.
The ancient trinitarian formula says it best: *opera trinitatis ad extra
indivisa sunt*. Romans 8, for instance, equates being "in Christ" (vv.
1, 2) with being "in the Spirit" (v. 9), and Christ's being "in you" (v.
10) with the Spirit's being "in you" (vv. 9, 11).

In the scant theological literature produced by classical
Pentecostalism one can find a declaration such as this: "All believers
have the Holy Spirit."[8] This statement is all the more remarkable
because in practice it is so little recognized and integrated with a total
theological view. All too often the oral tradition seems to forget this
basic doctrine and implies that one has not "received" the Spirit
unless he has received the filling with the Spirit evidenced by
glossolalia. This ambiguity concerning what is received and when is
not peculiar to Pentecostal theology in the twentieth century,
however. In the post-apostolic era the fathers of the church likewise
"were greatly confused about the manner in which Christians received the Spirit," according to patristic scholar J. N. D. Kelly.[9]
Non-Pentecostal churches that practice infant baptism are faced with
the same difficulty in deciding between baptism and confirmation as
the event in which the Spirit is received.

The whole church—Protestant, Pentecostal, Catholic, Orthodox—
needs to make a fresh inspection of the climax of John's Gospel. The
pericope, John 20:19-23, depicts a post-resurrection meeting of Jesus
with a group of His followers. This is not the place for me to exegete
the passage, but let us focus momentarily on the heart of it as Jesus ex-
claimed following, or simultaneous with, a symbolic bestowal of His
breath: *labete pneuma hagion*—"Receive [the] Holy Spirit" (John
20:22).

In Bruce Metzger's sizeable *Index to Periodical Literature on Christ
and the Gospels* only one article is to be found dealing with John

---

8. Ralph M. Riggs, *The Spirit Himself* (Springfield, MO: Gospel Publishing House,
1949), p. 44; cf. Myer Pearlman, *Knowing the Doctrines of the Bible* (Springfield, MO:
Gospel Publishing House, 1937), p. 307: "One of the most comprehensive definitions of
a Christian is that he is a man in whom the Holy Spirit dwells."
9. *Early Christian Doctrines* (New York: Harper and Row, [2]1970), p. 340.

20:22,[10] and the author of that article treats the whole passage as a "popular legend" not traceable to "apostolic reminiscence."[11] This write-off of the passage is wholly gratuitous, and equally speculative is the literary criticism that dubs the pericope "the Johannine Pentecost"[12] with the intent of discrediting it in favor of Luke's account of the outpouring of the Spirit in power from heaven. Since John's Gospel closes with no mention of the ascension other than Jesus' statement that it had not yet transpired (John 20:17),[13] it makes no literary sense to foist the Pentecost "form" on that which is certainly an Easter event.

If one looks critically at the climax of Luke's Gospel, he will find that it is the resurrection appearance of Jesus to the larger group of disciples (Luke 24:33-49)—after having "opened" the Scriptures to two of them in a seven-mile Bible study—that is the literary and theological high point of the Gospel. Central in that pericope are these words that speak of an act Jesus performed *in the minds* of the disciples: "Then he opened their minds to understand the scriptures" (Luke 24:45). His resurrected presence resulted in their spiritual illumination as the light of the gospel flooded them with truth. This illumination took place especially in their inner being as Christ touched their minds, and commissioned them as witnesses (Luke 24:48). This Lucan pericope meant for a Greek-thinking constituency harmonizes beautifully with the Johannine parallel (John 20:19-23) that specifies in Hebrew idiom the actual divine inbreathing of the Spirit (cf. Gen. 2:7) that changed precisely the mind of these people and nothing else.

Thus we can say that the third and fourth Gospels reveal to us the *birth* of the church as the result of Jesus' resurrection, and that Acts recounts for us the *baptism* of the church in power and glory as the result of Jesus' ascension. Here is a model for Pentecostal theology; it is the same kind of model as is found in our Lord's *advent* by the Spirit in Mary's womb (Luke 1:35) and His *anointing* by the Spirit in the world (Luke 3:22; Acts 10:38).

Problem two. "What is the nature of modern glossolalia? This

10. Frank W. Beare, "The Risen Christ Bestows the Spirit," *Canadian Journal of Theology*, 4 (1958), 95-100, cited on page 367 in Bruce Metzger, *Index to Periodical Literature on Christ and the Gospels* (Leiden: Brill, 1966).

11. Beare, "The Risen Christ," p. 100.

12. James D. G. Dunn, *Baptism in the Holy Spirit*, Studies in Biblical Theology, Series 2, 15 (Naperville, IL: Allenson, 1970), pp. 173-82.

13. Note how Dunn, *Baptism in the Holy Spirit*, p. 174, postulates with a number of European interpreters a secret ascension between John 20:17 and 19, but then later in his discussion backs off from this view as "not entirely satisfactory" (p. 176).

question seldom seems to pose a problem for Pentecostals in terms of their own experience.[14] But it does constitute a problem for Pentecostal theology, since the nature of such speech provokes skeptical curiosity in non-Pentecostals generally. Within the oral tradition there is no fixed answer.

Humanists and Jungians interpret the phenomenon as the antics of the human spirit and/or of a "collective unconsciousness" of the human race. They see the speaking as sort of an oral dream, only in this instance sounds rather than sights are being brought together out of the human psyche in fresh combinations.

To date, the linguists who have analyzed glossolalia have not accorded what they have heard the dignity of status with any modern languages they know.[15] And remarkable as it may seem, there are many classical Pentecostals who would not quarrel with the view that there is a "tongue" that has none of the components of language. Basing their supposition on the italicized word, "unknown," supplied in the sacrosanct antique version of A.D. 1611, they take it as being descriptive of the essence of the "tongue" rather than being descriptive of the relation of the mind of the speaker to the content of his speaking. Yet one cannot overlook the fact that such an answer is likely to be equivocal, for as soon as it is given, one may hear a qualifier that even though the glossolalia has no language character, God somehow understands it. Suddenly it has become "language" again, albeit by the miracle of God's omniscience.

The alternative to understanding glossolalia in the "ecstatic" sense is the etymological sense of "speaking a language."[16] The rationale for the latter is sufficiently simple to sketch. It is the Holy Spirit and not the human spirit that furnishes the materials of the holy speech. Since He is a God of order and infinite intelligence, the content of the speech He inspires cannot but be meaningful and ordered. From that small percentage of modern instances of glossolalia in which the speaker is understood as speaking in a language known by an

14. *The Glossolalia Phenomenon*, ed. Wade H. Horton (Cleveland, TN: Pathway, 1966), in some 300 pages written by men with an aggregate of approximately 300 years of the Pentecostal experience, never inquires into the linguistic nature of the glossolalia manifested in the authors.

15. Letter of August 31, 1959, from Eugene A. Nida to Robert F. De Haan *et al* (copy in my possession), and William Samarin, *Tongues of Men and Angels* (New York: Macmillan, 1972).

16. William G. MacDonald, "Glossolalia in the New Testament," *Bulletin of the Evangelical Theological Society*, 7 (1964), 67; Robert H. Gundry, " 'Ecstatic Utterance' (NEB)?" *Journal of Theological Studies*, ns 17 (1966), 299-307.

auditor,[17] one can extrapolate to the strong probability that all glossolalia bears the character of language.

Problem three. This next problem is very much an intramural one: "Does speaking in other tongues bear the character of a 'message' to men?" The major portion of the tradition would answer affirmatively on the basis of 1 Corinthians 14:5, which equates tongues and the interpretation thereof with prophecy. But another look at the passage might reveal that the equivalency is in *power to edify* and not in content as a message to man. In fact, no word meaning "message" is ever found in conjunction with glossolalia.[18]

One strand of the classical tradition views glossolalia as fundamentally a speaking by man *to* God[19] —and not *for* God as in prophecy. This means that all glossolalia would have the character of "praise" or "prayer," a concept in complete harmony with Acts and Corinthians.[20] Though I am at pains to document it, I think it can be shown that this idea of speaking "in the Spirit" *to* God underlies much of current Neo-Pentecostal thinking as well.

Let us take a case in point at a Pentecostal meeting. If one speaks in tongues and his utterance is properly interpreted (as defined here), it will be regarded as a praise of God's mighty works or a prayer to God. All will receive some edification for having heard this interpretation of the speaker's otherwise ineffable communion with God. They will be edified to the same degree they would have, had they heard him pray publicly in the common language or offer praise to God in spiritual testimony in the common language.

Suppose no interpreter is present—and Paul considered interpretation a rare gift by comparison (1 Cor. 14:13, 28). Suppose further someone else seizes upon the freedom in the service to prophesy. The "prophecy" is then looked on by the congregation as the "interpretation" of the tongue uttered, especially if the local tradition is heavy on

17. Ervin, *These Are Not Drunken*, p. 127; Horton, *The Glossolalia Phenomenon*, pp. 151f., 210-12; Ivor Rosser, *Charismata Grace Gifts* (Monmouthshire, South Wales: Published by the author, ca. 1936), pp. 105f.; articles in *The Pentecostal Evangel:* January 26, 1958, p. 5; August 9, 1959, p. 32; February 12, 1961, p. 28; January 21, 1962, p. 19; *Voice* (Full Gospel Businessmen's Fellowship International), Jan.-Feb. 1970, p. 12; Ralph W. Harris, *Spoken by the Spirit. Documented Accounts of "Other Tongues" from Arabic to Zulu* (Springfield, MO: Gospel Publishing House, 1973), pp. 5-127. These recorded instances only represent the top of the iceberg when one considers the *testimonia* at large.

18. As, for instance, the ordinary term for "message," *angelia*, in 1 John 1:5; 3:11.

19. W. I. Evans, *This River Must Flow* (Springfield, MO: Gospel Publishing House, 1954), p. 37.

20. Cf. Acts 2:11; 10:46; 1 Cor. 14:2, 4, 15, 16, 17.

"messages" in tongues. Now whereas the true interpretation of glossolalia as prayer or praise tends not to be sensational in itself, when young Christians hear the strange speech of glossolalia followed by a supposed interpretation that begins, "Hear, O my people, I say to you . . . ," it becomes quite sensational, and glossolalia is heightened to a place of public glamour it was not meant to have. It is thought of as *God's special speaking* in a manner superior to His speaking in prophecy.

It is proper, then, we would assert, for a man to speak by the Spirit of God in him to God transcendent in a language he (the man) does not understand; but it is improper—in terms of God's considerations for man—for God to deliver His messages to man in a language other than the man's own customary language. Once, God threatened to do this as a judgment on the backslidden nation that would not listen to what He was saying to them through the prophets in their own tongue (Isa. 28:11). When their Assyrian captors arrived jabbering in a tongue alien to them, they knew it was God's strange way of speaking to them in judgment.

My purpose here has been to reopen the question as to the *directional* nature of glossolalia—to God as worship, or to man as a message—and to elicit a biblical answer, for the tradition must always be open to the biblical correctives.

Problems four and five. "What shall we do for the 'chronic seeker' for spiritual fullness?" Does the Neo-Pentecostal answer drawn from a discarded strand of the older Pentecostal tradition[21] meet all the needs?

Akin to the problem of the chronic seeker is the fifth and final problem we shall broach here. It is what the tradition speaks of as a "shallow baptism." The recipient has no freedom in the Spirit and none of the glorious aftereffects of such an experience as cited earlier in this paper. He no longer seeks to be filled or shows any evidence of being "full." He may in all likelihood have been seeking tongues instead of the Lord. By almost any assessment the "shallow baptism" seems to be a euphemism for a pseudo-baptism.

Conclusion

We search for answers in the persuasion that those who seek shall also find. The problems we have are the spin-off of dynamic forward

21. Harold Horton, *Receiving Without Tarrying* (Bournemouth West, England: Published by the author, n.d.), pp. 1-14; J. E. Stiles, *The Gifts of the Holy Spirit* (Burbank, CA: Published by the author's wife, ca. 1951), pp. 94-121.

momentum. The big question the Pentecostal movement raises is that of the depth of the experience of Christ.

In the New Testament period the Pentecostal outpouring was upon *all* the church. Now today there is a fresh rain of the Spirit on believers in virtually all denominations. If this sprinkling should become a downpour, the classical Pentecostal denominations will have served their catalytic *raison d'être*.

The Pentecostal "movement" creates impetus in two directions. It moves the church centripetally closer to Jesus at its center, and coordinately it moves the church out centrifugally into the world in evangelism. The motive for these movements is the love of Jesus, and their *modus operandi* is the power of His Holy Spirit.

J. Rodman Williams

J. Rodman Williams is president of Melodyland School of Theology in Anaheim, California. He is a graduate of Davidson College (B.A.) and holds two theological degrees (B.D. and Th.M.) from Union Theological Seminary (Virginia). His Ph.D. in philosophy of religion was granted by Columbia University and Union Theological Seminary (New York).

After more than a decade as a member of the faculty of Austin Presbyterian Theological Seminary, Austin, Texas, Dr. Williams came to Melodyland Christian Center. There he set up an experimental school serving both undergraduate and graduate students in an academic setting committed to both charismatic and ecumenical principles in the evangelical tradition. Widely active as a leading charismatic theologian, Dr. Williams serves on the Faith and Order Commission of the World Council of Churches. He is a core member of the Catholic-Pentecostal International Dialogue.

In this mature and suggestive essay, Dr. Williams seeks to draw together features of the evangelical, sacramental, and Pentecostal traditions in such a way as to advance toward a new theology of Pentecostal reality. In this respect, his earlier work in *The Era of the Spirit* (Plainfield, NJ: Logos, 1971) and *The Pentecostal Reality* (Plainfield, NJ: Logos, 1972) may be consulted.

Pentecostal Theology: A Neo-Pentecostal Viewpoint

5

In this paper I propose to deal with only one aspect of Pentecostal theology, namely, the customary view of "baptism in (or with) the Holy Spirit." I am not here concerned to deal with the "initial evidence" of this baptism, but to discuss the Pentecostal schema of the place of Spirit-baptism in the Christian life. While noting what I deem to be Pentecostalism's positive contribution, I should like to make certain criticisms and suggest a way of possible advance.

Pentecostal Perspectives

Pentecostalism has traditionally understood baptism in the Holy Spirit as distinct from and subsequent to conversion. In the early Pentecostal movement stress was often laid on baptism in the Holy Spirit as a third separate work of God's grace. According to the very first issue of *The Apostolic Faith*, published in 1906, the first work is *justification*, "by which we receive remission of sins"; the second is *sanctification*, "by which He makes us holy"; the third is "the Baptism with the Holy Ghost [which] is a gift of power upon the sanctified life."[1] Later Pentecostal teaching, however, has tended to minimize, or even disregard, the work of sanctification as a prerequisite to Spirit-baptism. For example, the Assemblies of God officially says: "All believers are entitled to and should ardently expect and earnestly seek the promise of the Father, the baptism in the Holy Ghost and fire. . . . This experience is distinct from and subsequent to the experience of the new birth. . . ."[2] One Neo-Pentecostal writes: "The baptism in the Holy Spirit is a second encounter with God (the first is conversion) in which the Christian begins to receive the supernatural power of the Holy Spirit into his life."[3] Thus baptism in the Holy Spirit is viewed as something that occurs to those who are already Christians: it is the additional gift of power.

Pentecostals therefore go beyond many other evangelicals, who likewise stress conversion, by adding a subsequent experience of Spirit-baptism. Evangelicals frequently identify conversion with Spirit-baptism; accordingly, to be baptized in the Spirit signifies that operation wherein a person is united to Christ through the Holy Spirit. Until this work of the Spirit occurs there is no salvation, and any so-called Christianity is nominal or formal at best. Pentecostals, on the other hand, while affirming the evangelical emphasis upon the necessity of conversion, do not identify this experience with baptism in the Spirit. Spirit-baptism is an additional work of grace and serves a purpose other than that of relating a person to Jesus Christ.

Evangelical Perspectives

Thus we move into the critical area of tension between evangelical and Pentecostal theology. From the evangelical perspective all Christians—of course, those truly converted—are therein baptized with the Holy Spirit. There is no place, or need, for an additional work of Spirit-baptism. In the traditional Pentecostal view the Christian may have been baptized in the Spirit, even simultaneously with his conversion, but, on the other hand, this Spirit-baptism may not yet have happened. It is an additional work beyond that of a new life in relation to Jesus Christ, and one that many Christians may not yet

---

1. Quoted in Nils Bloch-Hoell, *The Pentecostal Movement, Its Origin, Development, and Distinctive Character* (Oslo: Universitetsforlaget; London: Allen and Unwin, 1964), p. 45.

2. Point seven of the "Statement of Fundamental Truths," *Minutes of the Thirty-fifth General Council of the Assemblies of God* (Miami Beach, Florida, August 16-21, 1973), p. 120.

3. Don W. Basham, *A Handbook on Holy Spirit Baptism* (Monroeville, PA: Whitaker Books, 1969), p. 10.

have experienced. Hence generally in evangelical thought all Christians are Spirit-baptized; in traditional Pentecostal thought there are both Christians *and* Spirit-baptized Christians.

Now this Pentecostal viewpoint often comes as a shock when the evangelical first encounters it. The evangelical may already have found himself at odds with so-called "nominal" Christianity, and insists that—regardless of church membership, water-baptism, and the like—a person to be a true Christian must be born again. Thus the evangelical sees the existing church as composed of both the unregenerate and the regenerate, the outwardly Christian and the truly Christian. But there is no room in his thinking for two categories of Christians. Accordingly, the Pentecostal position on Spirit-baptism often rouses the antagonism of the evangelical.

Sacramental Perspectives

If we turn from the evangelical viewpoint to what may be termed the "sacramental" there is another kind of difference. In the sacramental tradition there is little or no emphasis on such crisis categories as "conversion" or "baptism with the Holy Spirit." Rather it is assumed that through the proper sacramental action there is conversion-regeneration and the gift (or baptism) of the Holy Spirit. This sacramental action may be twofold: baptism and confirmation (or chrismation). Through this double action regeneration and the gift of the Holy Spirit are understood to be conveyed. Or the sacramental action may be single—baptism alone—wherein all that God gives in terms of salvation (whether or not differentiated into regeneration and the gift of the Spirit) is thought to be bestowed. Thus the baptized, or baptized/confirmed, person is fully initiated; he needs look no further for some special experience—an event of new birth and/or baptism in the Holy Spirit.

From what has just been noted, the sacramentalist may see Spirit-baptism either as occurring in and with water-baptism, or as taking place at the moment of the second rite (confirmation/chrismation). But in either case this is a far remove from the traditional understanding of baptism in the Holy Spirit as a crisis experience which has essentially nothing to do with water-baptism or confirmation. The sacramentalist, on the contrary, cannot understand how any action of the Holy Spirit outside the sacraments may be properly viewed as baptism in the Holy Spirit.

The sacramental position, moreover, contrasts with both evangelicalism and Pentecostalism in opposing their idea of a nominal Christianity. From the sacramentalist perspective all on whom the proper sacramental action has been bestowed are thereby Christians. Rebirth occurs in baptism: one does not need later to be regenerated. Spirit-baptism occurs with water-baptism or in the sacrament of confirmation/chrismation. There is no nominal Christianity: through the power of the sacraments the full Christian reality is conveyed.

One important similarity, however, between Pentecostalism and a sacramentalism that sees in confirmation/chrismation the gift of the Holy Spirit is that Pentecostalism also views Spirit-baptism as distinct from regeneration. In such a sacramental view regeneration is not Spirit-baptism. Rather regeneration occurs in the waters of baptism, whereas Spirit-baptism, or the Pentecostal gift of the Spirit, only happens in the subsequent sacramental rite. In the Pentecostal view likewise regeneration is not Spirit-baptism, for regeneration belongs to the moment of saving faith; whereas Spirit-baptism, though it *may* occur with regeneration, happens only when there is openness, submission, yielding to the fullness of God's coming in the Holy Spirit.

Even as "two-stages" sacramentalism (baptism and confirmation/chrismation) is thereby similar to "two-experiences" Pentecostalism, so the sacramental thought and practice that centers in baptism (thereby disregarding or minimizing any second act) has its parallel with evangelicalism. For in the latter case there is no view of a second or later moment of baptism in the Spirit; rather such Spirit-baptism occurs in water-baptism sacramentally or in the experience of conversion-regeneration. One ought not therefore to look beyond water-baptism or regeneration for baptism in the Holy Spirit.

A Constructive Proposal

The question now before us is, How are we to adjudicate these sharp differences between evangelicalism and Pentecostalism on the one hand and sacramentalism and Pentecostalism on the other? The point of my paper is that Pentecostalism needs a restatement that can speak to the criticisms of both evangelicalism and sacramentalism and move it to assume a more adequate theological position of its own.

First, I would urge that Pentecostalism, contra evangelicalism, is right in recognizing that there may be two distinct moments in Christian experience: both conversion and the gift (or baptism) of the Holy Spirit. These moments correspond to two distinct acts of God's grace: the "Christ-event" (His life-death-resurrection) and the sending of the Holy Spirit. There is, I believe, ample biblical evidence to support the contention that it is not proper to merge Spirit-baptism with conversion. The Book of Acts, especially in chapter 8:12-17 (but also less directly in other places), shows the non-identity of the two; and passages such as Ephesians 1:13f. point to a difference between redemption and the subsequent sealing of the Holy Spirit. Also the long history of ecclesiastical recognition (especially in Eastern Orthodoxy and Roman Catholicism) of two sacramental moments in Christian initiation cannot be disregarded. Whether the second moment follows directly upon the first (as in Eastern baptism-chrismation) or many years thereafter (as in Roman baptism-confirmation), in both cases there is recognition of a distinction between the two. Of verifying importance for the Pentecostal is the empirical fact that he testifies to there having been two distinct experiences in his own life: one wherein he was converted to Christ, another in which he received the fullness of the Holy Spirit. All of this evidence—biblical, historical, experiential—gives significant support to the Pentecostal claim of a differentiation between conversion and Spirit-baptism.

Second, I would submit that Pentecostalism, contra sacramentalism, is right in not binding conversion-regeneration and Spirit-baptism to particular sacramental actions. Biblically, for one thing, such binding is difficult to justify. Though, to be sure, there are verses here and there that, for example, might suggest that regeneration occurs only in water baptism, there is much about new birth (regeneration, redemption) that includes no reference to water-baptism. Moreover, it is very difficult to sustain the position that baptism in the Holy Spirit has any necessary connection with a sacramental action: for example, note Acts 1:5—2:4 and 10:44—11:17 (especially 11:15-17). Historically, it is also the case that the gift (or baptism) of the Holy Spirit has sometimes been associated with baptism, sometimes with confirmation/chrismation—and there is some suggestion in early patristic writing that Spirit-baptism has no connection with any sacramental action. For the Pentecostal there is frequent personal testimony that his experiences of conversion and Spirit-baptism have had no obvious connection with sacramental practice. Water-baptism is understood rather as a sign of a preceding experience of rebirth; and though there may be the laying-on of hands for the Holy Spirit, it is not viewed sacramentally or as essential to baptism with the Spirit. Many people of Pentecostal experience testify that Spirit-baptism occurred without any human mediation.

Third, I would hold that both evangelicalism and sacramentalism have important contributions and corrections to offer to Pentecostal theology and practice. Evangelicalism is rightly offended by the Pentecostal view of two kinds or levels of Christians: born-again Christians and Spirit-baptized Christians. Evangelical thought and experience sense that "baptism with the Holy Spirit" belongs to the reality of becoming Christian, and not to some additional event or experience. The view of two kinds, or levels, of Christians bears more kinship to Gnosticism than to New Testament Christianity. Sacramentalism is rightly disturbed by Pentecostal failure to recognize that the sacraments are means of grace, and therefore may serve as channels for God's gracious actions. In other words, sacraments are not simply signs or seals of spiritual reality but through them God deigns to convey that grace by which Christian existence comes into being.

A Suggested Synthesis

Now let me proceed to suggest a theological position that will seek to bring together some of the preceding matters. What is needed, *first* of all, is an understanding of baptism with the Holy Spirit that views this baptism as an aspect of Christian initiation. That is to say, Spirit-baptism is not an addition to becoming Christian (which view sets up two categories of Christians), but is the climactic moment of entrance into Christian life. It is not to be identified with redemption (cleansing, forgiveness), but with the gift of God's presence and power. The two, while belonging together in the totality of Christian initiation, often are separated in their actual occurrence. This may be understood from the perspective of Christian initiation as a process involving both forgiveness of sins (redemption) and the gift of the Holy Spirit (cf. Acts 2:38). Thus it is not proper to speak of Christians and Spirit-baptized Christians but only of persons in process of Christian initiation.

Here two mistaken positions are to be avoided: one that would identify becoming Christian with either the first or second moment, the other that would devalue such moments so that they are viewed as unimportant in the process of becoming Christian. In the former case, if identification is made with the first moment, there is the resulting situation of two categories of Christians; or if the identification is made with the second moment, this signifies that until the time of Spirit-baptism one is not really a Christian. In the case of devaluation of such moments there is the tendency to say that it does not matter whether or not there is a significant experience of conversion and reception of the Holy Spirit. Again, the former position lays overemphasis on a given moment, and as a result confusion and divisiveness may occur. The latter position so levels out distinctive moments in

Christian faith-experience that the important element of crisis or decision is seriously neglected. A proper theological position should maintain balance between crisis and development, between differentiation
and unity in Christian experience.

Second, in moving toward some theological understanding, it is important to recognize that, while baptism in the Holy Spirit is not confined to sacramental action, such action may serve as an instrument
for the giving of the Spirit. According to Acts, neither baptism with
water nor the imposition of hands is essential to conversion or to the
gift of the Holy Spirit; however, both actions frequently serve as
media of the reality to which they point. Water-baptism is "for" the
forgiveness of sins (Acts 2:38); thus such baptism may not only be sign
but also vehicle of the grace of forgiveness. The same thing is true of
the laying-on of hands; this is not merely a sign of God's gracious gift
but also frequently a channel through which the Holy Spirit is given
("given through the laying-on of the apostles' hands," Acts 8:18).
Thus there is a kind of objective *donum* in each of these sacramental
actions; both are conveyers of the reality which they symbolize.
Hence, whoever receives the sacrament thereby receives the reality
which the sacramental action symbolizes. One may have already
received the reality without such sacramental action, but whenever
such action occurs, the reality is present and objectively given.

But now we come to the crucial point: if, however, there is little or
no active and personal faith on the part of the recipient something
vital may yet be lacking, namely the appropriation of what has been
objectively given. Thus while the reality is at hand, the fulfillment
may not yet have occurred. A separation in time may therefore exist
between the sacramental action and the full expression of what it
signifies and conveys.

What Pentecostals witness to in terms of personal experience
therefore cannot be wholly lacking for those of sacramental participation. Those who have received water-baptism and the laying-on of
hands are not without the reality thereby symbolized. Accordingly,
such persons are not actually called to an altogether new
experience—for example, baptism in the Holy Spirit—which is completely foreign to them. They are rather being invited to that kind of
faith and openness wherein what has been given may be actualized
and fulfilled. This fulfillment, however, may well have about it the
freshness and liveliness of the totally new. Thus baptism in the Holy
Spirit while already present in the sacramental reality often breaks
out with tremendous vividness and power.

But the matter of the laying-on of hands raises another question.

What of the Christian traditions that have no such practice; are their members lacking in the sacramental reality of the gift of the Holy Spirit? Though the question is complex, and needs much more consideration than can be given here, the answer, I believe, is in the negative. The reason: Christian baptism in the name of the Father, Son, and Holy Spirit is entirely adequate for the full conveying of the sacramental reality. In the Book of Acts water-baptism is in the name of Jesus Christ, or the Lord Jesus, only (2:38, 8:16, 10:48, 19:5); there is no reference to the Holy Spirit. However, the additional action of imposition of hands for the gift of the Spirit often occurs. Christian baptism has seldom followed the pattern in Acts; it has rather been in accord with Matthew 28:19, "in the name of the Father and of the Son and of the Holy Spirit." Furthermore, this triune form of baptism was understood in the early church to be the only action needed for the fullness of Christian initiation. (A study of church history affords scant evidence that the early post-Apostolic church had an additional practice of laying-on of hands for the reception of the Holy Spirit.) Thus one may say that baptism in the triune name became the one sacramental action incorporating both baptism in the name of Jesus Christ and baptism in the Holy Spirit. Hence, whenever triune baptism is practiced there is no lack of the sacramental reality of the gift of the Holy Spirit.

The conclusion that may be drawn is simply this: the reality is there, whatever the sacramental practice. But the fact that the gift has been transmitted is by no means the last word. The critical question remains: has it been appropriated; has it been fulfilled? One may have been baptized in the name of Jesus Christ, but has Christ become a living reality? Indeed, one may have been baptized in the name of the Holy Spirit, but has the Spirit become a dynamic presence and power?

Summary

Finally, I shall make a brief theological statement that will embody some of what has already been said, but also add a few further thoughts.

Two major realities are attested in Pentecostal thought and experience: first, the event of Christ's life, death, and resurrection; second, the effusion of the Holy Spirit. In the first of these there is the forgiveness of sins; in the second there is the endowment of power. While closely related, they are clearly not the same. Conversion—turning from sin to Christ—is one thing, the gift or baptism of the Holy Spirit for empowering is another. The fullness of Christian faith and life includes both.

Also there is ample scriptural, historical, and empirical justification for recognizing that these two aspects of Christian reality may be separated from each other. The record in Acts (especially), the long ecclesiastical history of two sacraments of initiation, and the twofoldness in the Christian experience of many—all substantiate a distinction or separation. This by no means rules out the possibility—perhaps even the ideality—that these two aspects of experience happen in immediate conjunction. But whether they are separated or simultaneous it is important to stress the need for both in the fullness of Christian life and practice.

The emphasis on conversion is good and important, but there is particular need today to supplement this with concern about the gift of the Holy Spirit: the promise of God the Father through Christ to all those who turn in faith and repentance to Him. Without this supplementation the Christian life lacks fullness of power for witness and mission. The emphasis on sacraments is also good and important, but there is particular need today to supplement this with concern about the appropriation of what is objectively given: the new life in Jesus Christ and the renewing power of the Holy Spirit.

I might add that what may be most needed today theologically is the recovery of a sound trinitarianism wherein the one God—Father, Son, and Holy Spirit—is properly recognized and known. There is both a unity in Christian experience—"one God, one faith, one baptism"—and a manifoldness—"Go . . . baptizing in the name of the Father and of the Son and of the Holy Spirit." We must learn better how to emphasize the oneness of God, and the need for all of life to center in Him. We must also move ahead with deeper understanding of what it means to say that there are "three persons" in the unity of the godhead, and that to be truly Christian is to encounter God in His full tri-personal reality. Since, however, our single greatest neglect (especially in Western theology) has been in the area of the Holy Spirit, it is possible that, in the context of a comprehensive trinitarian theology and experience, we shall need to focus on the Holy Spirit for some time to come.

Donald L. Gelpi, S.J.

Donald L. Gelpi was ordained a Jesuit priest in 1964. After earning four degrees at St. Louis University, he completed a Ph.D. at Fordham University in 1970. For several years he served on the faculty of Loyola University, New Orleans. He became in 1973 professor of theology at the Jesuit School of Theology in Berkeley and co-director of the Berkeley Institute for Spirituality and Worship. His book *Pentecostalism: A Theological Viewpoint* (New York: Paulist Press, 1971) presents a high-level charismatic theology from a thoroughgoing Roman Catholic viewpoint carried further in *Charism and Sacrament: A Theology of Christian Conversion* (New York: Paulist Press, 1976). Besides *Pentecostal Piety* (New York: Paulist Press, 1972) and several other books, he has published scholarly articles on philosophical and theological themes in such journals as *Thought* and *Concilium*.

Here, Fr. Gelpi argues that charismatic presuppositions are not only suited but necessary to both the sacramental and hierarchical aspects of Roman Catholic thought and practice.

Pentecostal Theology: A Roman Catholic Viewpoint

6

The "new Pentecost" among Roman Catholics, like every genuine religious revival, is a complex event. Many Catholics have found in the charismatic renewal of their church a deeper conversion to Christ and a deeper knowledge and love of God. In my own experience with Catholic prayer groups, prayer for Spirit-baptism and openness to the gifts of the Spirit has borne positive fruit in a variety of ways.

Through the renewal, many Catholics have come to feel a sense of the reality of God and of His call. They acquire a growing sensitivity to the gifts of the Spirit. The words of Scripture take on a new meaning and life for them. People grow in an expectant faith in God's saving and healing power. They experience His healing as a fact in their own lives and in the lives of others. There is a rediscovery among Catholics of the gift of tongues, of prophecy, of healing. The fruits of the Spirit are also abundantly manifest: love, joy, peace, patience, and all the other signs of the Spirit's presence.

Along with these positive fruits, the Catholic charismatics I know also experience a renewal of their devotion to sacramental worship. In the Catholic prayer groups with which I am familiar, Spirit-baptism is presented as a renewal of one's confirmation. And for many believers the practice has given new meaning to the sacraments of initiation. Eucharistic worship becomes more Spirit-filled. There is also renewed loyalty to the official leaders of the church and a desire to follow their pastoral guidelines.

In my own life I can testify that involvement in the Catholic charismatic renewal has changed my whole approach to the ministry. I find that I no longer try to save people, as I once did. I am instead more inclined to leave that to God. In proclaiming His Word I rely more now upon God's gifts and His anointing than I did in the past. The academic work I do has become more of a spiritual ministry, rather than a purely scholastic enterprise.

But despite the many signs of God's presence within it, the "new Pentecost" among Catholics remains, nevertheless, a source of alarm for many. Some, like Fr. Andrew Greeley, fear it as a wave of irrational emotionalism. Others cannot relate to the style of prayer practiced at the meetings and are in fact threatened by it. Others are alarmed by some of the pastoral problems which occur in the movement.

Still, the American Catholic bishops' Committee on Doctrine has investigated the movement and given it initial approval. And more and more bishops and priests are taking an active and sympathetic interest in it.

I would like in these limited remarks to address myself to two fears common among Roman Catholics as they first approach the renewal. Some see the renewal as a threat to the traditional sacramental worship of the Roman Church. Others see it as a threat to the traditional forms of hierarchical government.

Since, moreover, in these remarks, I have been asked to speak from a specifically Catholic viewpoint I have for the most part derived my reflections from sources peculiar to the Roman Catholic tradition.

My remarks will fall into three parts. I would first like to establish a general theological context by summarizing the doctrinal stance of the Second Vatican Council on the gifts of the Holy Spirit. Second, I would like to reflect on the relation between charism and sacrament. Third, I would like to discuss the relation between charism and hierarchy.

If what I say seems impersonal at times, the tone of my remarks has nothing to do with my attitude toward the renewal. It reflects rather the customary function of the theologian within my particular religious tradition. For strict theological discourse is the attempt to reflect in a public manner about a shared faith experience. Therefore, it differs in its mode of expression both from personal professions of faith and from personal witness to God's activity in one's life.

Vatican II and the Holy Spirit

The Catholic charismatic renewal has from the beginning drawn a certain amount of inspiration from the Second Vatican Council. From the earliest days of the renewal, charismatic Catholics felt that the sudden and, for Catholics at least, often startling outpouring of spiritual gifts was the answer to Pope John's prayer during the council for a "new Pentecost" in the Catholic Church. And in point of fact, an analysis of the documents of Vatican II provides a solid resource for understanding and interpreting the renewal.

It is clear, for instance, that the conciliar decrees look upon the Holy Spirit as an active force in human religious experience, as a power to be contended with. His mission makes a pragmatic difference in the lives of men.

The work of the Spirit is described in the council documents as one of sanctification, inspiration, and unification.

Sanctification

The Spirit's sanctifying activity is manifest in the "obedience of faith" which He inspires. This obedience consists of heartfelt assent to the divine revelation. The inner freedom to give such an assent is presented in conciliar documents as the product of the Spirit's "anointing." And this anointing is described as an illumination of the mind which is accompanied by an ease and joy in actively assenting to God in His saving Word.

The illumination which the Spirit brings is, moreover, not static but dynamic. It involves a growing active penetration into the meaning of God's plan of salvation. It demands, therefore, constant openness to the gifts of the Holy Spirit (Rev, 5; Miss, 15; Ch, 15).[1]

As sanctifier, the Spirit acts in the name of Jesus. He inspires men to

---

1. Abbreviations refer to the following conciliar decisions of Vatican II (1962-65), a convenient English translation of which may be found in *The Documents of Vatican II*, ed. Walter M. Abbott (New York: Guild Press, 1966):

Ap	Decree on the Apostolate of the Laity *(Apostolicam actuositatem)*	**Or**	Decree on Eastern Catholic Churches *(Orientalium ecclesiarum)*
Ch	Pastoral Constitution on the Church in the Modern World *(Gaudium et spes)*	**Pr**	Decree on the Ministry and Life of Priests *(Presbyterorum ordinis)*
Eccl	Dogmatic Constitution on the Church *(Lumen gentium)*	**Ren**	Decree on the Appropriate Renewal of the Religious Life *(Perfectae caritatis)*
Ep	Decree on the Bishops' Pastoral Office in the Church *(Christus Dominus)*	**Rev**	Dogmatic Constitution on Divine Revelation *(Dei verbum)*
Lit	Constitution on the Sacred Liturgy *(Sacrosanctum concilium)*	**Un**	Decree on Ecumenism *(Unitatis redintegratio)*.
Miss	Decree on the Church's Missionary Activity *(Ad gentes)*		

glorify and praise the Father for His saving action in Christ. Hence, the sanctifying activity of the Spirit becomes visible in the very acts of praise which believers offer to God (Ep, 1).

The sanctification of the Holy Spirit is also experienced as a purification and as a renewal of life. That is to say, the Spirit inspires men with a desire to abandon sinful selfishness and to live the beatitudes: to be poor with Christ's poor, to eschew empty honors, to leave all for Christ's sake, and to suffer persecution in love for the sake of the gospel (Ap, 4; Ch, 21; Or, 30).

The Spirit is experienced as a source of life because He inspires living deeds of faith, of love, of trust in God, and of praise (Eccl, 4). By His gifts, He inspires men to devote themselves to life-giving services to their fellow men (Ch, 38). He fills the church with an eschatological longing for the fullness of life (Eccl, 4; Ch, 22). He strengthens men to live their lives according to the Christian law of love (Ch, 22), and He teaches men to relate to God intimately as God's own children (Ch, 27).

Hence, by the active indwelling of the Spirit, the Christian community is transformed into a theophany, a visible manifestation of the divine presence. "For it is the function of the Church, led by the Holy Spirit who renews and purifies her ceaselessly, to make God the Father and His Incarnate Son present and in a sense visible" (Ch, 21).

The theophantic character of the activity of the Holy Spirit is presented in the council documents as extending not only to individual persons but to ecclesiastical institutions as well. In dealing with this point, the language of the documents is, moreover, strong. The institutions of the believing community are described as "quasi-incarnations" of the Spirit in His activity. The *Dogmatic Constitution on the Church (Lumen gentium)* observes, for instance:

> Just as the assumed nature inseparably united to the divine Word serves Him as a living instrument of salvation, so, in a similar way, does the communal structure of the Church serve Christ's Spirit, who vivifies it by way of building up the body. (Eccl, 8; cf. DS 3328[2])

Inspiration

Among the visible forms of Christian life and worship which the Spirit illumines and transforms by His activity are: the written Word of Scripture, the sacraments, the church's missionary activity,

---

2. Henricus Denzinger and Adolfus Schönmetzer, *Enchiridion symbolorum definitionum et declarationum de rebus fidei et morum* (Freiburg im Breisgau: Herder, [32]1963).

religious orders, the apostolate of the laity, and the hierarchical structures of the church.

The Scriptures were, of course, originally inspired by the Holy Spirit (Rev, 11). And in each generation of believers, the Scriptures "impart the Word of God Himself without change, and make the voice of the Holy Spirit resound in the words of the prophets and apostles." When illuminated by the Spirit, the Word of Scripture becomes a "living and efficient Word" transforming the hearts and lives of men (Rev, 21).

Not only the Word of Scripture but the sacramental words of the church as well derive their power and efficacy from the inner anointing of the Holy Spirit. For it is by the power of the Spirit that sacramental worship (especially eucharistic worship) sanctifies the faithful and nourishes charity in their hearts (Ap, 3).

The council documents also depict the church's missionary activity as a continuation of the first Pentecost. Having commanded His apostles to go and make disciples of all nations, Jesus continues to send His Spirit as a force impelling Christian evangelists to the four corners of the world. The council documents insist, moreover, on the charismatic character of the missionary vocation. "The Holy Spirit uses manifold means to arouse the mission spirit in the Church of God, and often anticipates the action of those whose task it is to rule the life of the Church" (Miss, 29).

Religious orders and congregations too are presented as the institutional expression of charismatic impulses from the Holy Spirit. They are "spiritual families" gathered into unity by the Spirit of Jesus. And the same Spirit impels religious to spend their lives in devoted public service of Christ and of His people (Ren, 1, 15). Appropriately, then, the renewal of religious life and of its institutional structures must proceed under the impulse and guidance of the Spirit (Ren, 2).

The movements and anointing of the Spirit also provide the basis for the apostolate of the laity (Ap, 1, 29). Indeed, the charismatic call of the Spirit establishes the basic rights and duties of each individual within the worshiping community. The *Decree on the Apostolate of the Laity (Apostolicam actuositatem)* observes:

> For the exercise of this [lay] apostolate, the Holy Spirit who sanctifies the People of God through the ministry and the sacraments gives to the faithful special gifts as well (cf. 1 Cor. 12:7), "allotting to everyone according as he will" (1 Cor. 12:11). Thus may the individual "according to the gift that each has received, administer it to one another," and become "good stewards of the manifold grace of God" (1 Pet. 4:10), and build up thereby the whole body in char-

ity (cf. Eph. 4:16). From the reception of these charisms or gifts, including those which are less dramatic, there arise for each believer
the right and duty to use them in the Church and in the world for the
good of mankind and for the upbuilding of the Church. In so doing,
believers need to enjoy the freedom of the Holy Spirit who "breathes
where he wills" (Jn. 3:8). At the same time, they must act in communion with their brothers in Christ, especially with their pastors.
The latter must make a judgment about the true nature and proper
use of these gifts, not in order to extinguish the Spirit, but to test all
things and hold fast to what is good (cf. 1 Thes. 5:12, 19, 21). (Ap, 3)

This important text hints at a key distinction made in the council
documents between "hierarchical" and "charismatic" gifts. Pius XII
hinted at such a distinction in *Mystici corporis* (DS 3801). And Pope
Paul used it in an allocution during the council on September 14,
1964. It reappears in the conciliar documents themselves. And it provides a useful insight into the council's approach to the charismatic
gifts.

Unfortunately, the terminology in which the distinction is couched
is potentially confusing. Since "gift" and "charism" are elsewhere
used synonymously, the phrase "charismatic gift" is a redundancy.
Moreover, the division of gifts into "hierarchical" and "charismatic"
seems to set up an irreconcilable opposition between them. From this
seeming opposition, one might be tempted to infer, erroneously I
think, that hierarchical leaders are by definition precluded from being charismatic persons, and vice versa.

The real intent of the distinction is, however, nothing of the sort. It
is an attempt to affirm at one and the same time both the need for official church leadership and the organic interdependence of all of the
gifts of the Spirit, including those granted to hierarchical leaders.
Hence, the council documents do observe that the apostles enjoyed
outstanding spiritual gifts, for the exercise of other charisms in the
early church was subject to their authority (Eccl, 17; Ap, 17). And the
documents also speak of the bishops as the successors of the apostles
and insist on episcopal responsibility to test every charismatic movement and to preserve what is truly from the Lord.

But the documents are equally clear that it is the Spirit of Christ
who leads the church, not the apostles and bishops. Those, moreover,
who exercise hierarchical gifts have no right to suppress the Spirit's
activity. If, therefore, those with hierarchical gifts have the duty, and
therefore the right, to pass discerning judgment on the origin of different charismatic impulses which occur in the community, they also
have the responsibility to judge those impulses correctly. By the
same token, those authentically inspired by the Spirit have the right

and the duty to follow that inspiration without hindrance from church leaders (Ap, 3; Miss, 4).

At the same time, those in positions of hierarchical leadership are also promised special gifts of teaching. As successors to the apostles they are anointed to be true and authentic teachers of the faith (Ep, 2). In exercising this teaching office, however, church leaders do not stand above the Word of God but serve the Word. They must listen to God's Word devoutly, guard it scrupulously, and explain it faithfully. But in expounding the Scriptures, those endowed with the gift of teaching give expression to the inspired tradition of the church. As a result, sacred Scripture, church tradition, and the teaching authority of church leaders stand in such an organic relationship that they cannot be adequately understood independent of one another. The Word of Scripture was consigned to writing under the inspiration of the Spirit. Sacred tradition is the process by which God's Word is handed on from generation to generation under the guidance and gifts of the Spirit through the instrumentality of official church teachers.

By the hierarchical gifts, therefore, the council means those spiritual gifts which enable official church leaders to exercise the ministerial responsibilities demanded by their office. The exercise of these gifts should bear fruit in a deep love on the part of the hierarchy for the church, zeal for worship, and genuine apostolic flexibility (Pr, 9, 10; Lit, 43). The most outstanding of the hierarchical gifts are the gifts of teaching and discernment. And significantly the latter gift is presented as the key to church government.

Unification

In addition to the work of sanctification and inspiration, the Holy Spirit effects the unification and reconciliation of all who are open to His activity. The ultimate ground for unity within the process of salvation is God Himself in His inner triune life. But within the Godhead, it is the Holy Spirit who, through His very work of sanctification and inspiration, acts in a special way as the bond of union among men (Un, 2; Eccl, 4).

Through the anointing of the Holy Spirit, God's salvific call goes out to all men (Ch, 27). Hence, the activity of the Holy Spirit did not begin for the first time on Pentecost Day. He was already at work before the coming of Christ (Miss, 4). He prepared the coming of Jesus, who was conceived by the power of the Spirit and was "impelled" to apostolic activity through the Spirit's anointing at the Jordan (Miss, 4).

The descent of the Spirit upon the apostles at the first Pentecost had as its purpose to reverse the effects of the tower of Babel by confounding the tongues of men anew, but this time in order to unite them in the praise of God (Eccl, 4; Miss, 4).

In His final eschatological outpouring, the Holy Spirit of God is revealed to be the Spirit of Jesus. For it is by breathing forth His Spirit on every generation of Christians that Jesus leads men to the "obedience of faith" and exercises His Lordship (Ch, 1, 38; Eccl, 4; Ap, 7).

Nevertheless, the activity of the Spirit of Jesus cannot be confined to His activity in the hearts of believers. The *Pastoral Constitution on the Church in the Modern World (Gaudium et spes)* affirms clearly that God's Spirit not only "directs the unfolding of time and renews the face of the earth" but that He is "not absent" from the social and political movements which seek to procure justice and a humane mode of life for the disadvantaged members of society (Ch, 26). Moreover, the Spirit seeks to lead all men to unity in Christ (Eccl, 31).

More to our present purpose, the Spirit summons men to unity through His charismatic gifts (Eccl, 7). For the same Spirit dwells in Christ and in the members of His mystical body, and by gifts of sanctification and of service unites them in faith and love to their Lord and to one another (Eccl, 4, 7).

These seem to me to be some of the insights offered by Vatican II into the activity of the Holy Spirit. Two particular points made in the documents deserve special reflection: the theophantic character of the Spirit's activity in the church and the organic interrelation of the gifts.

Charism and Sacrament

The fuller implications of the council documents can, I believe, be illuminated by reflection on some of the trends in theology which led up to the conciliar decrees. I would like to focus specifically on Catholic sacramental theology. And I would like eventually to draw both on these reflections and on the council documents in order to begin to discuss the question of the relation of charismatic and sacramental piety.

In the post-Tridentine church Catholic theology was couched in the logic and vocabulary of scholastic thought. And it derived its problematic largely from the polemics of the Reformation.

Scholastic theological manuals attempted to give a "scientific" explanation of the sacraments by reducing them to the four Aristotelian causes: efficient, final, formal, and material. This "causal" analysis of the sacraments proved to be extremely artificial, a fact which became apparent in the attempt to assign a specific matter and form to each of the sacraments. Finding the "matter" and "form" of the sacraments of matrimony and of orders, for example, proved to be a perplexing puzzle.

At a more practical level, preoccupation with defining the "metaphysical essence" of each sacrament reinforced the legalistic rubricism that came to characterize so much of Catholic ritual worship. Fixed essences invite codification.

At the same time Reformation polemics often focused the attention of Catholic theologians in a rigid sort of way upon a limited number of theological questions; for example, Are the sacraments numerically seven? Were they all instituted by Jesus? Are the seven sacraments in fact efficacious?

Polemic preoccupation with one particular set of theological problems can easily lead the theologian to overlook or devaluate other important aspects of the Christian faith experience. This is particularly so when theological thinking is carried on at a high level of abstraction. Abstractions are apt to obscure more than they explain. Now, scholastic theology, based as it is on a reductionist logic of classification, is nothing if not abstract. The combined effect of abstractionism and embittered polemic on post-Tridentine Catholicism was then, not infrequently, the production of a certain imbalance in popular Catholic religious attitudes.

For instance, belief in the efficacy of the sacraments was and is in many ways a consoling doctrine for many Catholics, for it speaks to them of the gratuity of God's grace and salvation. But exaggerated emphasis on the efficacy of the sacramental minister's prayer tended to blind many Catholics to the fact that the total "pragmatic effectiveness" of any sacrament also depends on the personal attitudes of the sacramental worshiper. In the day-to-day piety of many Catholics, the notion of "sacramental efficacy" began to imply a kind of "mechanical efficiency."

Unfortunately, the more Catholics began to relate to the sacraments as "grace machines," the more formalistic their worship became. In other words, oversimplified explanations of the meaning of sacramental efficacy and exaggerated concern with the prayer of the sacramental minister tended to obscure in the minds of many Catholics the prophetic character of sacramental worship. Many Catholics seemed to forget that sacramental worship, when properly understood, is in fact a covenant renewal which challenges each sacramental worshiper to a daily, personal, public witness to Christ.

At the same time, with the development of exegesis and the growth of a hermeneutical sense among Catholic theologians, the historical

arguments for the divine institution of the seven sacraments traditionally elaborated by Catholic apologists were gradually revealed to
be, in many cases, historically, exegetically, and hermeneutically
naive.

Dissatisfaction with a strict scholastic theology of the sacraments
combined with concern over the shallowness of a great deal of popular sacramental worship in order to produce a reformulation of
Catholic sacramental theology.

Much of this reformulation developed under the inspiration of German, and especially of Heideggerian, existentialism. Heideggerian
polemic against "ontic" patterns of thinking was used effectively by
theologians like Karl Rahner to mount a critique of the scholastic
theological manuals.

In sacramental theology one important result was a diminished
preoccupation with the "metaphysical essence" of each sacrament
and a growing preoccupation with the sacrament's historical meaning and symbolic structure. On the one hand, preoccupation with
sacramental symbolism fed the liturgical renewal. And, on the other,
the theological "retrieve" of the historical development of sacramental worship alerted Catholic theologians to the possibility of far more
creative flexibility in the forms of Catholic worship than had been
possible under the old legalistic rubricism.

One of the most important concepts to emerge from this trend in
Catholic speculation was the notion of "primordial sacramentality"
(Ursakrament). Theologians began to realize that Catholic use of the
term "sacrament" had been far too restrictive and ritualistic. They
began to realize that the full meaning of the seven sacraments could
not be grasped until these formal acts of worship were resituated in a
broader context.

The traditional notion of a "sacramental" as a grace-filled and
quasi-sacramental act of personal piety had in some ways hinted at
the idea of "primordial sacramentality." But even the theology of
"sacramentals" had remained so preoccupied with excluding
"sacramental efficacy" from the acts of private devotion that it
precluded in practice a fuller insight into the quasi-sacramental symbolism of acts of personal devotion and faith. As in the case of the
sacraments themselves, then, the question of the symbolic meaning of
extra-sacramental acts of worship tended to be neglected (DS 3844).

Among the theologians of the council, Karl Rahner did more
perhaps than anyone else to remedy these lacunae in Catholic
sacramental thought. In his theology of symbol, he attempted to pro-

vide a speculative basis for an expanded notion of the "sacramental."[3]

In this expanded definition, "sacramentality" is characteristic of any concrete event within human experience which both reveals and conceals the power and presence of God. This notion of primordial sacramentality is closely connected with Rahner's reflections on the Trinity and on the theology of mystery. For the realm of primordial sacramentality correlates with the historical missions of the Son and of the Holy Spirit.[4]

The event of the incarnation is the normative instance of primordial sacramentality, because the concrete human experience of the man Jesus is the visible historical embodiment of that relation of sonship which is the second person of the Trinity. Since, however, all men are called to abandon their sinful state and to enter into a relation of adopted sonship analogous to the relation which Jesus has with the Father, the incarnation is the real-symbolic, primordially sacramental expression both of who the Son of God is and of what man, in God's saving mercy, is called by God to be.

Moreover, the incarnation mediates the final eschatological outpouring of the Holy Spirit. The union of the Spirit and the church is not a hypostatic, or personal, union, as the incarnation is. But to the extent that the Christian community experiences the call of the Spirit of Jesus and responds to His anointing, it is conformed to Jesus and becomes the real-symbolic and primordially sacramental expression of God's saving presence in the world.

As we have seen, this sense of the primordial sacramentality of the church as a concrete living symbol of the divine presence finds occasional expression in the documents of Vatican II. The documents teach that through the anointing of the Spirit, the Father and Son are rendered, as it were, "visibly present" in human history. Such a statement makes theological sense, if the Son is the real-symbolic, primordially sacramental expression of the Father and if the community of believers is the real-symbolic and primordially sacramental expression of the relation of adoptive sonship.

One important consequence of the notion of primordial sacramentality is, of course, that for Catholic theologians it provides a suggestive, speculative alternative to an essentialistic, scholastic approach to the sacraments. For it shifts theological attention away

3. Karl Rahner, *The Church and the Sacraments*, trans. W. J. O'Hara (New York: Herder and Herder, 1963).

4. Karl Rahner, "The Concept of Mystery in Catholic Theology," *Theological Investigations*, vol. IV in *More Recent Writings*, trans. Kevin Smyth (Baltimore: Helicon; London: Darton, Longman, and Todd, 1966), ch. 2, pp. 36-73.

from the material and formal "essence" of the sacrament and raises the broader question of each sacrament's historical and salvific meaning. In this context, the seven sacraments are seen to be public acts of worship which recall the normative revelation of God in Jesus Christ. They are covenant renewals in which the sacramental worshiper is challenged to renew his commitment to Christ in the strength and efficacious power of Christ's prior commitment to him. In other words, the sacramental character of these seven acts of public worship is grounded in the symbolic significance of the Christian community as that historical community of faith which emerges consciously from the historical revelation of God's Word and which is formed in its historical progress by the guidance and gifts of His indwelling Spirit.

You will, I hope, pardon this rapid and necessarily cryptic recapitulation of a number of abstract and complex theological notions. But they are, I believe, important for any speculative theological assessment of the Catholic charismatic renewal. For they provide an important key to understanding at a speculative theological level the relationship between sacramental and charismatic piety as it has developed in the Catholic renewal, at least as I have experienced it.

For if it is true that the seven sacraments derive their symbolic significance from the primordial sacramentality of the Christian community as the historical prolongation of the revelation of God's Son, it is also true that at an existential level the primordial sacramentality of the Christian community is largely grounded in the gifts of the Holy Spirit. This last point deserves, I believe, some further reflection.

The experiential correlate to the word "gift" is, I would suggest, a religious call. The new Israel is by the gift of God ideally a prophetic community in which each individual is open in his heart to the illumination and anointing of God's Spirit. The call of the Spirit is twofold: a call to sanctification and a call to service.

One is sanctified, made holy, set apart from the rest of men, by the experience of "putting on the mind of Christ." That is to say, through the gifts of sanctification, the Spirit summons each believer to penetrate more and more deeply into a lived experience of the meaning of Jesus' message, His mission, His life, and His relation to the Father (DS 178; Leo XIII, *Divinum illud munus*, 38).

Assimilation to Jesus bears fruit in the active service of others (Phil. 2:1-11). And through the gifts of service, one is called by the Spirit to a specific vocation within the Christian community.

There is, I would suggest, a threefold sense in which the gifts of the Spirit are integral to the primordial sacramentality of the church.

First, when the visible forms of Christian life develop as a conscious response to the call of the Spirit, they are a theophany and a summons to faith. A selfless act of love and service done in the name of Jesus is a visible sign of the anointing of the Spirit. It is a challenge and an invitation to all who witness it for them to believe and then go and do likewise. Similarly, a community of faith truly dedicated to the service of the needy and to the rejects of society is a living sign of the power and the anointing of the Spirit. The council documents make this point in a variety of ways, but most strikingly, perhaps, in referring to the visible forms of Christian life as though they are "quasi-incarnations" of the Holy Spirit.

Second, the gifts of the Spirit are, I would suggest, integral to any thorough theological understanding of the purpose of the seven sacraments. By baptism, the Christian not only publicly seals his covenant with God and is incorporated into a eucharistic community of faith, but he is summoned sacramentally to put on the mind of Christ by growing in openness to the gifts of sanctification. By confirmation the adult Christian is summoned to mature service in the Christian community. The sacrament summons him particularly, therefore, to a prayerful discernment of the specific gift of service to which the Spirit of Jesus summons him.

The vocational sacraments of orders and matrimony are a public, ecclesiastical, sacramental seal upon the call felt by individual Christians to a specific kind of service within the community. And together they provide the community with a pastoral paradigm for discerning the gifts of service.

The sacraments of reconciliation and anointing of the sick are the sacramental ritualization of the faith-healing practiced in the early Christian community. For healing is the sign of divine forgiveness (DS 1323, 1324).

The Eucharist should be both the Spirit-filled proclamation of God's Word and a solemn covenant renewal in which each community as a community prays for greater openness to the gifts of the Spirit and the full release in their lives of His saving power. It is for this reason that the Holy Spirit is invoked in every eucharistic canon.

In other words, to overlook the charismatic dimension of the Christian experience is to overlook the fundamental purpose of the sacramental system so carefully preserved and defended within the Roman tradition.

There is a *third* sense in which the gifts of the Spirit are integral to any theological understanding of the primordial sacramentality of the church. For in any sacramental community in which the gifts of the

Spirit are *not* operative, the ritual celebration of the sacraments will tend to be experienced as empty and formalistic, as a rite without purpose.

There is, then, a certain historical irony in these theological conclusions. For if the charismatic is integral to the primordial sacramentality of the church, then many Roman Catholics, as a result of their polemic concern to vindicate the legitimacy of ritual sacramental worship, have, by opposing sacrament to charism, in practice if not in theory, lost a true sense of the full salvific meaning of ritual sacramental worship. And on the other hand many Protestants, who have in some instances at least devalued the importance of ritual sacramental worship, have often—perhaps without realizing it consciously—felt and preserved a better sense of primordial sacramentality than many Roman Catholics.

It seems to me, moreover, that one might draw a similar conclusion concerning the average Roman Catholic's understanding of the hierarchical gifts and their function in the church.

Charism and Hierarchy

The hierarchy are those who are called to leadership in the eucharistic community's service of worship. The service of worship is a public service which culminates in the celebration of the Lord's Supper as a public, communal profession of faith in the Lord and of dependence on Him. That celebration is an act of recall. In it we remember the Lord's love and mercy in dying for our sins. But recalling the love and forgiveness of the Lord in living faith is different from recalling a dental appointment. For it is an act which is performed under the power and anointing of the Spirit of Jesus. The community leader who summons the people of God to such a Spirit-filled act of recall must then do so himself in the power and under the anointing of the Spirit. Hence, only those should lead the community in such an act who have been spiritually gifted with the call to leadership in the service of worship. And those are most certainly called whose vocation has been thoroughly tested and discerned by the community and its ordained leaders.

Now to lead a community of worship in the recall of the love of God revealed in the new covenant is to lead the community in a covenant renewal. That is to say, it is to remind the community in the name of Jesus, in the efficacious power of His Spirit, and with the authority which comes from the Spirit's call and anointing, that the Father's love goes out to each individual. Hence, the sacrament summons each believer to a response of living and expectant faith and trust in God, and a love of God and of one's neighbor.

One cannot, however, responsibly summon a community to such a covenant renewal without making sure that each worshiper understands the meaning of the act he performs. As a public ordained leader of covenant worship in a charismatic community, one also has the responsibility to challenge his community prophetically to live with a day-to-day openness to the gifts of the Spirit.

The hierarchical gifts of which Vatican II speaks are then the Spirit's call to such service in a eucharistic community. The hierarchical gifts bring with them the responsibility to ensure the public instruction of the faithful in the Word of God and the discerning evaluation of the movements of the Spirit within the community.

Now because such sacramental leadership is public, it endows one's life with a special visibility, and therefore with a special sacramental meaning. For one who assumes a public responsibility becomes a public person. And one who functions as a public person ceases to live purely and simply as a private individual. He finds instead that the meaning of his official actions is of necessity colored by the public responsibilities he has assumed. This experience is common enough in ordinary human affairs. The mere fact that a man is President of the United States means that he must suppress many of his personal feelings in his public statements and actions. For what in another man would be the expression of personal pique or preference would in his public statements be an expression of policy.

There is a similar transformation in the meaning of a man's life in the case of a public religious leader, except of course that the meaning in this case is salvific. One called to leadership in the service of covenant worship is called to set an example of faith and practical service for the community he leads. What might be sin in another becomes scandal in him.

Similarly, the positive salvific meaning of his ministry of worship is also affected by his public position. When he prays as an official leader, as one ordained to preside over a public act of covenant worship, he confronts the community not merely as an individual but as one called by the Spirit to be the community's leader and official representative (1 Tim. 6:2-16; 2 Tim. 1:6; 2:1-19).

Now the religious meaning of a life of leadership in worship has a sacramental character precisely because it is an expression of God's call and anointing and not of mere human preference. The sacramental ordination of leaders in the Christian community presupposes, therefore, a period in which one's call to the ministry has been tested and discerned to be truly from the Spirit. And the rite of sacramental ordination publicly confirms and completes that call. Now a call is a charism. Hence the sacramental meaning of a life of hierarchical service in the church is rooted and grounded in the charismatic. And the rite itself cannot be properly understood except in that context.

These reflections throw some light, I believe, on the difference between the "hierarchical" and "charismatic" ministries affirmed by Vatican II. Take, for example, a ministry of prophecy or a ministry of teaching. In many instances the difference is not a difference in the concrete act. A bishop or a priest may utter the same words of prophecy which an individual prophet might speak. A bishop or priest may teach the same truths as any catechist. But if his prophecy and teaching are truly expressive of his call to hierarchical ministry, then the social and ecclesiastical significance of his words, the sacramental visibility of his ministry, is altered by the fact that he has been summoned by the Spirit to a role of official leadership in the community. For as a result of that call, he speaks not merely as an inspired individual but as the official, spiritually anointed representative of the entire community.

Moreover, if the organic interdependence of the gifts of the Spirit means anything, then one should expect that just as a "charismatic" prophecy will elicit a response in a Spirit-filled community, including its official leaders, so an authentic Spirit-filled "hierarchical" prophecy or teaching, expressed by an official church leader, will find a response among Spirit-filled believers, if it truly proceeds from the Spirit. If any teaching fails to elicit the appropriate response, then the matter should be subjected in love to careful scrutiny and discernment.

In addition, not only is the sacramental visibility of a hierarchical ministry rooted in a charismatic anointing but the practical leadership of the Christian community presupposes a charismatic context. There is no way to understand church leadership truly or adequately by employing a bureaucratic or political model. What is needed is a charismatic model. And on this point, it seems to me the council documents are quite clear.

The council documents teach that in addition to basic human rights common to all men, the Christian possesses spiritual rights and duties which are rooted in his charismatic call to service. Vatican II teaches that one called by the Spirit to a particular form of service has the consequent right and duty to answer responsibly to the anointing of the Spirit. The council also teaches that the Spirit dispenses His gifts where He wills and often inspires individuals who are not members of the ordained hierarchy to particular leadership roles.

Legal and bureaucratic structures which stifle charismatic growth usurp the role of the Spirit. Paradoxically, then, official church leaders can lead the Christian community effectively only when they themselves follow the lead of the Spirit. The self-effacement which Jesus inculcated in His apostles is not accidental to ecclesiastical leadership; it is at its very heart (Matt. 20:24-28; Luke 9:46-48). At the same time, responsibility for deciding what is and what is not of the Spirit rests with the leaders, who must test all and hold fast to what is good (1 Thess. 5:21).

It is, then, simply impossible for the most orthodox Catholic to understand the role of the hierarchy in the church without simultaneously acknowledging its charismatic basis and the larger charismatic context in which hierarchical leadership is to be exercised. If this comes as a surprise to some Catholics, perhaps they should re-examine their theological understanding of the meaning and practice of church government. For the Church of God is neither the Holy Roman Empire nor General Motors.

If the preceding reflections are sound, then those religious values which Roman Catholics have traditionally prized most highly, namely, sacraments and hierarchy, are in the last analysis unintelligible apart from a theology of charism. And their integral preservation as elements of the Catholic tradition depends on the openness of the Catholic community to the charismatic anointing of the Spirit of Christ.

It would seem, then, that the Spirit who summoned Catholics to ecumenical openness in the decrees of Vatican II is effecting that openness in the Catholic charismatic renewal. Not only are charismatic Catholics and Protestants learning that they do indeed share in the same spiritual anointing, but many Catholics are discovering that by openness to the charismatic gifts long cherished and preserved by their Protestant brethren, they themselves are beginning to understand, for the first time it seems, the real meaning of their own religious traditions. One can only hope that a similar transformation of attitudes is occurring in other Christian communions, so that by mutual openness to the gifts that characterize our respective traditions, we may grow into the union to which we are called in Christ Jesus.

PART THREE
Analytic Assessments

R. Hollis Gause

R. Hollis Gause was associated for over twenty-five years with Lee College, Cleveland, Tennessee, which has granted him an honorary doctorate in humane letters. He served as dean of the college and dean of the division of religion. He holds a B.A. from Presbyterian College, Clinton, South Carolina (1945), a M.Div. from Columbia Theological Seminary, Decatur, Georgia (1949), and the Ph.D. from Emory University in Atlanta (1975). Among his publications is an exegesis of John 17 contributed to *Kirchen der Welt—Der Pfingstkirchen*, ed. Walter J. Hollenweger (Stuttgart: Evangelisches Verlagswerk, 1971). In 1972, he was president of the Society for Pentecostal Studies. He was ordained by the Church of God (Cleveland, Tennessee) in 1954. Dr. Gause now serves as dean and director of the Church of God Graduate School of Christian Ministries.

In this article Dean Gause reflects, as a traditional Pentecostal, on current interrelations between the Pentecostal and charismatic movements.

Issues in Pentecostalism

7

The term "Pentecostalism" as a specific sectarian designation is of recent origin. In the United States the word "Pentecostal" apparently was originally associated with Wesleyanism. This was the product of the Wesleyan identification of the experience of sanctification with the infilling of the Holy Spirit. For instance, the term "Pentecostal" was at one time a part of the denominational title of the Church of the Nazarene, one of the stronger communions committed to the Wesleyan doctrine of sanctification. At that time the term "Pentecostal" was not specifically associated with the experience of speaking in tongues.

The strong revival of the experience of speaking in tongues in the late nineteenth and early twentieth centuries came basically from a holiness milieu; consequently, the tongues movement used a religious vocabulary very much similar to the religious vocabulary already standardized in Wesleyanism. For the most part, however, the Wesleyan churches and the other established churches rejected the doctrine and practice of speaking in tongues.

The groups that emphasized speaking in tongues came to be distinguished from other churches by their emphasis on a repetition of the Day of Pentecost: hence, the designation "Pentecostal." The term

"Pentecostal" was, at least in some circles, an opprobrious term. Most churches disassociated themselves from the experience and doctrine; the Pentecostal Church of the Nazarene dropped the term "Pentecostal" from its denominational title.

This kind of distinction within the Christian church (and Protestantism in particular) is a product of the "tongue-speaking" movement. The term "Pentecostal," then, is (or at least has been until recently) a particular designation of a segment of the Christian profession. Unfortunately it has become a denominational designation. This segment of the Christian profession has the following characteristics: (1) It is basically a product of the Protestant tradition. It has taken basically the formal character of the Protestant Reformation by an affirmation of justification by faith alone, of the infallibility of Scripture as the written revelation of God, and of the universal priesthood of believers. (2) While often denouncing creeds, it has adopted the traditional beliefs of the Protestant churches (many of which are common to all Christendom). I have in mind such theological points as are affirmed by the Apostles' Creed. (3) It has generally been identified with the holiness movement. A large segment of the Pentecostal movement is in the direct heritage of the Wesleyan holiness movement. That part of Pentecostalism that does not have this direct heritage does have the heritage of a "separated life" movement.

Pentecostalism, then, in the sense in which it has normally been used is a designation of a segment of the Protestant tradition that is distinguished from other Protestant groups by the following beliefs: (1) the belief that the experience first recorded in Acts 2 is to continue in the life of the Christian church; (2) the belief that this experience is distinct from regeneration (or conversion generally) and subsequent to it; (3) the belief that this experience is the baptism of the Holy Spirit and that its initial outward sign is speaking in other tongues as the Spirit gives utterance; (4) the belief that this is the normal experience to be expected in every believer.

I offer these points of historical review in order to show that the term "Pentecostal" does have a historical identity, though admittedly of rather recent origin. This historical identity is primarily within the Protestant tradition. This historical identity does not give the Pentecostal churches a copyright on the term "Pentecostal." For the most part, however, other Protestant bodies have been delighted to yield this term to Pentecostal churches.

More recently the term "Pentecostal" has been applied to any who profess to speak in tongues, even though they cannot be identified under the terms above. Still more recently the term "Neo-Pentecostal" has been employed to designate those who speak with tongues but who wish to dissociate themselves from some aspect of traditional Pentecostalism.

Scriptural Bases

A more fundamental identification of Pentecostalism must be found in the Scriptures. This identification may be established in John 20:19-23 (KJV). This is one of the recorded appearances of the resurrected Jesus. In this appearance, Jesus demonstrated: (1) that He was alive, by His visible and physical appearance; (2) that He had been raised up in the body of the crucifixion; (3) therefore, what He bestows as risen Lord is what He had purchased as dying Lord. All that He had gained in His humiliation He is and He bestows in His glory.

In this appearance as risen Lord, Jesus bestows His legacy of redemption. This legacy is represented in the three statements recorded of Jesus in this appearance: (1) "Peace be unto you." The peace gained at Calvary is bestowed in resurrection. (2) "As my Father hath sent me, even so send I you." The witness can go forth only if he is in Christ redemptively, and only if he goes forth in the same Spirit that anointed Christ. (3) "Receive ye the Holy Ghost." The breathing is the symbol of bestowal. The words "Receive ye the Holy Ghost" are the command to be receptive. This command and bestowal are acts of the crucified and risen Lord. They represent the indication of His will. The bestowal is the redemptive bequest of the risen Lord. It is this command that is the authority for Paul's exhortation in Ephesians 5:18 (KJV), "And be not drunk with wine, wherein is excess; but be filled with the Spirit."

With this background of command and provision, there are certain conclusions that may be made about the New Testament church's experience in the outpouring of the Holy Spirit. The baptism and infilling of the Holy Spirit are essential to New Testament Christianity. This is shown by the relatively inactive condition of the church from the Day of Ascension until the Day of Pentecost. They had the same commission on the Day of Ascension that they had on the Day of Pentecost. However, the church was not prepared to fulfill the Great Commission without first having the equipment of the baptism in the Holy Spirit. The church was not fully prepared for existence as the church, because the Holy Spirit is the Spirit of worship and of witness.

We must conclude, then, that the baptism in the Holy Spirit is not an optional or decorative experience in the life of the church or the believer. It is significant that the New Testament attitude toward the baptism in the Holy Spirit is that this experience is the normal expectation of one who is in Christ. The idea of remaining a Christian without the baptism in the Holy Spirit was considered an abnormality. In practice, this experience should never have become a basis of denominational distinction. Pentecost is Christian and Christianity is Pentecostal; Pentecostalism should never have become a distinctive denominational designation.

Another aspect of the identification of Pentecost from the Scriptures is the statement of Acts 2:4, which may be translated as follows: "And all were filled of the Holy Spirit, and they began to speak with other tongues because[1] the Spirit was giving[2] to them to speak." There are causal connections here between the following: (1) When the tongues of fire sat upon the members of the worshiping body, they were filled with the Holy Spirit. (2) When they were filled with the Spirit, they began to speak with other tongues. (3) They began to speak with other tongues as and because the Holy Spirit was giving them to speak.

This identification of Pentecost continues in the subsequent events recorded in Acts 2. Probably the heart of the matter lies in what was preached on the Day of Pentecost and what became the distinctive proclamation of the early church. The sermon that is recorded of Peter in Acts 2 deals with the defense of the phenomena there witnessed. His defense is based on prophetic promise and on his claim that Jesus of Nazareth had given the experience then being witnessed. From this defense Peter moves to an enunciation of the motif that is characteristic of all the addresses recorded in Acts—designated the *kerygma* by New Testament students. His message is: Jesus of Nazareth was crucified, God raised Him from the dead, He has ascended to the right hand of God, and He is coming again to judge the quick and the dead. It is significant that this message is the center of New Testament preaching and literature. Though Paul makes quite a defense of the ministries of the Holy Spirit both in the church and in his own experience, his greatest emphasis is upon the cross and the resurrection.

Why do we pursue these two lines of thought? The first intends to delineate Pentecostalism in its recent historical origin. The second intends to identify Pentecostalism with normative New Testament church life.

1. For this use of *kathōs*, see F. Blass and A. Debrunner, *A Greek Grammar of the New Testament and Other Early Christian Literature*, trans. Robert W. Funk (Chicago: The University of Chicago Press, 1961), #453 (2) = p. 236.

2. Imperfect tense, *edidou.*

The conclusions that may be drawn are these:

1. Pentecostalism has its origins in a conservative Protestant milieu.

2. Pentecostalism has its origins in a holiness or separatist milieu.

3. Pentecostalism has adopted the beliefs of the milieu in which it originated. It has traditionally been a Trinitarian, evangelical movement.

4. Pentecostalism is distinct from the milieu in which it arose primarily in two respects: (a) its practices of worship, and (b) its doctrine of the baptism and manifestation of the Holy Spirit. Of these, the former is not really that distinctive. Such practices as weeping, shouting, and physical exertion (jerking, or however our world likes to characterize such) are common to most Protestant churches. These phenomena are usually treated as aberrant and undesirable, but the Pentecostal revivalists treated them as desirable and normative for a "good service."

The more specific point of distinction of Pentecostalism is that it distinguishes the baptism in the Holy Spirit from other religious experiences in the order of salvation. The Pentecostals who had a Wesleyan holiness background broke away from that background by making sanctification and the baptism in the Holy Spirit two distinct experiences. In similar fashion Pentecostals who were not so closely tied to a Wesleyan doctrine of sanctification made the baptism in the Holy Spirit distinct from the experience of conversion. These interpretations constitute a specific doctrinal break with other churches in the Protestant community.

I emphasize Pentecostalism's break with Protestantism because it arose from within Protestantism. There is an equally distinctive break with the traditions of the Roman Catholic Church. It lies in Pentecostalism's rejection of most of the sacramentalism of the Roman Catholic Church, and particularly in Pentecostalism's order of the experience of salvation and its baptism in the Holy Spirit.

Pentecostalism also added the doctrinal distinction of treating the experience of speaking in tongues as the Spirit gives utterance as the initial evidence of the baptism in the Holy Spirit.

The fundamental conclusion that may be drawn from the distinctions stated above is that Pentecostalism is *not* a "third force," distinct from Protestantism and Roman Catholicism. In its historical connections, it is fully identifiable with the Protestant tradition.

All of these points are offered on the assumption that it is legitimate to identify a term by its historical development. This is more impor-

tant actually than its etymology. Both historical development and
etymology may be subject to much evolution. But if the term and the
movement come to take on a normative character and to correspond
to each other, the term (or terms) and its definition become fairly well
identified and stable. It is my contention that this has happened with
the word "Pentecostal" and its derivatives.

One has to know that such a terminology is subject to change, and,
in fact, is in the process of change. This fact calls for a clear use of terminology. We cannot carry on dialogue unless our use of terms is
meaningful. The terms must be specific and not purely personal in
content.

The more important purpose of our study to this point is the one
associated with the New Testament literature and its recognition of
what we have called "Pentecostal phenomena." In keeping with the
biblicism of its background, the Pentecostal movement has
understood the manifestation of experiences such as speaking in
tongues, interpretation of tongues, prophesying, and other ministries
and gifts of the Holy Spirit to be normative in the New Testament
church. I would point out that the very existence of rules for governing the ministries of the Holy Spirit is tacit approval of their operation. Paul's instructions on the control of the spiritual gifts presupposes their legitimacy. To find in rules of operation a prohibition
against existence is to reveal one's own prejudices. With reasoning of
this type, what is aberrant or special to a unique situation is not
understood as normative; hence, there is no expectation of its continuing regularity in the church. But given the Pentecostal presupposition,
those things that are regulated—and hence normative—may be expected to continue regularly in the life of the church. Hence, they may
take on a doctrinal significance.

Doctrinal Norms

What are those doctrinally related norms that may be discovered in
the New Testament? The first is that the experience of the baptism in
the Holy Spirit is distinguishable from conversion. The second is that
the initial outward manifestation of the baptism in the Holy Spirit is
the experience of speaking with other tongues as the Spirit gives utterance. The third is that the practice of holiness is normative for professing Christians and particularly for those seeking or professing the
indwelling presence of and baptism in the Holy Spirit. The controlling
motif for these doctrines, however, is not the person and work of the
Holy Spirit—but the person and work of the Son as the Redeemer,
who is revealed by the word and Spirit of God.

The facts, then, lead us to the conclusion that Pentecostalism is not the central concern of the Pentecostal. He has become predominantly identified by an aspect of his religious experience that is not central to his theology or message. His concern is the centrality of Jesus Christ.

Problematic Issues

There are certain problematic issues within Pentecostalism. These are created by the history of Pentecostalism and the present tension between the so-called "classical Pentecostals" and the so-called "Neo-Pentecostals" (or "charismatics"). Some of these problems are distinctive of one side or the other; some are common to both.

The *first* issue is the use and meaning of our terms. What is the meaning of the terms that we are dealing with? The key terms are our nomenclature: Pentecostal, Neo-Pentecostal, and—more recently—charismatic. Earlier in this paper, an attempt was made to give a historical and biblical basis for the use of the term "Pentecostal." Whatever the word "Neo-Pentecostal" means, I would suggest that it must submit to some kind of analysis that defines its character as something other than a negative attitude toward the so-called *classical* Pentecostal position. More recently, the term "charismatic" has been used. This seems to be an outgrowth of the popular use of the word *charisma* and its plural, *charismata*, as designations of the extraordinary ministries of the Holy Spirit described in 1 Corinthians 12. I personally question the use of the term because I doubt that Paul intended a technical use of his term. But the essential question is, Are we using the term with biblical content or with existentialist content? If the latter, then no hearer knows if he is hearing what any speaker is saying. If we expect to communicate, we cannot use words (like the Mad Hatter in *Alice in Wonderland*) to mean only what we want them to mean, nothing more, nothing less.

Our *second* problematic issue, it seems to me, lies in the fact that we have attempted unification on the assumption of a common experience. A common experience is exactly the sort of thing that permits identity of phenomena to hide differences of commitment. It is no new observation that persons not even Christian (professing the worship of other gods) have had experiences which are similar to "speaking in other tongues" (and in fact are called glossolalia). Additionally, virtually all religious movements have had "prophets" who professed to give divine oracles. So the phenomena of Pentecostalism cannot unify, or for that matter, even identify.

The *third* fundamental problem is to designate a common ground of authority for religious experiences, belief, and practices. Unification must have a common ground of authority as a basis of commitment and vocabulary. Can we come to designate an authority for the use and definition of terms? I would suggest that such an authority must begin with Scripture, analytically studied. If we cannot come together under this banner and authority, there are theological and ideological differences that forbid any unification of our efforts, and in fact, our fraternity.

The *fourth* issue to be faced by Pentecostals is the matter of theological identity. Pentecostalism has not faced the necessity of such an identity. This fact is in evidence from several points: (1) the nebulous character of creeds within the Pentecostal communions; (2) the theological hodgepodge now coming together under the banner of "charismatics" and the use of tongue-speaking (or other charismatic expressions) as the unifying motif; (3) the unwillingness of Pentecostals to support advanced theological training as strongly as they do advanced training in other areas. This is not a problem seen only among the traditional Pentecostals. Pentecostals tend to place their religious commitments and experiences in an unanalyzed vacuum unaffected by other intellectual developments. Traditional Pentecostals want a slicked-up evangelistic and hortatory professionalism but not an analytical and systematic theology. The charismatics want an experience that does not interfere with doctrinal and traditional commitments already made.

The *fifth* issue here is that Pentecostalism has not faced the dangers of an emotion- and experience-centered theology. This difficulty is, in fact, an outgrowth of the points just mentioned. This is a theological stance, but it is one that has "happened to us" rather than one that we have arrived at by study of Scripture.

This kind of development has produced an anti-intellectualism that revolts against education, rejects intellectual analysis of religious experience, and rejects a biblical examination and analysis of religious experience.

Experience (often a charismatic manifestation) is used to affirm a doctrine or a decision, approve or vindicate a man, sanctify a communion, or canonize a mode of worship. In traditional Pentecostalism, this has led to emotional excesses in worship, erroneous doctrinal affirmations, and false personal judgments. Among charismatics, the new-found experience apparently does not lead to an examination of traditionally held views; instead, the experience of speaking in tongues is used to confirm the rightness of all of the personal conditions, beliefs, and practices which prevailed at the time.

In making emotion so central, we are often unwilling to submit to scriptural government of the manifestations of the Holy Spirit. Many Pentecostals do not consider 1 Corinthians 14 their favorite passage of Scripture. We fail to recognize that one of our favorite passages ("Quench not the Spirit"—1 Thess. 5:19, KJV) is as much violated by excesses as it is by suppression.

The use of emotional experience as a basis for our critiques has also served to develop a sort of incipient gnostic level of judgment. Morality is decided on the basis of what seems appropriate and this judgment is then translated into the leading of the Holy Spirit. It appears in man-made ordinances which say, "Touch not; taste not; handle not" (Col. 2:21, KJV). It also appears in the "imitation of Jesus" motif which judges all things by the question, "What would Jesus do in this situation?" The subjective answer to this is taken as the answer of the Holy Spirit. This problem also surfaces in another extreme—libertinism. Here it is assumed that the Holy Spirit (as understood emotionally and experientially) confirms as good whatever one is and whatever one does when he is being "blessed." This is a shallow form of emotional pragmatism that is passed off as the guidance of the Holy Spirit.

The *sixth* problematic issue to be faced within the Pentecostal movement is that we have not always kept a biblical perspective of what the baptism in the Holy Spirit is to do for us. We sometimes exalt the secondary benefits of the Spirit-baptism to a primary level. Charismatic manifestations are used (and sought) as emotional cathartics. Charismatic manifestations are made the tool of the individual and are subjected to his will.

We do not take seriously enough the fact that the Holy Spirit is the Spirit of Christ. Hence we tend to make the Holy Spirit central to testimony, religious experience, and preaching. The relationship of the gift of the Holy Spirit to Christ's redemptive work indicates the centrality of Christ and His cross to the Pentecostal experience.

The surest evidence of the Holy Spirit-filled life is the Christ-filled life. It is a superficial emphasis to talk about the baptism in the Holy Spirit as giving power only for witnessing. It is empowerment for godly living. This is evident from the fact that the spiritual graces that identify holy living are called the fruit of the Spirit.

In this light we fail to take into account that the Holy Spirit-filled life is a contradiction and condemnation of this world order. The Paraclete comes to convict the world of sin, of righteousness, and of judgment. This threefold convicting has Christ as its center (John 16:8-11). The Holy Spirit is the Spirit of Christ and, as the Spirit of Christ, He is opposed to the spirit that now works in the children of disobedience (Eph. 2:2). We must not be deceived by a new-found popularity of the Pentecostal experience. The cross and all that proceeds from the cross are still an offense to and condemnation of the world. The baptism in the Holy Spirit is equally offensive because it proceeds from the cross. This is true in spite of the present modishness of speaking in tongues. We must not imply any removal of the offense which the cross gives to the world.

Gordon D. Fee

Gordon D. Fee was ordained in 1959 as a minister of the Assemblies of God. He is a graduate of Seattle Pacific College (B.A., 1956; M.A., 1958) and of the University of Southern California (Ph.D., 1966). After a pastorate in the state of Washington, he served on the faculties of Southern California College (Costa Mesa) and Wheaton College before assuming his present position as associate professor of New Testament at Gordon-Conwell Theological Seminary, South Hamilton, Massachusetts. He is a member of the Studiorum Novi Testamenti Societas and serves on the American executive committee of the International Greek New Testament Project, co-chairing its patristics section. His publications, often on textual criticism, have appeared in *Biblica*, *Journal of Biblical Literature*, *New Testament Studies*, and *Novum Testamentum*. His doctoral thesis was a study of *Papyrus Bodmer II—Its Textual Relationships and Scribal Characteristics*, now published as *Studies and Documents 34* (Salt Lake City: University of Utah Press, 1968).

In this essay, Dr. Fee surfaces an issue basic to the ongoing discussions of Pentecostal theology. He pleads for careful notice of the historical character of Acts, on which much of classical Pentecostal doctrine is based. In what way, he asks, may historical precedent be normative?

Hermeneutics and Historical Precedent – a Major Problem in Pentecostal Hermeneutics

8

Walter J. Hollenweger offers this interesting dedication in his comprehensive survey of Pentecostalism in the churches: "To my friends and teachers in the Pentecostal Movement who taught me to love the Bible and to my teachers and friends in the Presbyterian Church who taught me to understand it."[1] This statement by a former Pentecostal reflects the strength of Pentecostalism in general and its weakness in hermeneutics in particular.

Pentecostals, in spite of some of their excesses, are frequently praised for recapturing for the church her joyful radiance, missionary enthusiasm, and life in the Spirit. But they are at the same time noted for bad hermeneutics. Thus, in the more recent irenic treatments of Pentecostals and their theology—such as those by James D. G. Dunn,[2] Frederick D. Bruner,[3] Hollenweger,[4] and Clark H. Pinnock[5]—one finds

1. *The Pentecostals, The Charismatic Movement in the Churches* (Minneapolis: Augsburg, 1972), p. xvi.

2. *Baptism in the Holy Spirit, Studies in Biblical Theology*, Series 2, 15 (London: SCM, 1970).

3. *A Theology of the Holy Spirit, The Pentecostal Experience and the New Testament Witness* (Grand Rapids: Eerdmans, 1970).

4. See n. 1.

5. With Grant R. Osborne, "A Truce Proposal for the Tongues Controversy," *Christianity Today*, 16 (Oct. 8, 1971), 6-9. See Pinnock's essay in the present volume.

words of appreciation for the Pentecostal contribution alongside a critical assessment of the exegetical base for its distinctive teaching on Holy Spirit baptism.

The Problem

Although other exegetical and theological problems are sometimes noted, the crucial issue for Pentecostals in hermeneutics lies at their very heart, namely, with their "distinctives": (1) the doctrine of subsequence, i.e., that there is for Christians a baptism in the Spirit distinct from and subsequent to the experience of salvation, a doctrine which Pentecostals share with many "non-tongues" expressions of Christianity, and (2) the doctrine of tongues as the initial physical evidence of baptism in the Spirit.

An example of the formulation of these distinctives may be found in articles 7 and 8 of the "Statement of Fundamental Truths" of the General Council of the Assemblies of God:

7. The Baptism in the Holy Ghost

All believers are entitled to and should ardently expect and earnestly seek the promise of the Father, the baptism in the Holy Ghost and fire, according to the command of our Lord Jesus Christ. This was the normal experience of all in the early Christian Church . . . . This experience is distinct from and subsequent to the experience of the new birth (Acts 8:12-17; 10:44-46; 11:14-16; 15:7-9) . . . .

8. The Evidence of the Baptism in the Holy Ghost

The baptism of believers in the Holy Ghost is witnessed by the initial physical sign of speaking with other tongues as the Spirit of God gives them utterance (Acts 2:4). The speaking in tongues in this instance is the same in essence as the gift of tongues (1 Cor. 12:4-10, 28), but different in purpose and use.[6]

It will be noted that the sole biblical support for these teachings consists of passages from the Book of Acts. It is important to note further that in the literature of the movement the experience of the apostles in Acts 2:4 is often seen as subsequent to their "conversion" experience in John 20:22. One also finds the doctrine of subsequence supported by the example of Jesus, who was conceived of the Holy Spirit, but endued with power by the Spirit at His baptism.[7] Thus for

---

6. *Minutes of the Thirty-fifth General Council of the Assemblies of God* (Miami Beach, Florida, August 16-21, 1973), p. 102.

7. See especially Ralph M. Riggs, *The Spirit Himself* (Springfield, MO: Gospel Publishing House, 1949), pp. 47-61. Cf. Dennis and Rita Bennett, *The Holy Spirit and You* (Plainfield, NJ: Logos International, 1971), pp. 23-25.

Pentecostals the baptism in the Holy Spirit subsequent to conversion
and evidenced by tongues is "the clear teaching of Scripture," based
on biblical historical precedent. The Acts of the Apostles is the normative record of the normative primitive church. Therefore, the
apostolic experience is the normative model for all Christians.[8]

Those who disagree with Pentecostals on these points usually argue
in two closely related veins. First, they argue that one must
distinguish between *didactic* and *historical* portions of Scripture, and
that for the formulation of Christian doctrine and experience one
must go primarily to the didactic portions, and only secondarily to
the historical.[9] Secondly, what is *descriptive history* of the primitive
church must not be translated into *normative experience* for the ongoing church. Pinnock and Osborne have put these two arguments
together thus: "Didactic portions of Scripture must have precedence
over historical passages in establishing doctrine," and " . . . the Book
of Acts does not establish a normative experience for the believer
today."[10]

The issues raised here have to do with the hermeneutics of the
historical passages of Scripture, especially with the concept of
historical precedent. Is there a way in which biblical historical
precedents speak to us as God's Word? And in what way, if at all, is
such a Word to be regarded as normative?

Some Preliminary Observations

Two observations should be made about hermeneutics within the
traditional Pentecostal movement. First, their attitude toward Scripture regularly has included a general disregard for scientific exegesis
and carefully thought-out hermeneutics. In fact, hermeneutics has
simply not been a Pentecostal thing. Scripture is the Word of God and
is to be obeyed. In place of scientific hermeneutics there developed a
kind of pragmatic hermeneutics—obey what should be taken literally;
spiritualize, allegorize, or devotionalize the rest. Pentecostals, of
course, are not alone in this. Furthermore, gifted men tend to apply
this hermeneutic with inspired common sense. Therefore, although exegetical aberrations abound in Pentecostal pulpits and sometimes in

---

8. Hollenweger, *The Pentecostals*, p. 321, cites a Swiss Pentecostal confessional statement which says: "The apostolic church is its obligatory model."

9. See, for example, John R. W. Stott, *The Baptism and Fullness of the Holy Spirit*
(Downers Grove, IL: Inter-Varsity, 1964), p. 8, and Anthony Hoekema, *Holy Spirit Baptism* (Grand Rapids: Eerdmans, 1972), pp. 23f.

10. "A Truce Proposal," p. 8.

their pamphlets, the mainstream of traditional American Pentecostalism has treated Scripture in very much the same way as have other forms of American fundamentalism or evangelicalism. The differences have been over *what* is to be literally obeyed.

Secondly, it is probably fair—and important—to note that in general the Pentecostals' experience has preceded their hermeneutics. In a sense, the Pentecostal tends to exegete his experience. For example, the doctrine of Spirit-baptism as distinct from and subsequent to conversion did not flow naturally out of his reading of Scripture. What happened was that he himself had spent a considerable time after his conversion sensing a lack of spiritual power. He saw the dynamic, life-transforming quality of the apostolic experience in Acts 2 and asked God for something similar. When he did have a dynamic experience in the Holy Spirit, he said with Peter, "This is that." The fact that it happened after his conversion helped him to see this very pattern in Scripture: he saw the analogy with Jesus and the apostles, and the precedent in Samaria (Acts 8) and Paul (Acts 9). What followed was perfectly natural. He took the scriptural pattern he had now found, supported by his own personal experience and that of thousands of others, and made it normative for all Christians.

In defense of the Pentecostal, it should be observed that although he has tended to arrive at the biblical norm by way of his experience, he is not alone in establishing norm on the basis of historical precedent rather than on the explicit teaching of Scripture. The practice of infant baptism and the theology of its necessity are based first of all on the exegesis of some historical passages in Acts and one in 1 Corinthians (7:14); they are made normative on the basis of the historical precedent.[11] (Roman Catholic theologians would prefer the word "tradition.") The Baptists' insistence on baptism by immersion is based on no clear statement of Scripture, but rather on the exegesis of certain passages (including word study: "to baptize" = "to immerse") and historical precedent.[12] The partaking of the Lord's Supper every

---

11. See especially the debate between Joachim Jeremias and Kurt Aland: Jeremias, *Infant Baptism in the First Four Centuries* (Philadelphia: Westminster, 1960), and *The Origins of Infant Baptism* (London: SCM, 1963); Aland, *Did the Early Church Baptize Infants?* (London: SCM, 1961); Pierre Ch. Marcel in *The Biblical Doctrine of Infant Baptism* (London: James Clarke and Co., 1953) bases his argument on the related hermeneutical principle of the analogy of faith.

12. It is interesting to see the Bennetts assume a moderate stance on this issue of historical precedent: "It is assumed that you who are reading this book and who accept Christ will receive or have received baptism with water in the manner of the particular Christian fellowship to which you belong, and in accordance with your understanding of what the Scripture teaches about it" (*The Holy Spirit and You*, pp. 25f.).

Sunday is required by some Christians on the basis of historical precedent (Acts 20:7).[13] Likewise, on the basis of Acts 2:44f. some groups in the Jesus movement require the selling of possessions and having all things in common. Even such fringe groups as the snake-handlers argue for their distinctive practices partly on the basis of historical precedent (Acts 28:3-6).

The hermeneutical problem, therefore, is not unique to Pentecostals. It has to do with the interpretation and appropriation of the historical sections of Scripture. The problem may be posed in several ways. *How* is the Book of Acts the Word of God? That is, does it have a Word which not only describes the primitive church but speaks as a norm to the church at all times? If there is such a Word, how does one discover it, or set up principles in order to hear it? If the primitive church is normative, *which* expression of it is normative? Jerusalem? Antioch? Philippi? Corinth? That is, why do not all the churches sell their possessions and have all things in common? Or further, is it at all legitimate to take descriptive statements as normative? If so, how does one distinguish those which are from those which are not? For example, must we follow the pattern of Acts 1:26 and select leaders by lot? Just exactly what role does historical precedent play in Christian doctrine or in the understanding of Christian experience?

Already this paper has raised more questions than its author is capable of answering. Unfortunately, one looks in vain in the standard works on hermeneutics for answers, because for the most part these questions are not asked. Under the rubric of "special hermeneutics" one finds suggestions or principles on how to deal with prophecy, typology, parables, apocalypses, etc., but nothing on the manner in which one is to understand the historical sections as a normative Word for today.[14] This is all the more surprising when one considers how often the Old Testament and New Testament historical

13. It is of interest that the Assemblies of God sees baptism by immersion as "commanded in the Scriptures," but makes no statement on the frequency of the Lord's Supper. Most Assemblies, therefore, observe the Supper monthly, although daily or weekly seems to be the biblical "pattern."

14. Paul D. Wieland offered a thesis to the Graduate School of Wheaton College entitled "Criteria for Determining the Normative in New Testament Church Government" (1965). But he scarcely comes to grips with the issues raised here. He does have a long section on hermeneutics, which simply goes over much-plowed ground. In his (all too short) section on the hermeneutics of history he fails to distinguish between history as the mighty acts of God and as the mere recording of narrative events per se. He suggests that events in New Testament history may be exemplary, serving as models or warnings (p. 15), but he offers no discussion of the criteria to be used in determining in what way, if any, they are normative for us.

and biographical sections are preached from not simply for illustrative value, but also somehow by analogy for normative value.

Since this is an exploratory essay, what follows is a potpourri of general hermeneutical observations and specific suggestions for the hermeneutics of historical precedent. These are not offered as definitive, but as an invitation to further dialogue both with my own Pentecostal brethren as well as with other evangelicals.[15]

Some General Principles

1. It should be an axiom of biblical hermeneutics that the interpreter must take into account the literary genre of the passage he is interpreting, along with the questions of text, grammar, philology, and history. Such a principle would appear to be self-evident, yet it is seldom applied to the New Testament except for the Apocalypse. However, the Gospels, Epistles, and Acts are also distinct literary types, and awareness of this fact must become a part of valid hermeneutics.

The point is that not every biblical statement is the Word of God in exactly the same way. The fact that the Psalms are poetry, that the prophets are primarily a collection of spoken oracles, that Ecclesiastes and Job are Jewish wisdom literature, that Daniel and the Revelation are apocalyptic, that the epistles are letters, and that the Acts is historical narrative must be a primary consideration in interpretation in order to avoid the non-contextual, "promise box" approach to Scripture.

For example, the epistles must be taken seriously as letters, not treated primarily as theological treatises. Theology obviously abounds, and frequently is the primary intent; but they are not systematic treatises on theology. Paul's theology is related to his special task as missionary to the Gentiles, and it is worked out accordingly.[16] This does not diminish the theological value of the epistles—indeed, I think it enhances it—but it does demand that the interpreter be aware of the genre and *not* treat the writings of Paul in the same manner he would the treatises of Augustine or the *Summa* of Aquinas.

So also with the Acts. However much of the "theology" of Luke one

15. Much of what follows may seem irrelevant to some of my Roman Catholic brethren, since historical precedent (as tradition) has for them a fixed role in establishing what is normative for Christian faith.

16. Cf. G. W. Barker, W. L. Lane, J. R. Michaels, *The New Testament Speaks* (New York: Harper & Row, 1969), pp. 148f.

finds in the book, it is *not* an epistle, nor a theological treatise. Even if one disregards its historical value, he cannot, indeed must not, disregard the fact that it is cast in the form of historical narrative. This, it seems to me, is the great fault of the monumental works of Dibelius and Haenchen.[17] They tend to treat Acts first as theology and only secondarily as history. I demur. Theology there is aplenty, and theology is most likely a part of Luke's intent; but it is cast as history, and the first principle of hermeneutics here is to take that literary genre seriously.

The significance of this principle for our problem is that in the hermeneutics of biblical history the major task of the interpreter is to discover the author's (I would add, the Holy Spirit's) *intent* in the recording of that history. This, of course, is a general maxim of hermeneutics and applies to the other literary genres as well. But it is of crucial importance to the hermeneutics of the historical narratives. For it is one thing for the historian to include an event because it serves the greater purpose of his work, and yet another thing for the interpreter to take that incident as having didactic value apart from the historian's larger intent.

Although Luke's "broader intent" may be a moot point for some, it is a defensible hypothesis that he was trying to show how the church emerged as a chiefly Gentile, world-wide phenomenon from its origins as a Jerusalem-based, Judaism-oriented sect of Jewish believers, and how the Holy Spirit was ultimately responsible for this phenomenon of universal salvation based on grace alone.

An event such as the conversion of Cornelius serves this broader interest not simply to "represent a principle . . . of higher historical truth" (so Dibelius), nor simply to illustrate Christian conversion in general or the baptism in the Holy Spirit in particular (so Pentecostals). Rather, Cornelius serves for Luke as the first-fruits of the Gentile mission, and he is important to Luke's purpose because his conversion is by direct intervention of the Holy Spirit through one of the Jerusalem apostles (Acts 15:7; cf. 10:19, 44; 11:12; 15). Through these combined circumstances the eyes of the church were opened to the fact that "even to the Gentiles God has granted repentance unto life."

Whatever else one gleans from the story, whether it be the place of visions in Christian guidance (!) or the nature of Christian conversion, such gleanings are *incidental* to Luke's intent. This does not mean that

---

17. Martin Dibelius, *Studies in the Acts of the Apostles* (London: SCM, 1956); Ernst Haenchen, *The Acts of the Apostles* (Philadelphia: Westminster, 1971).

what is incidental is false, nor that it has no theological value; it does mean that God's Word *for us* in that narrative is primarily related to what it was intended to teach.

On the basis of this discussion the following principles emerge with regard to the hermeneutics of historical narrative:

a. The Word of God in Acts which may be regarded as normative for Christians is related primarily to what any given narrative was *intended* to teach.

b. What is *incidental* to the primary intent of the narrative may indeed reflect an author's theology, or how he understood things, but it cannot have the same didactic value as what the narrative was *intended* to teach has. This does not negate what is incidental, nor imply that it has no word for us. What it does argue is that what is incidental must not become primary, although it may always serve as additional support to what is unequivocally taught elsewhere.

c. Historical precedent, to have normative value, must be related to *intent*. That is, if it can be shown that the purpose of a given narrative is to *establish* precedent, then such precedent should be regarded as normative. For example, if it could be demonstrated on exegetical grounds that Luke's intent in Acts 1:15-26 was to give the church a precedent for selecting its leaders, then such a selection process should be followed by later Christians. But if the establishing of precedent was *not* the intent of the narrative, then its value as a precedent for later Christians should be treated according to the specific principles suggested in the next section of this paper.

2. Closely related to the foregoing discussion is the observation that not all doctrinal statements derived from Scripture belong to the same categories, nor are they on the same level within those categories.

In general, doctrinal statements fall into three categories: (a) Christian theology (what Christians believe), (b) Christian ethics (how Christians ought to behave), and (c) Christian experience or practice (what Christians do). Statements within these categories may further be classified as primary or secondary, depending on whether, on the one hand, they are derived from what are "propositions" or "imperatives" (i.e., what is *intended*), or whether, on the other hand, they are derived incidentally, by implication or by precedent.[18]

For example, in the category of Christian theology such statements as God is one, God is love, all have sinned, Christ died for our sins,

18. This, of course, does not rule out the didactic nature of the historical portions of Scripture. What we learn of God from His acts is every bit as important as what we learn from "propositions." These acts, which teach us of His reality and grace, are usually *interpreted* as having didactic or saving significance. Thus we have Gospels, not

salvation is by grace, and Jesus Christ is divine are derived from passages where they are taught by intent, and are therefore primary. At the secondary level are those statements which are the logical outflow of the primary statements, or are derived by implication from Scripture. Thus the fact, or "that-ness," of the deity of Christ is primary; *how* the natures concur in unity is secondary. A similar distinction may be made with regard to the doctrine of Scripture: that it is the inspired word of God is primary; the nature of inspiration is secondary. This is not to say that the secondary statements are unimportant. Quite often they will have significant bearing on one's faith with regard to the primary statements. In fact, their ultimate theological value may be related to how well they preserve the integrity of the primary statements.

Similar distinctions may be made in the category of Christian ethics. At the primary level are the general maxims, the imperatives, the absolutes: love for one's enemy, unlimited forgiveness, temperance, etc. From these may be derived concrete principles and applications for specific situations.

The concept of levels of doctrinal statements seems to apply as well to the category which is of special interest in this paper: Christian experience and practice. For example, the necessity of the Lord's Supper is at the primary level, based on an imperative; but the frequency of its observance, which is based on precedent alone, is surely not as binding. So also with the necessity of baptism and its mode, or the practice of Christians "assembling of themselves together" and the frequency or the day of the week. Again, this is not to say that the secondary statements are unimportant. For example, one will surely be hard pressed to prove that Christians must meet to worship on Saturday or Sunday; but in either case one is saying something of theological significance by his practice.

The doctrine of a baptism in the Holy Spirit as subsequent to conversion and accompanied by tongues seems to belong to the secondary level of doctrinal statements in my third category. That the Christian is to be (or keep) filled with the Spirit, that he is to walk and live in the Spirit is at the primary level and normative. When and how he enters that dimension of Christian experience, although not unimportant, is not of the same "normative" quality, because the "when and how" is based solely on precedent and/or analogy.

simply collections of the sayings of Jesus. The saving events of history are a deed-word complex—not simply deed, nor simply word. Cf. George E. Ladd, *The New Testament and Criticism* (Grand Rapids: Eerdmans, 1967), pp. 19-33.

Specific Principles for the Use of Historical Precedent

With these general observations and principles in view, I would offer the following suggestions as to the hermeneutics of historical precedent:

1. The use of historical precedent as an analogy by which to establish a norm is never valid in itself. Such a process (drawing universal norms from particular events) produces a *non sequitur* and is therefore irrelevant. Thus, to urge the necessity of water baptism as an act of obedience to Jesus' example is bad exegesis. John's baptism and Christian baptism, though the latter is probably rooted in the former, are different things, and the meaning and necessity of Christian baptism must be made of sterner stuff.

Likewise the analogies of Jesus and the apostles as having been "born" of the Spirit and later "baptized" in the Spirit may be interesting as analogies, but they are of such different kind from succeeding Christian experience that they can scarcely have normative value. The Day of Pentecost is a great line of demarcation; it marks the beginning of the age of the Spirit. Surely valid patterns of *Christian* experience must follow that Day, not precede it.

2. Although it may not have been the author's primary purpose, historical narratives do have illustrative and, sometimes, "pattern" value. In fact, this is how the New Testament people used the historical precedents of the Old Testament. Paul, for example, used certain Old Testament examples as warnings to those who had a false security in their divine election (1 Cor. 10:1-13); and Jesus used the example of David as an historical precedent to justify His disciples' sabbath actions (Mark 2:23-28 and parallels).

Whether we can reproduce the manner of exegesis which the New Testament authors applied to the Old Testament may be a moot point.[19] It should be noted, however, especially in cases where the precedent justifies a present action, that the precedent does not establish a norm for specific action. Men are not to eat regularly of the show-bread or to pluck grain on the sabbath to show that the sabbath was made for man. Rather, the precedent illustrates a principle with regard to the sabbath.

A caveat is in order here: for a biblical precedent to justify a present action, the principle of the action must be taught elsewhere, where it

---

19. Richard N. Longenecker, in "Can We Reproduce the Exegesis of the New Testament?" *Tyndale Bulletin*, 21 (1970), 3-38, has argued that because of the revelatory character of the New Testament its exegesis should "once-for-all" be considered not normative, and in some cases not even repeatable.

is the primary intent so to teach. For example, to use Jesus' cleansing of the temple to justify one's so-called righteous indignation—usually a euphemism for selfish anger—is to abuse this principle. On the other hand, the Pentecostal may justify his speaking in tongues not only from precedent (in Acts) but also from the teaching about spiritual gifts in 1 Corinthians 12—14.

3. In matters of Christian experience, and even more so of Christian practice, biblical precedents may be regarded as repeatable patterns—even if they are not to be regarded as normative. This is especially true when the practice itself is mandatory but the mode is not.

The repeatable character of certain practices or patterns should be guided by the following considerations:

a. The strongest possible case can be made when only one pattern is found (although one must be careful not to make too much of silence), and when that pattern is repeated within the New Testament itself.

b. When there is an ambiguity of patterns or when a pattern occurs but once, it is repeatable for later Christians only if it appears to have divine approbation or is in harmony with what is taught elsewhere in Scripture.

c. What is culturally conditioned is either not repeatable at all, or must be translated into the new or differing culture.

Thus, on the basis of these principles, one can make the strongest kind of case for immersion as the mode of baptism, a much weaker case for the observance of the Lord's Supper each Sunday, and almost no case, except on other grounds, for infant baptism.[20] By the same token, the Mormon practice of baptism for the dead fails on all counts.

It is in the light of such principles, and in keeping with the careful exegesis of all passages involved, that one must examine the Pentecostal "distinctives."

Pentecostal Distinctives and Historical Precedent

The question of a baptism in the Holy Spirit distinct from and subsequent to conversion remains a thorny one. In the first place, the Pentecostal has indeed experienced such a "baptism," and for him it has had a dynamic quality similar to the life in the Spirit one finds in the Acts. But apart from the analogies of Jesus and the apostles (ruled out as irrelevant), his biblical support for this baptism as "subsequent

20. Infant baptism, of course, may be argued from historical precedent, but not so easily from biblical precedent, which is the issue here.

to and distinct from" rests on the "pattern" of Samaria (two weeks?), Paul (three days), and Ephesus (several minutes?). When faced with the Cornelius episode, he has argued either that Cornelius was already a Christian as a god-fearer (surely a case of exegetical gymnastics) or that "this visitation was God's ideal, His perfect pattern: believe Christ, receive the Holy Spirit in immediate succession."[21]

His strongest case is the episode at Samaria (Acts 8), but whether Luke intended to imply an experience "distinct from" conversion is debatable. Some indeed have argued against the Pentecostals (weakly, it seems to me) that the Samaritans were not even Christians until the advent of the Spirit (8:17). However, there are too many terms denoting Christian experience prior to verse 17 to give this view much support. Such terms as "[they] with one accord gave heed to what was said" (v. 6), had "much joy" (v. 8), "believed Philip as he preached the good news" (v. 12), "were baptized" (v. 12), and "had received the Word of God" (v. 14) are used elsewhere by Luke to describe the *Christian* experience of conversion. To argue on the basis of Romans 8:1-17 that they do not do so here is a case of special pleading.

Yet the Holy Spirit "had not yet fallen on them" (v. 16). Is Luke thereby intending to teach "distinct from and subsequent to"? Probably not. It is furthermore questionable whether he is teaching it incidentally—at least the notion that a baptism in the Spirit is distinct from conversion. In a carefully argued exegetical study of all the relevant passages in Acts, Dunn *(Baptism in the Holy Spirit)* concluded that for Luke the real evidence (and chief element) of Christian experience was the presence of the Spirit. What seems to be important for Luke in this narrative is that the validation (and completion) of Christian experience in the initial spread beyond Jerusalem is tied to the Jerusalem church and signified by a dynamic quality similar to theirs. If Dunn is correct, and it surely is defensible exegesis, then the concept of subsequence is irrelevant. What is of consequence is the experiential, dynamic quality of the gift of the Spirit.

If, however, a baptism in the Spirit "distinct from and subsequent to" is neither clearly taught in the New Testament nor necessarily to be seen as a normative pattern (let alone the *only* pattern) for Christian experience, there is a pattern in Acts which *may* be derived not only from historical precedent but also from the intent of Luke and Paul.

As Dunn (who is non-Pentecostal) has shown, for Luke (and Paul) the gift of the Spirit was not some sort of adjunct to Christian ex-

21. Riggs, *The Spirit Himself*, p. 111.

perience, nor was it some kind of second and more significant part of Christian experience. It was rather the chief element in the event (or process) of Christian conversion. Everywhere for Luke it is the presence of the Spirit that signifies the "real thing." And Paul asks the Galatians as to their Christian experience, "Did you receive the Spirit by works of the law, or by hearing with faith?" (Gal. 3:2). Furthermore, in Acts the recurring pattern of the coming (or presence) of the Spirit has a dramatic, or dynamic, element to it. It was experienced, or to use contemporary parlance, it was very often *charismatic* in nature.

If in his attempt to recapture this New Testament pattern, the Pentecostal saw the dynamic element as "distinct from and subsequent to," he should not thereby be faulted. The fault perhaps lay with the church which no longer normally expected or experienced life in the Spirit in a dynamic way.

The question as to whether tongues is the initial physical evidence of the charismatic quality of life in the Spirit is a moot point. The Pentecostal sees speaking in tongues as a repeated pattern and has argued that it is *the* normal pattern. Others agree that it is a repeated, and therefore repeatable, pattern; but to insist that it is the only valid sign seems to place too much weight on the historical precedent of three (perhaps four) instances in Acts.

What, then, may the Pentecostal say about his experience in view of the hermeneutical principles suggested in this paper?

1. In the New Testament the presence of the Spirit was the chief element of Christian conversion and the Christian life.

2. In Acts, as well as in the Pauline churches (cf. 1 Thess. 5:19-21; 1 Cor. 12—14, a charismatic dimension was a normal phenomenon in the reception of the Spirit.

3. Speaking in tongues, if not normative, was a repeated expression of the charismatic dimension of the coming of the Spirit.

4. Even though most contemporary Christians no longer expect a charismatic dimension *as an integral part of their conversion*, they may nevertheless—on the basis of the New Testament pattern—still experience such a dimension of life in the Spirit. That this dimension is now usually subsequent to conversion is ultimately irrelevant. The charismatic dimension is a repeatable, and--the Pentecostal would argue--valuable dimension of life in the Spirit.

5. Since speaking in tongues was a repeated expression of this dynamic, or charismatic, dimension of the coming of the Spirit, the contemporary Christian may expect this, too, as a part of his ex-

perience in the Spirit. If the Pentecostal may not say one *must* speak in tongues, he may surely say, why *not* speak in tongues? It does have repeated biblical precedent, it did have evidential value at Cornelius' household (Acts 10:45-46), and—in spite of much that has been written to the contrary—it does have value both for the edification of the individual believer (1 Cor. 14:2-5) and, with interpretation, for the edification of the church (1 Cor. 14:5, 26-28).

William J. Samarin

William J. Samarin is a Phi Beta Kappa graduate of the University of California at Berkeley (B.A., 1950), where he also earned (in 1962) a Ph.D. in linguistics. Since 1968 he has been professor of linguistics and anthropology at the University of Toronto. A specialist in socio-linguistics and in African languages, he has served as a special consultant to governments, not only of the United States, but also of African nations. The recipient of numerous grants and fellowships, Dr. Samarin has conducted linguistic field research in more than a dozen little-known languages and has published over fifty articles, reviews, and books. His interest in glossolalia dates from his youth, but it was his academic concern with the study of language in religion (within the field of the sociology of language) that led to his *Tongues of Men and Angels: The Religious Language of Pentecostalism* (New York: Macmillan, 1972).

In this article, Dr. Samarin reports a scientific study of the motives of a group of New Pentecostals in a non-charismatic church, concluding that becoming a glossolalist is not necessarily the consequence of conflict.

Religious Goals of a Neo-Pentecostal Group in a Non-Pentecostal Church

9

The study reported here was stimulated by a colleague who was asked
to give a critical reading to the first draft of my *Tongues of Men and
Angels*.[1] He felt, in spite of the fact that my avowed goal was a
socio-linguistic one (to describe what glossolalia is and how it is used
in the Pentecostal movement), that I should have said more about the
culture in which speaking in tongues takes place. What he wanted
was an ethnography of Pentecostal groups. In explaining his criticism,
he made claims based on impressions he had received from observing
certain local Pentecostal groups. To test his hypotheses is the goal of
this investigation.

But first, I should like to admit the desirability of an ethnography of
Pentecostal culture. It is good to have an understanding of the
cultural matrix in which any kind of behavior takes place. Yet a moment's thought reveals how rash that response of his was. His position
would require that all socio-linguistic studies—not to mention anthropology, folklore, musicology, economics and perhaps all other
studies of man—would have to be postponed until all cultures every-

1. William J. Samarin, *Tongues of Men and Angels: The Religious Language of
Pentecostalism* (New York: Macmillan, 1972).

135

where have been described. (And we do not even raise the problems of distinguishing one culture from another and of deciding which "subcultures" deserve separate descriptions.)

Another criticism of his position is specific to Pentecostalism. Which of its many exponents would one describe in the ethnographic monograph? It would be easiest to restrict oneself to an established Pentecostal denomination, like the Assemblies of God or the Pentecostal Holiness Church. It would be even easier to focus on a local church affiliated with one of those denominations. But glossolalia is verbal behavior that transcends all varieties of Pentecostalism. It is in fact one of the diacritic features of the Pentecostal movement. And this is the really substantive point: in dealing with Pentecostalism we are confronted not by a single "culture" but by a social movement.

Because Pentecostalism is a movement, there is a continuum on which are located different kinds of social entities. At one end of the continuum is the bureaucratized Pentecostal church, which is structurally and in some cases ideologically (or doctrinally) indistinguishable from evangelical Protestant Christianity.[2] (The pastor of one Pentecostal Holiness church in Canada said of his denomination, "We are the Presbyterians of Pentecostalism.") At the other end are loosely organized, small, sometimes religiously unaffiliated groups of close friends who meet for Bible study, prayer, and "sharing" (that is, talking about their faith, their problems, and their victories: what American Blacks would call "rap" sessions). In between are many different kinds of groups. Categorizing them will be arbitrary, or it will be determined by research goals.

Since glossolalia is pan-Pentecostal I could not limit myself to one segment of the movement, no more than Gerlach and Hine[3] could when they tried to describe the process inherent in all movements of social transformation. This is, of course, not to deny significant differences (even in the statistical sense) between various realizations of

2. By "evangelical" I mean something like orthodox or historical Christianity as manifested in Protestantism. This is a term evangelicals in the English-speaking world use of themselves: note the National Association of Evangelicals (in the United States). They contrast themselves with liberals. In this taxonomy "evangelical" is also used at a lower level to contrast with "fundamentalist." The latter would differ in, for example, his understanding of what biblical inspiration is and the extent to which evolution is part of the creative process. These are fairly clear and useful terms. In what follows, as in other treatments of contemporary Pentecostalism, "charismatic" is used synonymously with "Pentecostal."

3. Luther P. Gerlach and Virginia H. Hine, *People, Power, Change: Movements of Social Transformation* (New York: Bobbs-Merrill, 1970).

the movement. For example, glossolalia has different functions and frequency among second- or third-generation Pentecostals than it does among neo-Pentecostals. (The latter term designates participants in the movement who are "recruited" from outside traditional Pentecostalism, for example, from Presbyterian, Lutheran, and Roman Catholic churches. This is, however, not a term they use of themselves. They prefer to be known as Spirit-filled Christians, and they will use "Pentecostal" only as a last resort.)

In faulting me for not describing Pentecostal culture, my colleague says that I gave the impression that glossolalia can happen in just about any kind of Christian group in North America. This, he says, is simply not so. Although one finds the use of glossolalia among New Pentecostals from the larger denominations, it occurs, he says, only among nomiral members of those denominations, and "only within a context of defiance of the traditional culture of these larger groups." He cites one clergyman from a "mainline" denomination, a leader in the charismatic movement not only in his denomination but ecumenically, whose most "enthusiastic audiences are the Pentecostals; and his following is rather severely limited to these and to certain very estranged members" of his own denomination. He deduces therefore that the culture in which glossolalia takes place is one in which there is "conflict with the whole of liberal Protestantism." This is, in fact, a culture of "conflict and struggle."

I take these assertions seriously, because they were intended to challenge the validity of my socio-linguistic interpretation of speaking in tongues. In my colleague's opinion, I had failed to explain why people engage in glossolalia, because I had failed to see it as a sign of hostility and separatism.

The testing of the hypothesis could very well be a large-scale one, involving competence in psychological and sociological as well as anthropological methodologies. There are several reasons why I was not able to undertake an investigation of this magnitude at this time. Besides, my competence lies only in linguistics and anthropology. Nevertheless, I engaged myself in one study that resources and time permitted.

The Church Setting

What I needed was a group of neo-Pentecostals affiliated with a mainline church. It was not difficult to find such a group, for they abound in North America as well as England and in certain parts of the European continent. The group I studied were members of a mainline church in a large urban center in Canada. Ten years ago evangelicals would have considered the church liberal, its minister not preaching salvation. The denomination includes both evangelical (but probably no fundamentalist) and liberal ministers and churches. It was the pastor, as in many other cases in the contemporary scene, who had brought the new teaching to this congregation, after he had experienced the filling of the Holy Spirit. This experience took place about six months after his arrival.

Over a period of several years, a large number of his parish were "converted" to the new teaching, many of whom were active in the church and held responsible lay offices (see below). Communication took place mostly at the level of personal interaction or in small groups, not through pulpit propagandizing. Perhaps because of the pastor's example, intra-church "proselytizing" created very little strain on the church. The pastor has not been called on the carpet for his beliefs; there has been no significant emigration of church members because of the charismatic nucleus; and the church program has not suffered in any way. By all counts the church is doing as well as, if not better than, the average church of its rank in this denomination.

Moreover, when I began the study, the church had just called a new minister, evangelical but not charismatic (although charismatics were well represented on the search committee), to replace the other who was leaving voluntarily ("because the Lord led") to initiate a specialized and nondenominational ministry for "deeper spiritual" life. At the time of his leaving, one of the parishioners said, "Things were very good for him." He was admired as a person and respected for his ministry even by those who had not been converted to either the evangelical or charismatic emphases that he had introduced into the church. There appears to have been no criticism that he had become hostile to his denomination (that he was anti-establishment). At the time of this writing, it has been almost two years since the transition from one minister to the other.

The study was carried out by the use of a questionnaire returned anonymously at my request. The names of the prospective informants were provided by the pastor. The explanatory letter that accompanied the questionnaire mentioned the pastor's endorsement. The list contained the names of 105 people, 65 of whom were at that time in regular attendance at the church. Twenty-five were or had been linked closely to this church but were now going to other churches, and 15--now in full-time Christian service or training for such--were or had been related to the church or were products of its ministry. Of these, 44 or 41.9% returned the questionnaire. The family status of those who received the questionnaire is indicated in Table 1.

Table 1: Neo-Pentecostals in a Mainline Canadian Church

Couples (25 x 2)	50
Children of Couples	3
Mother and child (2 x 2)	4
"Mr."	12
"Mrs."	23
"Miss"	13
	105

Characterization of the Subjects

The respondents, as one might expect from a superficial acquaintance with the congregation, are from what is casually designated "middle class." Sixty per cent of the annual salaries, computed for single persons and for households (in the case of the married people), are, for example, in the $5,000 to $15,000 range (see Table 2).

Table 2: Annual Salaries of Respondents

Under $5,000	18.2%	(8)
$5,000 to $10,000	31.8%	(14)
$10,000 to $15,000	27.3%	(12)
$15,000 to $20,000	6.8%	(3)
Over $20,000	13.6%	(6)
Not indicated	2.3%	(1)

For present occupations 11 registered housewife or student; 20 indicated secretary, teacher, or nurse. There was one dentist, one in the civil service, one systems analyst, and so forth. The salaries, if not the occupations, are suggested by the subjects' education: 10 have one university degree or more; 13 have a high school diploma as well as some special training or university course work; 7 have only a high school diploma; 14, surprisingly (since only one person was less than 20 years old), have less than a high school diploma.

This, then, is a mature group. Thirty-five (79.5%) of them are married. The average age is 40.3 years (19 or 43.2% in the 31-50 age range). Most of them (31 or 70.5%) are female.

Although it was not possible to undertake any kind of psychological testing with this group, the subjects were asked to describe the kind of person they considered themselves to be by choosing one or the other of the following characterizations or by marking an intermediate grade. The scores are indicated in Table 3.

Table 3: Self-characterization by Neo-Pentecostals*

Emotionally stable	27.2%	Affected by feelings	25.0%	±	50.5%
Shy	15.9%	Uninhibited	29.5%	±	50.0%
Nervous	9.1%	Relaxed	45.4%	±	45.4%
Serious	31.8%	Happy-go-lucky	4.6%	±	56.8%
Reserved	22.7%	Outgoing	43.2%	±	29.5%
Suspicious	0.0%	Trusting	63.6%	±	29.5%
Practical	36.4%	Artistic	15.9%	±	45.4%

* The symbol ± means in between the two opposites.

Although the subjects obviously preferred to play it safe by standing in the middle ground, the following picture of them seems to emerge: stable, uninhibited, relaxed, serious, outgoing, trusting, and practical.

In religious affiliation also this is a stable group. They had all been church members for a long time (the average is 22 years), and their church affiliation seems to have been stable. The first church membership for 56.8% of the subjects was in the United Church. But other mainline churches are also well represented: 13.6% for both Methodist and Anglican. The other churches are Baptist, Presbyterian, Evangelical Lutheran, and Pilgrim Holiness (one each for the last two). A good number of the subjects, however, became members about seven years before this study, that is, about the time when Pentecostal teaching began to have an effect in the church. (It is remarkable how quickly the new teaching took root in the church. Within a year after the pastor had had his own experience there was apparently a strong contingent of like-minded people. Since transitional periods in Protestant churches, unlike the legendary first hundred days of an American presidential administration, are reported to be sluggish and stressful, the success of the movement within this church is noteworthy. It is curious that Gerlach and Hine, in their otherwise very commendable work, say nothing at all about the rate of growth of a movement, except to link it to opposition. In their sense of the term—a very specific sense—there was, of course, "opposition" in the church.)

This group is well suited to an analysis of their motives for adopting Pentecostal teaching, because on an average they became members of this church 7.4 years ago (although the range is from 1 to 31 years). Seventeen of the 44 came to this church from other denominations, of whom 11 came in the last three years and 14 in the last 7. These figures would suggest that they joined because of or in connection with their new beliefs. This is confirmed by answers to the question "In what year did [the baptism in the Spirit] take place?": for 41 of them this was 7 years before the study.

Several kinds of data reveal that in spite of the change in church membership there were for most people no drastic changes in religious belief. (But see below.) They were and still are at the "evangelical" rather than "liberal" end of the Protestant continuum. Conversion, for example, is an important evangelical doctrine and one of its distinguishing characteristics. When asked if they remembered the specific time when they were converted, 86.3% replied yes, 9.1% no, and the rest gave no reply. Twenty-three of the subjects were converted 7 years before the study. We can assume that conversion and Spirit-baptism took place in the same year and as the result of the same witnessing. This would, of course, mean that many of these people were "saved" or "became Christians" some time after they had become church members. This is, however, no anomaly to evangelicals. They recognize that it is easy to be a church member, but only God can transform a person's soul as he accepts for himself personally the sacrifice of Jesus Christ. In fact, when asked if they could remember a time when they were *not* Christians, 88.6% replied yes; for 34 of the subjects this was an average of 10.2 years before the study (10 people did not provide this information). All of them, of course, now considered themselves Christians, as was indicated in answers to a specific question.

Discontent, Aspirations, and Realization

Conflict or dissatisfaction would seem to be implied in religious conversion and church switching. Two specific questions tried to discover the motivation for adopting the Pentecostal teaching. The first had to do with their local church: "Before the Spirit-baptism, to what extent were you dissatisfied with the local church of which you were a member?" Their answers fell into four categories:

> Not at all. 38.7%
>
> A little. 15.9%
>
> Quite a bit. 22.7%
>
> Extremely so 13.6%
>
> (No reply . . . . 9.1%)

It was fortunate, however, that the next question asked them to describe their dissatisfaction, for the responses reveal no ideological conflict:

—I felt there was more to being a Christian than I knew, but I couldn't find the key.

—Lack of teaching about life of Christ

—Hypocrisy

—Indifference to the person of Christ

—It didn't seem to be doing anything.

—I felt so much of religion was superficial.

—Dead

—The basic social problems in the community and the needs of the parishioners for answers to their problems were not being met.

—A feeling that the clergy were not convinced of the truth of what they taught.

—There is a warmth and fellowship lacking.

—I was trying to find a much deeper faith, a close relationship to God, and there just was no help or teaching for my age group. Church work business doesn't help you, neither does running rummage sales and luncheons.

—Much talk, too little action

—People seemed to be cold, not interested in newcomers.

—Sermons were interesting but didn't seem real.

—I was searching for meaning to life. I left each service still searching. The minister couldn't tell me *how* to find Christ.

—To me it seemed a meaningless ceremony addressed to something I had no hope of contacting.

—There seemed to be no supply for my needs, no answers to my problems, no real contact with the Lord.

—No fellowship in Christ; unable to share Christ with others.

—I was very discouraged with what I classified as the "ineffectiveness" of the universal church.

—No life or power that could encourage my children to be involved and want to embrace Christianity.

—I felt on the outside, inadequate, wanted a closer walk with the Lord.

—Some of the things that was [sic] taking place in the church, reaction of the Christians in the church.

—Too many people opposing conversions.

—Christ was given a back seat; current events, politics seemed to come first.

—People's attitudes—intolerance, etc.

That deep frustration or hostility was absent or minimal in their motives is also indicated by the fact that 70.4% of the subjects indicated that they had *not* considered attending or becoming a member of a church other than the one they were attending before the Spirit-baptism; 25% said they had, but I did not ask for further reasons.

As the preceding statements indicate, dissatisfaction was religiously defined. This was further revealed in answers to a parallel question: "Before your Spirit-baptism, to what extent were you dissatisfied with yourself as a Christian?"

Not at all...................... 15.9%

A little........................ 25.0%

Quite a bit..................... 34.1%

Extremely so................... 22.7%

(No reply .... 2.3%)

Religious aspirations, as judged by the subjects themselves and as revealed by religious behavior, seem to have been fulfilled. When asked to give graded responses (more, less, or same) to the question "What do you think of the following aspects of your life since your baptism in the Spirit?" they replied as indicated in Table 4.

Table 4: Christian Life Following the Spirit-baptism

	More	Less
(a) Faithful in church attendance	59.1%	36.4%
(b) Active in church work	50.0%	38.6%
(c) Open and free in talking with non-Christians about religion	90.0%	11.4%
(d) Conscious of the presence of God	100.0%	0.0%
(e) Expectant of God helping you personally	90.9%	9.1%
(f) Enthusiastic about your Christian faith	97.7%	2.3%

Only for (a) and (b) did 1 and 2 persons indicate less intensity. Notice that the categories that received the highest scores are subjective ("conscious," "expectant," "enthusiastic"), but activism is certainly indicated in (c).

Activism is also indicated in answers to a question about church responsibilities that they had held in the last five years: 93.2% had held some position, 77.3% more than one, and 47.7% more than two. It would appear from the designations given that most of these were in the local church, not for the denomination at large. However, the amount of volunteer social or religious work independent of the home church carried on in the preceding five years is high: 77.3% had done such work. Some of it might be considered typical of the middle-class society represented by this group (such as Scouts, Red Cross, cancer society), but much of it is not.

Another interesting fact about the effect of the Spirit-baptism is that 61.4% of the subjects felt that their relationships with their spouses were better and only 13.6% felt that they were the same. (Eight were not married, and 2 did not reply.) Improvement is also indicated in the extent to which they actually tell about or share their experience with others who have had no such experience: 34.1% said "a little," and 56.8% "as much as I possibly can."

Christian activism is revealed also in various types of focused activity or fellowship with other Spirit-baptized Christians: 86.3% said they met with others. This was for Bible study (76.3%), prayer (97.4%), and for other purposes (63.2%). These activities were undoubtedly carried on in addition to regular church functions, and some of them included people from other churches: 18.4% met with people from a different church but the same denomination, 34.2% a different church and denomination, and 68.4% the same church.

The preceding characterization of this group of believers— Pentecostal features of baptism and tongues set aside—could easily apply to any evangelical segment of Protestantism regardless of denominational affiliation. Evangelicals say, in fact, that it is belief and behavior, not church membership, that counts. "Evangelical" is indeed what this group seems to consider itself. When asked "Which of the following 'labels' would you NOT want applied to yourself?" they replied in the following way (ranked in Table 5 for the sake of presentation).

Table 5: Percentage of Respondents Disfavoring Religious Labels

Liberal	59.1%
Modernist	56.8%
Traditional	43.2%
Fundamentalist	40.9%
Neo-Pentecostal	36.4%
Mainline	34.1%
Pentecostal	25.0%
Evangelical	2.3%

But were they "evangelical" to begin with? This was determined by asking them to register their belief on certain matters that I happened to know characterize evangelical groups or Pentecostal groups or both. The answers to the question "Do you today believe that . . . ?" are given in Table 6.

Table 6: Religious Beliefs of Neo-Pentecostal Group

	Yes	No	Uncertain
(a) God is a personal being	97.7% (43)	0%	2.3% (1)
(b) Jesus was born of a virgin	88.6% (39)	2.3% (1)	9.1% (4)
(c) Jesus rose from the dead	100.0% (44)	0%	0%
(d) The Bible is God's inspired Word	93.2% (41)	2.3% (1)	4.5% (2)
(e) The apostles miraculously spoke in different languages on the Day of Pentecost	97.7% (43)	2.3% (1)	0%
(f) Demons can possess Christians or non-Christians	90.9% (40)	2.3% (1)	6.8% (3)
(g) God can heal the sick if Christians pray	97.7% (43)	0%	2.3% (1)
(h) A Christian should be enthusiastic about his faith	100.0% (44)	0%	0%

What is significant here is that 25% of the people had held all these beliefs before their baptism in the Spirit: 6.8% had had no set opinion. Further specification settles the matter. When asked *which* of these they did not believe before their experience, they replied (here ranked again):

(f) Demons.	50.0%
(e) Tongues	36.4%
(g) Healing	29.5%
(a) God as person.	15.9%
(h) Enthusiasm	13.6%
(d) God's Word	11.4%
(b) Virgin Birth	9.1%
(c) Resurrection.	4.6%

This is an interesting gradation: the last three doctrines are shared by all evangelicals (and Pentecostals naturally), although there are different ways of interpreting the doctrine of inspiration. The top three are Pentecostal doctrines; although evangelicals generally believe in healing, Pentecostals "practice" it. Evangelicals in general would consider change in (h) evidence of Christian growth or maturity. Perhaps (a) also indicates more personal communion with God, but I simply intended to contrast belief in a personal deity with disbelief.

The belief that miracles and visions occur today can also distinguish Pentecostalism from the rest of evangelicalism. For the Pentecostal this is an active belief, for the others a passive one. There are, in other words, very few evangelicals who would report having had a vision or having been personally involved in a miracle. This difference is seen in our subjects. In fact, 75% reported that they had been personally involved in a miracle (no, 15.9% and no reply, 9.1%); 90.0% of those who had been involved had this experience after they were Spirit-filled (24.2% before). Similarly, 50% of the subjects had had a vision (40.9% not), 12 of them after their baptism.

Conclusion

Impressions derived from the observation of local participants in the charismatic movement led my colleague to the hypothesis that hostility was a determinant factor in their conversion or recruitment. This study is sufficient to invalidate that hypothesis. There is no evidence in this mainline church that either the pastor or the parishioners who accepted the Spirit-filled way were rebelling against a different ideology, in this case "modernistic" in nature. To this day, even though the minister has extended his ministry beyond his parish, he is considered by his fellow clergymen, as one of them volunteered, a "real good guy." That this remark came from a minister rather far to the liberal side makes the comment even more significant than it superficially appears.

One *ad hoc* study is, of course, no better than another one. But this examination does more than simply invalidate a hypothesis. It adds to the already considerable body of knowledge that contradicts simplistic explanations about conversion to the Pentecostal movement. The explanations are numerous, but they are largely based on some form of deprivation or deviancy theory. The literature has been examined from two different points of view by W. Samarin[4] and V. Hine,[5] but our conclusions are the same. They are shared by Johannes Fabian, an anthropologist who has written an ethnographic analysis of an entirely different religious movement, the Jamaa.[6] It arose within the fold of the Catholic church, among urbanized Katangese in what used to be the Belgian Congo. By all reports its participants in 1971 still considered themselves faithful believers of the Catholic church. The anthropologist writes:

> We did not find any millenarian, nativistic, or separatist motives [in joining] . . . . The constitution of the group could not be traced to any specific impulse from the environment, such as an economic crisis, a political event, a natural catastrophe, a sudden change in the population--events which have often been linked with the rise of prophetic-charismatic movements.[7]

It should also be noted that Catholic Pentecostals in North America, far from being fundamentalist or radical, appear to be more faithful to the culture of their church than some other Catholics who have been active in underground movements of one type or another. This is the judgment of one Catholic theologian who has followed both the Protestant and Catholic movements rather closely.[8]

To replace deviancy explanations Gerlach and Hine, among other things, stress the importance of personal contacts in recruitment to

---

4. W. Samarin, *Tongues of Men and Angels*, ch. 2.

5. Virginia H. Hine, "Pentecostal Glossolalia: Toward a Functional Interpretation," *Journal for the Scientific Study of Religion*, 8 (1969), 211-26.

6. Johannes Fabian, *Jamaa: A Charismatic Movement in Katanga* (Evanston, IL: Northwestern University Press, 1971).

7. Ibid., p. 200.

8. Kilian McDonnell, "Catholic Pentecostalism: Problems in Evaluation," *Dialog*, 9 (Winter, 1970), 35-54. (Reprinted in 1970 under the same title by Dove Publications, Pecos, NM.)

social movements whether they be Pentecostal, Black Power, or Communism.[9] With this explanation, as with most of the analysis of their book, I am in entire agreement. To my mind, however, Gerlach and Hine fail to place sufficient emphasis on religious aspirations as being conducive to conversion to the Pentecostal point of view. But they do not ignore this factor. For example:

> Christians who attend church out of purely social needs, who are not particularly interested in the Bible, and who take their religion with a grain of salt [people whom evangelicals in general and Pentecostals in particular regard as nominal, lukewarm, immature Christians], can remain impervious to the Pentecostal ideology. It is the serious Christian who feels he should read more of the Bible, who is vaguely aware of its "impossible ethic," and who has come to expect some sort of meaningful experience to occur within his religious institution, who can be touched by Pentecostal witnessing.[10]

That this was not obvious to social scientists before is due in large part to the fact that their data were determined by their hypotheses. They failed to find out enough about the people themselves; they failed to listen to what Pentecostals said about themselves and about what they wanted in life. (Much of this testimony could have been obtained from Pentecostal literature—which has hardly been tapped by social scientists.)

This very restricted study only confirms what I have long known about that part of Protestant Christianity (namely evangelicalism) from which Pentecostalism arises: that it is fed by the holiness stream which places great value on personal commitment and piety and is ever experimenting with processes ("exercises," Catholics would call them) that lead to "the deeper Christian life." Pentecostalism is only part of this movement. Or one might say that it is that part of the stream where the current flows strong. Because it is strong, it carries away people who are ready to fall into it. They already want to be, as they say, "100% Christians." And the movement, through its positive personal interrelations (kinship and friendship networks), through its compelling symbols, and through its rituals, only provides them with the means for realizing their aspirations.[11] For all this I find un-

---

9. Gerlach and Hine, *People, Power, Change*, especially ch. 4.

10. Ibid., pp. 177f.

11. Becoming a Pentecostal—living out "the experience"—is a process. For many individual converts it leads in directions that were not anticipated. We often find that people become more orthodox (as this study illustrates) or heterodox. It is not unusual for neo-Pentecostals to move into spiritism or occultism. (And Fabian found that even while Jamaa doctrine was explicitly Christian, it returned to traditional culture for some of its

mistakable parallels in Fabian's analysis of what he calls the prophetic event or encounter that brings a person into the Jamaa (the "family" or "tribe")—like Pentecostalism it answers fundamental questions about life.[12]

symbolism.) It would be a serious mistake, however, to confuse the end with the beginning.

12. Appreciation is here recorded for help I had from Stan Skarsten and Henry Regehr (both professional social workers) in preparing the questionnaire. Skarsten also commented on an early draft of this paper.

Richard A. Baer, Jr.

Richard A. Baer, Jr., is a Phi Beta Kappa graduate of Syracuse University (A.B., 1953). He attended Princeton Seminary (B.D., 1957) and Harvard University (Ph.D., 1965). From 1966 to 1973 he was associated with Earlham College in Richmond, Indiana, where teaching in his doctoral field of New Testament led to a growing interest in environmental ethics. Publications, lectures, and consultancies in the field of conservation eventually led to his appointment as associate professor in the department of natural resources at Cornell University.

Dr. Baer describes in this article common ground between the glossolalia of Pentecostalism, the silence of Quaker worship, and the liturgy of the Catholic traditions. In each case, he argues, the analytic intellect is surpassed and a divine reality thereby communicated.

Quaker Silence, Catholic Liturgy, and Pentecostal Glossolalia – Some Functional Similarities

10

Among non-Pentecostals, much of the recent discussion of glossolalia or speaking in tongues focuses on the strangeness of the phenomenon. Many leaders in mainline denominations see the current charismatic movement as a clear threat to the peace of the Christian community and the integrity of the church's witness. Scholarly papers raise the question, Are tongues basically a pathological religious practice? In not a few churches pastors have been dismissed when it was learned that glossolalia had become part of their personal religious experience.

Whereas even ten years ago it was possible for most Christian leaders to dispose of glossolalia with a few condescending remarks about "religious fanatics" and "lower class fringe sects," the explosion of the charismatic movement in the past few years among Catholics and mainline Protestants rules this out today. In a paper entitled "Personal and Situational Determinants of Glossolalia" presented at the September 1973 Los Angeles conference on *Religion and the Humanizing of Man*, H. Newton Malony of Fuller Theological Seminary argued that what little evidence there is regarding personality characteristics of glossolalics not only tends to rule out psychopathol-

ogy but may even suggest that as a group "glossolalics [are] better ad-
justed than members of a conventional denomination."[1]

I would argue that the "strangeness" of glossolalia to most people,
not least of all ministers and seminary professors, has blinded them to
a fundamental functional similarity between speaking in tongues and
two other widespread and generally accepted religious practices,
namely Quaker silent worship and the liturgical worship of the
Catholic and Episcopal churches. My thesis is that each of these three
practices permits the analytical mind—the focused, objectifying
dimension of man's intellect—to rest, thus freeing other dimensions of
the person, what we might loosely refer to as man's spirit, for a deeper
openness to divine reality. In their own distinctive ways I believe that
tongues, Quaker silence, and the liturgy of the church all contribute
powerfully to this goal.

Significantly, this goal is not achieved by a deliberate concentration
on the emotions as over against the analytical mind. Neither the silent
worship of the Quakers, the practice of glossolalia, nor the liturgical
worship of the Catholic or Episcopal church seeks to stimulate the
emotions as such in the manner of some revival meetings or some of
the more contrived celebrations in certain avant-garde Protestant and
Catholic congregations. Rather, in each of the three traditions I have
mentioned, the desire is to free man in the depth of his spirit to respond to the immediate reality of the living God. The intent is not to
play on the emotions either as an end in itself or as a means to some
other desired end—for example, deeper commitment to the beliefs and
practices of the church.

Speaking in Tongues

My thesis will become clearer as we examine in some detail these
three practices which on the surface appear so very much dissimilar.
Contrary to uninformed speculation and opinion, speaking in
tongues is not a form of religious hysteria or spirit possession. Nor is
it, except occasionally and quite incidentally, uncontrolled expression
of emotion. Not only is the glossolalic fully aware of what he is doing
when he begins to speak in a tongue but he also can stop at will. Although the glossolalic may be moved by deep emotion—as indeed he
often is in non-glossolalic experiences of prayer and worship—the act

1. H. Newton Malony, Nelson Zwaanstra, and James W. Ramsey, "Personal and Situa-
tional Determinants of Glossolalia: A Literature Review and a Report of Ongoing
Research" (paper presented at the International Congress of Learned Societies in the
Field of Religion, Los Angeles, Sept. 1-5, 1972), p. 1.

of speaking in tongues itself is not best characterized as emotional in contrast to intellectual. The actual speech can be only a quiet whisper or even subvocal; or, on the other hand, it can be loud and boisterous. At times the glossolalic feels a singular *lack* of emotion while speaking in tongues.

For the most part, the glossolalic makes use of tongues for praising God. But three other uses are also common: (1) the expression of deep anguish or inner sorrow, (2) intercession, and (3) petition. In each instance there may be something deep inside the individual which he simply is unable to express in words. For some people, and occasionally for almost everyone, silence seems appropriate at such moments. But others find that unpremeditated glossolalic speech best permits them to express their joy or sorrow. The use of tongues in such a case is similar to the fulfillment a person may find in spontaneous dancing; and, of course, the use of the dance for the expression of religious ecstasy is a well-known and virtually universal phenomenon.

In petition and intercession one may not really know *what* to pray for. Even though there may be a deep sense of need or an acute awareness of distress, the one praying may possess little intellectual understanding of what is wrong, of what needs changing, or of what "solution" or healing would be appropriate. In such cases praying in a tongue may well be the most satisfying religious response available. Recall Paul's words in Romans 8:26 about the Spirit helping us in our weakness as He "intercedes for us with sighs too deep for words." Glossolalic prayer is felt by many to be of particular value in relation to the healing of early childhood traumas which have become submerged in the depths of the unconscious. Frequently an individual will know that something from his early childhood is sabotaging his behavior in the present but he will neither know what the trauma was nor how to pray for deliverance. In such cases praying in a tongue for the "healing of the memories" may be thoroughly appropriate.

It should be noted that I am describing glossolalia mainly as it occurs in the context of a person's private devotions. Much of what I have written is also relevant to the employment of glossolalia in the gathered worship of the church, but I should prefer not to discuss this controversial topic in this paper. Suffice it to say that such a public manifestation of tongues as group singing "in the Spirit" can be an exquisitely beautiful and joyful experience for the participants and even for observers.

Quaker Silent Worship

Striking parallels exist between Quaker silent worship and the practice of glossolalia. At its best Quaker silent worship involves a kind of letting go, a lack of strain or effortful attention, a willingness to "flow" with the leading of the Spirit and with the larger movement of the entire meeting. In the course of the worship an individual may be led to speak to the gathering, but he retains the freedom either to yield to this urge or to fight it. In either case, however, it would seem quite inappropriate to describe this experience as hysterical or label it a form of spirit-possession in the classical mystical sense. The individual is quite aware of what he is about and retains definite control over his speech.

However, it is not a strained or forced control but rather more like that of the skillful dancer or lover. What is said will, to be sure, have intellectual content—but intellectual content is not the main element. One does not plan ahead of time what he will say, just as one does not invent a tongue in which to speak. There is rather a sharing out of the depths of one's self, or differently described, a speaking that is prompted by the leading of the Spirit. It is almost universally felt in Quaker circles that rational analysis and argument over what is spoken "out of the silence" is inappropriate. One is not to analyze or judge but rather to listen and obey.

As in the case of glossolalia, the process of speaking out of the silence and of listening in the silence involves a resting of the analytical mind, a refusal to let deliberative, objective thinking dominate the meeting. Rather, one tries to "center down" and become open to the "inner light" within himself, to "that of God in every man," to the "leading of the Spirit."

Silence is common among Quakers both in private devotions and in public worship. Although what one speaks out of the silence in the meeting needs no interpretation as such, others, as led by the Spirit, may add to what has been said, often in a manner not dissimilar to the Mishnaic commentary of the rabbis on the Torah. I find a rough parallel here to what is common practice among Pentecostals. The use of tongues in one's private devotions needs no interpretation. But in the public worship one should not speak in a tongue unless someone who can interpret is present (1 Cor. 14:28). Significantly, the interpretation usually appears to be less a word-for-word translation of what has been said than a kind of paraphrase of the tongue with particular emphasis on reproducing its spiritual tone and general direction.

The phenomenon of quaking or shaking is still found among some Friends and would seem to be religiously and psychologically similar to glossolalia. A significant difference, however, is that one seems to have less control over the quaking than one does over speaking in a tongue and cannot necessarily terminate the practice at will. Actually, quaking is extremely rare today among Friends, but there are other stylized physical manifestations which typically accompany speaking out of the silence. For example, one often speaks with a slightly lowered head and with little or no direct eye contact with fellow worshipers. Frequently the tone of voice has a decidedly subdued quality, probably reflecting what is the deep inner conviction among Friends that one does not try to persuade or convince others of the truth of what is said by human emotion, logic, or eloquence. Rather one speaks "out of the depth of silence" by the leading of the inner light, the divine Spirit. It is only this divine Spirit that can bring true conviction and response on the part of the hearer. In other words, the communication or revelation is immediately self-authenticating. It is a word spoken not primarily in order to change the ideas of the hearer or rouse his emotions but rather to confront him in the inner depths of his spirit.

It is noteworthy by comparison that in public Pentecostal-type worship what is spoken in a tongue, although usually more animated than the word spoken by Quakers out of the silence, nonetheless possesses something of the same quality. The speaker does not attempt to convince, persuade, or rouse people to action, perhaps in part because he is not himself rationally aware of the content of his speech. Also there is frequently a marked degree of inwardness on the part of the speaker, often reflected in the avoidance of direct eye contact (or closed eyes) and a tone of voice different from what he would employ in ordinary affairs.

The Liturgy

Similarities between glossolalia and the liturgical worship of the church are less obvious than those we have noted in relation to Quaker silent worship. But they are also significant. I shall refer mainly to the liturgical worship of the Episcopal Church, since this is the tradition I know best. Just as glossolalia and silent Quaker worship may at first be puzzling, frustrating, even irritating to the non-initiate, so to many outsiders the practice of liturgical worship sometimes appears to be little more than a mechanical exercise in futility. What good can possibly come of the repetition week after

week of the same prayer of confession, word of absolution, interces-
sions, and petitions? And how can one even focus on what is being
said when most of his attention is directed to turning pages and
deciding whether to stand or to kneel? Even though he remembers the
advice "When in doubt kneel!" the non-initiate is so preoccupied with
physical motions and the proper sequence and enunciation of prayers
and other responses that it is almost beside the point to talk of the
resting of the analytical mind and an encounter with God in the
depths of the human spirit.

But all of this is not really surprising and is not unlike the experience of the person first learning to dance. At that point even
walking seems far more graceful than those awkward, contrived
motions. But when one has mastered the dance steps, a kind of
"wisdom of the body" takes over which indeed permits the analytical
mind, the focused attention, to rest. One begins to "flow" with the
beat of the music, the rhythm of the dance.

So with the liturgy. The very repetition Sunday after Sunday of the
same prayers, responses, and creeds frees the individual from needing
to focus consciously on what is being said. To be sure, his mind and
heart are frequently stimulated by the theological content and the
aesthetic movement of the liturgy. Also the total aesthetic impact of
the environment—stained glass, wood carvings, Christian symbols,
singing, organ music, incense, candles—helps produce a sense of
awe and mystery.[2]

But as beautiful and moving as all of these elements are, there is yet
a deeper movement of the human spirit as it encounters the Spirit of
God, the presence of the risen Christ, the reality of the Holy Spirit.
The analytical, objectifying mind is permitted to rest and thus the
spirit of man is free to experience reality on a new level. Moreover,
although feelings are often heightened by liturgical worship, there is
no conscious attempt to manipulate the emotions to achieve some
desired effect. It is on the level of spirit that liturgical worship
becomes most significant.[3]

---

2. It is at this point that Quakers remain understandably cautious and choose for themselves utterly simple surroundings for worship. Their fear is that one can be so cap-
tivated by external form and beauty that worship will remain on the level of the
aesthetic. This has been perhaps a necessary corrective within the total life of the
church and reflects an austerity not unlike the Old Testament prohibition against
making graven images. At its worst, however, Quaker worship sometimes reflects a
Gnostic-like repudiation of the rich beauty and vitality of creation and man's somatic
existence.

3. Although I have been greatly helped by Romano Guardini, *The Spirit of the Liturgy*
(London and New York: Sheed and Ward, 1935), I cannot fully agree with him that

Furthermore, the very formality of the liturgy and the fixed nature of the responses may save the worshiper from undue introspection and thus help him to center more fully on the presence of God. Nor does he need to fear revealing more of himself than is appropriate in public. Romano Guardini writes that "the liturgy has perfected a masterly instrument which has made it possible for us to express our inner life in all its fullness and depth without divulging our secrets . . . . We can pour out our hearts and still feel that nothing has been dragged to light that should remain hidden."[4]

As has been frequently noted, a high level of sound, insofar as it insulates a person from ordinary auditory stimuli, has an effect in some ways similar to a complete absence of sound. There is a rough analogy here to the interrelationship between Quaker silence and liturgical worship. Also the fact that one knows the prayers and responses by heart (not, *by head!*) frees one to be open to ever-new and ever-changing leadings of the Spirit *during* the very act of repeating fixed prayers and predetermined responses.[5]

This same dynamic probably explains much of the value of Father Zossima's famous Jesus-prayer in *The Brothers Karamazov* and of the repetition of the Catholic Rosary. In some evangelical Protestant circles the repetition of a single-stanza chorus five or six times in a row would seem to have a similar effect. Even highly intellectual people frequently discover as much (or more) fulfillment in the singing of such choruses as they do in some of the great theological-doctrinal hymns of the church. Compilers of hymnals would do well to note this fact, for often they have reflected a kind of Calvinistic, ascetic, theological snobbishness in making up their collections.

---

thought is dominant over feeling in the liturgy. To be sure, as he argues, emotion in the liturgy is generally "controlled and subdued" (p. 129), but I have difficulty with his statement: "The heart speaks powerfully, but thought at once takes the lead" (p. 129). The more accurate contrast, I believe, is that between thought and feeling, on the one hand, and man's spirit (the dimension of depth or self-transcendence) on the other. Thus neither feelings nor the analytical mind is the dominant or controlling factor but rather the reality of the Spirit of God addressing man's spirit.

4. Guardini, *The Spirit of the Liturgy*, p. 131.

5. But, on the other hand, the fixed quality of the liturgy can be used by the individual to insulate himself from real change. In this case the regularity of the liturgy imprisons rather than frees the person. But it could be argued that roughly the same insulating effect can take place in Quaker silent worship and in glossolalic worship. Rather than using the silence to center down into a creative openness to the leading of the Spirit, the Quaker worshiper may simply become drowsy or retreat into a kind of numb withdrawal from reality. Likewise, glossolalic speech may be employed in a given situation to escape from a more reflective understanding of God's will or a specific decision of the will to be obedient to God's leading.

The argument can still be heard that the mass would be more effective in its religious impact if it were left in Latin. Authentic religious sensitivity, it is said, is reflected in the considerable resistance which many people—both young and old and from almost all social, national, and intellectual backgrounds—have shown to changing the mass into the vernacular. One could also point to the distress many Episcopalians today feel about "updating" the language of the liturgy.

It is too easy to dismiss these reactions with such labels as "conservative" or "reactionary." Perhaps the fact that one does not understand much of the Latin of the mass makes it easier for him to be open to God on the level of spirit, just as in the case of glossolalia and Quaker silent worship. In the latter the silence is experienced—or, more accurately, facilitates the experience of God—but is not as such "understood."

My own position is that to leave the mass in Latin rules out for most people an important element of ethical and theological content. In Pentecostal churches this dimension is achieved through the interpretation of the glossolalic speech, and in Quaker silent worship what is spoken out of the silence has ethical and theological content, even though it is not presented in a critical or analytical fashion.

Playfulness in Worship

So much for my basic thesis. It is an analysis which suggests or illuminates several subsidiary issues, to which I now turn in the second part of this paper.

People frequently ask me: But what is the value of speaking in tongues? I have already addressed myself to this question above, but here I am tempted simply to add: "Because it is a lot of fun." More and more I am impressed with the element of playfulness in glossolalia, the sheer childlike delight in praising God in this manner. It is a contagious delight, and in many charismatic prayer groups people will infrequently break out in a childlike, spontaneous, almost irrepressible (but not hysterical) laughter right in the midst of prayers. Such laughter suggests an absence of a heavy, super-seriousness about oneself and one's worship. It is the freedom a child has to burst into laughter even at an important family gathering. It reflects a lack of pomposity, an ability to see oneself (even one's serious praying) in perspective. My experience is that such laughter has almost always had about it a releasing quality; and although it may sometimes be occasioned by some slight awkwardness of speech or action on the part of someone in the group, it is almost always a sympathetic and joyful laughter, thus ultimately healing and redemptive.

How fascinating then that Romano Guardini refers to the "playfulness of the liturgy." In his book *The Spirit of the Liturgy* he contends that the liturgy, formally analyzed, is more like play than work. The liturgy, he writes,

> is life pouring itself forth without an aim, seizing upon riches from its own abundant store, significant through the fact of its existence . . . . It unites art and reality in a supernatural childhood before God . . . . It has no purpose, but it is full of divine meaning . . . . It is in the highest sense the life of a child, in which everything is picture, melody and song.[6]

Of all human activities such worship is the least goal-oriented. "The soul," Guardini concludes, "must learn to abandon, at least in prayer, the restlessness of purposeful activity; it must learn to waste time for the sake of God."[7] One is immediately reminded of the beginning sentence of the great Westminster Confession: "The chief end of man is to glorify God *and to enjoy him forever.*"

If it is not too presumptuous for a non-Friend to venture a judgment, I would suggest that present-day silent Quaker worship often manifests a kind of heaviness which comes from taking itself too seriously. The way of simplicity has in some instances become a life of drabness, and one could only wish that out of the silence laughter and playfulness might emerge as well as reverence and heightened moral sensitivity.

The Promise of Folly

It is noteworthy that each of the three phenomena we have examined—glossolalia, Quaker silence, and the liturgy of the church— exhibits a kind of strangeness or peculiar style as over against man's more usual religious and secular activities. This is perhaps most often felt in the case of glossolalia, but it is not absent from the other two.

Of particular interest to me is the resistance which the non-initiate often exhibits when confronted with this strangeness. Various faith healers point to the resistance often encountered by one who is seeking for healing. And John Sherrill, author of *They Speak with Other Tongues*, writes that "there seems to be a strange link between taking a seemingly foolish step—which God specifies—and receiving spiritual

---

6. Guardini, *The Spirit of the Liturgy*, pp. 179-81.

7. Ibid., p. 183.

power."⁸ Billy Graham refers to the same phenomenon and sees the value of the altar call at revival meetings as linked to it.⁹ John Sherrill describes his own considerable resistance to the seemingly foolish step of raising his hands to God in praise. Only when he risked his middle class decorum and respectability through actually praising God in this way did he break through to a deeper experience of the Holy Spirit.¹⁰

Paul's experience of coming to faith in Jesus as the Christ is, on a theological level, analogous. As a sensitive, educated Pharisee with all the proper credentials, he simply could not grasp how God's promises could have been fulfilled through a simple Galilean who was put to death on a cross as a common criminal. Indeed, the gospel was a scandal to him as it was foolishness to the Greeks. But after his encounter with Christ on the road to Damascus, Paul was able to write that:

> God chose what is foolish in the world to shame the wise, God chose what is weak in the world to shame the strong, God chose what is low and despised in the world, even things that are not, to bring to nothing things that are, *so that no human being might boast in the presence of God. He is the source of your life in Christ Jesus* . . . . (1 Cor. 1:27-30, italics supplied)

There appears to be a principle of the spiritual life that as long as man insists on keeping full control of himself he cuts himself off from a deeper relationship with God. I am reminded of Jesus' saying in Mark 10:15 (and parallels): "Truly, I say to you, whoever does not receive the kingdom of God like a child shall not enter it." Or we could point to the account in 2 Kings 5 of Naaman the Syrian, who was required to wash in the muddy waters of the Jordan in order to receive healing. Apparently many individuals are required to perform a seemingly foolish or ridiculous action in order to be released for a genuine spiritual breakthrough. Parenthetically I would want to add, however, that not every foolish act or belief is valuable. Perhaps it is just foolish!

It seems plausible to me that the attitude of the conservative evangelical towards the Bible also reflects a certain setting aside of the arguments of the analytical mind. Even though intellectually he may feel the force of evidence against the plenary or verbal inspiration of the biblical autographs, nonetheless experientially he has discovered that in submission to what he holds to be a verbally

8. John L. Sherrill, *They Speak with Other Tongues* (New York: Pyramid Books, 1964), p. 116.

9. Ibid.

10. Ibid., pp. 116f., 123.

inerrant Bible, growth and renewal have taken place in his spiritual pilgrimage. He may be willing to live with intellectual difficulties for the sake of the positive religious experience. So too with many Roman Catholics in relation to the doctrine of papal infallibility. One would need to ask in these instances, however, whether the intellectual price is not too high.

One final question on this subject: If my basic thesis is correct that there is an underlying functional similarity between glossolalia, Quaker silence, and the liturgy of the church, why then have so many Episcopalians and some Quakers sought and experienced glossolalia? I am not sure this question really can be answered. It may well be that these three types of religious practice complement and build upon each other, as indeed has been my own experience. Or, it could be the case that glossolalia for many people in our culture represents a more decisive break with the hegemony of the analytical mind than either Quaker silence or the liturgy of the church and thus opens the way to spiritual growth beyond what the individual has previously experienced.

Life as the Praise of God

Let me examine in somewhat greater detail a religious practice closely related to the phenomena we have just described, namely the discipline of praising and thanking God for all things that happen in one's life—for pain as well as joy, darkness as well as light, evil as well as good. This is an old theme in Christian piety. Eighteenth century English clergyman William Law, for example, writes:

> If anyone could tell you the shortest, surest way to all happiness and perfection, he must tell you to make it a rule to yourself to thank and praise God for everything that happens to you. For it is certain that whatever seeming calamity happens to you, if you thank and praise God for it, you turn it into a blessing.[11]

More recently, in our own century, the German poet Rainer Maria Rilke picks up the theme when he writes:

> Tell us, poet, what is it you do?
>   I praise.
> But the deadly and the monstrous things, how can you bear them?
>   I praise.
> But even what is nameless, what is anonymous, how can you call upon it?

11. Quoted by Merlin R. Carothers, *Power in Praise* (Plainfield, NJ: Logos International, 1972), p. v.

> I praise.
> What right have you to be true in every disguise, beneath every
> mask?
> I praise.
> And how is it that both calm and violent things, like star and storm,
> know you for their own?
> Because I praise.[12]

In our own day, in the book *Prison to Praise* (1970), which has sold
close to half a million copies in two brief years and has been lauded by
people of widely divergent backgrounds, Army Chaplain Merlin
Carothers develops this theme of praise for all things. He is careful to
avoid blurring distinctions between good and evil or denying the
reality of evil altogether, as is the case in Christian Science. Also, he
recognizes the danger of repressing anger, hurt, and disappointment.
One should not pretend that he likes everything that happens in his
life. Nonetheless, Chaplain Carothers presents a powerful statement
in favor of the discipline of praising not only *in* all circumstances but
for all circumstances. He describes dozens of case histories in this and
in two more recent books,[13] where learning to praise God for all circumstances in life has resulted in major personality change and
spiritual development.

My immediate interest in this practice of praising God for all things
is that it represents a kind of relaxing of the hegemony of the
analytical mind which is analogous to what happens in glossolalia,
Quaker silence, and liturgical worship. It involves the confession:
"Lord, I do not really understand *why* you have permitted these
things to happen, but I will submit to your will and the realities of the
world you have created nonetheless. I do not believe you sent or
caused this hurt or darkness or evil, yet I accept the fact that you permitted it."

Many who practice the discipline of praise for all things witness to
the fact that they had previously found it quite impossible fully to accept certain experiences and realities in their own lives and circumstances. They simply found the dynamics of full acceptance
beyond their ability. But in praising God for those very circumstances
which they could not accept, they frequently discovered that they
were able to accept and come to peace with the reality itself.

---

12. I cannot locate the source of this particular translation. For another translation of
this poem, which in the original is entitled "Für Leonie Zacharias," see Rainer Maria
Rilke, *Poems, 1906 to 1926*, trans. J. B. Leishman (Norfolk, CT: New Directions, 1957),
p. 258.

13. *Answers to Praise* (Plainfield, NJ: Logos International, 1972); *Power in Praise*
(Plainfield, NJ: Logos International, 1972).

The one theme that consistently runs through this paper is that the individual who insists on being fully in control of his own self insulates himself from divine reality.[14] To experience the presence and power of the Spirit of God necessitates a letting go, a being open to. The saints and mystics have witnessed to this from time immemorial. Such a letting go is not easy for modern Western man, not least of all because of an intellectual tradition dating back to Francis Bacon, Descartes, Leibnitz and others, which sees knowledge primarily as the ability to gain power over, to control, one's environment. Moreover, as Western man increasingly lost faith in a transcendent God and in the reality of the resurrection of the dead, death no longer was seen as a rite of passage to fuller life, but rather as a confrontation with nothingness, the abyss, and the final loss of self-control. To "let go" in a world without God was to risk chaos and the destruction of self.[15]

It is not surprising that the church has been influenced by this cultural framework and has also come to be wary of the loss of control, especially as this occurs in religious ecstasy. Tillich argues that the church "must avoid the secular profanization of contemporary Protestantism which occurs when it replaces ecstasy with doctrinal or moral structure."[16] However, both structure and ecstasy are needed in the church, according to Tillich, and "the church must prevent the confusion of ecstasy with chaos."[17]

---

14. See Reinhold Niebuhr's discussion of this theme in *The Nature and Destiny of Man* (New York: Scribners, 1949), II, 107-17. Man's self is shattered at the very center of its being "whenever it is confronted by the power and holiness of God and becomes genuinely conscious of the real source and center of all life" (p. 109). Niebuhr points to the Pauline dialectic, which makes clear that the self is not obliterated but rather for the first time finds true fulfillment when it is possessed by the Holy Spirit. "Yet such possession of the self is destructive," he concludes, "if the possessing spirit is anything less than the 'Holy Spirit' " (pp. 111-12).

15. In the secular context of psychotherapy and psychoanalysis the "letting go" motif is basic. If the client insists on censoring his thoughts and his speech, the therapist has little access to his repressed experiences and the realm of the unconscious. The therapist often encourages the client to "let go" and discover the powers of life emerging within him. The operative assumption is that reality is of such a nature that it tends towards integration and wholeness. By trying too hard to become whole the client may only impede the healing process. Some therapists and sensitivity group trainers, however, have perhaps overreacted to our cultural bias in favor of control and exhibit in their work a prejudice against clear ideas, conscience, will, and the analytical mind. My own position is that the individual must discover a balance between head and heart, mind and body, objectivity and subjectivity. Significantly, orthodox Christian theology has consistently held that the balancing, harmonizing, or centering of one's life is found outside of the self. It is realized only in the entrusting of oneself to God.

16. Paul Tillich, *Systematic Theology* (Chicago: University of Chicago Press, 1963), III, 117.

17. Ibid.

In a statement which J. Rodman Williams quotes in his book *The Era of the Spirit*, Tillich writes:

> This whole part of the present system [Part IV: "Life and Spirit"] is a defense of the ecstatic manifestations of the Spiritual Presence against its ecclesiastical critics; in this defense, the whole New Testament is the most powerful weapon. Yet, this weapon can be used legitimately only if the other partner in the alliance—the psychological critics—is also rejected or at least put into proper perspective.[18]

Such words cannot, of course, be used to validate glossolalia or other charismatic phenomena in the church. At the very least, however, they might encourage greater openness to such experiences among non-Pentecostals, and by God's grace a deeper experience of the richness of life God wants us to realize in our commitment to Jesus Christ as Lord and Savior.

18. Ibid., p. 118. See the excellent discussion of Tillich's position in J. Rodman Williams, *The Era of the Spirit* (Plainfield, NJ: Logos International, 1971), pp. 85-91.

PART FOUR
Personal Reflections

Ray H. Hughes

Ray Hughes now serves on the executive committee of the Church of God (Cleveland, Tennessee). Between 1972-74 he was General Overseer, the chief executive officer of his church. He has held numerous church leadership positions, including the chairmanship of the Pentecostal Fellowship of North America and posts with the Advisory Committee of the Pentecostal World Conference and the Board of Administration of the National Association of Evangelicals. He is a popular speaker at a wide variety of church and civic affairs.

Dr. Hughes holds the B.A. from Tennessee Wesleyan College and the M.S. and Ed.D. degrees from the University of Tennessee. He also holds an honorary doctorate granted by Lee College, where he served as president from 1960-66.

This essay delineates Dr. Hughes' critique of the New Pentecostalism from his standpoint as a leader among traditional Pentecostals.

The New Pentecostalism: Perspective of a Classical Pentecostal Administrator

11

My assignment is "The New Pentecostalism: Perspective of a Classical Pentecostal Administrator." I have been labeled as a classical administrator, but I am not sure what is meant by classical. One person has said, "It means that you got there first." However, I agree with Edward O'Connor that it is incongruous to use the term "classical" in connection with anything so free, spirited, and emotional as the original Pentecostal movement. Since classical connotes a rigidity and a formalism quite foreign to traditional Pentecostals, I feel that it is a misnomer. I hope that those who speak and write on the subject will discover a distinguishing term that will more clearly describe what I am.

These are exciting days, and we are privileged to live in the "pneumatic era." Without a doubt God is pouring out His Spirit upon "all flesh," "even as many as the Lord our God shall call." No one group can claim primacy or a monopoly on the Spirit. The Spirit is sovereign. He breathes where He wills, and Christ baptizes men severally as He wills. And I hasten to say that it is His will for all to receive the fullness of His Spirit (Acts 2:38f.; 1 Cor. 12:7).

167

The traditional, or classical, Pentecostal movement had its beginning just prior to the turn of the century.[1] Evangelical Christians,
with a desire to recapture God's plan for His church and to reaffirm
the cardinal principles and doctrines of historic Christianity in all of
their pristine power and glory, sought God for His fullness. As a result, they were greeted with an outpouring of the Spirit which was to
be the beginning of a world-wide movement.

Although the majority of those early believers had no desire to
leave the established church, they were ostracized because of their
Pentecostal experience. They had a broad area of agreement doctrinally with the evangelicals, but there was a strong resentment
toward the "tongues experience." Therefore, there was no alternative
but to establish Pentecostal fellowships where they could have freedom of expression of their new-found experience. Pentecostals in time
became a strong sector of evangelicalism.

In those days a non-evangelical (much less an anti-evangelical) who
claimed to be a Pentecostal was almost unheard of. But the picture is
quite different today. Some evangelicals have readjusted their level of
tolerance so as to accommodate Pentecostals within their fellowship.
The emergence of Pentecostal claimants among non-evangelicals has
been received with acceptance or tolerance. There is a claim to the
Pentecostal experience among the liberal movements and Roman
Catholics as well. Pentecostal adherents in these groups have been
labeled as the "New Pentecostals" or "Neo-Pentecostals."

Defining the term "New Pentecostalism" would be almost as difficult as defining Fundamentalism. In its brief existence it has been
given various interpretations corresponding to the religious backgrounds of its adherents. For example, to the Catholics it is a
"charismatic renewal," which implies that the baptism in the Holy
Spirit is not a new experience but an "actualization" of an experience
received objectively in the baptismal celebration. It is an experience
of reaffirmation rather than initiation, not necessarily accompanied
by speaking with tongues. Very simply, for them it is a renewal in
faith.[2]

For most evangelicals who embrace the New Pentecostalism, it is
an added dimension in spiritual living. They perceive the baptism in

---

1. The most publicized outpourings occurred in Topeka, Kansas, in 1901 and in Los
Angeles in 1906. But there was a significant outpouring in 1896 in Cherokee, North
Carolina. See Charles W. Conn, *Like a Mighty Army* (Cleveland, TN: Church of God
Publishing House, 1955), pp. 18-20.

2. Kevin and Dorothy Ranaghan, *Catholic Pentecostals* (New York: Paulist Press,
1969), p. 142.

the Spirit as a crisis experience subsequent to the new birth, and not a renewal of a previous experience.

To many liberal church people who have known Christ only nominally prior to their contact with the New Pentecostalism, it has an altogether different meaning. It is an act of regeneration or a conversion experience which has transformed their lives. Therefore, we have a problem of terminology.

When Pentecostalism was confined mostly to evangelicals, the issues with which we dealt were not, by and large, of a fundamental nature. But since non-evangelicals have become claimants of the Pentecostal experience, new questions have arisen which must be faced and answered. Let us consider a few of these questions.

The Question of Doctrine and Commitment

A concept accepted by many New Pentecostals is that since Pentecostalism is not a denomination, nor a doctrine, but an experience, it can be accommodated within the framework of any doctrinal persuasion. Therefore the doctrinal persuasion is not the concern, but the experience. If this theory holds true, one could conceivably possess the Pentecostal experience regardless of his belief or doctrine.

The serious question then arises, "Does belief or doctrine have any bearing on experience?" For if doctrinal beliefs do not have any bearing on experience, then does it matter what one believes? I would submit that one cannot separate faith and commitment. For what one believes determines his experience. We proceed from doctrine to experience. The apostle declared, " . . . ye have obeyed from the heart that form of doctrine which was delivered you" (Rom. 6:17, KJV). A serious problem arises if we divorce experience from doctrine.

The Word of God is the means by which experience is authenticated. On the Day of Pentecost, when the one hundred twenty received the infilling of the Spirit, Peter related the experience to the Word, " . . . this is that which was spoken by the prophet Joel" (Acts 2:16, KJV). While the observers focused on the experience, Peter presented the scriptural basis for the experience. Any experience that falls outside the framework of the Scripture must be identified as spurious, regardless of how supernatural it might seem or of how impressive it might appear.

The Word of God does not set forth an experience-oriented Pentecost, but rather a Word-centered Pentecost. Scripture is not verified by experience, but experience is tested by Scripture. Since man is an emotional being, it is a safeguard for him to validate his experience by the Word. The Scripture provides guidelines for the experience to be translated into avenues of effective service. God does not give one an experience for experience' sake; therefore, the necessity of the balance of experience and doctrine. One's experience can always be challenged on the authority of the Scripture. If this is not the case, man is the ultimate authority. And his experience becomes unchallengeable or the last word.

The Corinthian church was somewhat experience-centered, and the apostle Paul pointed them back to the Word: "If any man thinks himself to be a prophet, or spiritual, let him acknowledge that the things that I write unto you are the commandments of the Lord" (1 Cor. 14:37, KJV). The Holy Spirit is the Spirit of Truth, "Howbeit when he, the Spirit of truth, is come, he will guide you into all truth . . . " (John 16:13, KJV).

Admittedly, those who receive the experience must be given time for growth and development. But when the Spirit possesses one, He guides him into all truth. He will not remain in error. "If any man will do his will, he shall know of the doctrine, whether it be of God . . . " (John 7:17, KJV). Christianity itself is based upon doctrine; and where there is the absence of doctrine and teaching, error occurs. First century Christians based their experience on the doctrine of the apostles and continued steadfastly in this doctrine, so much so that a complaint rose against them that they had filled Jerusalem with their doctrine.

So then I would submit that the baptism in the Holy Spirit is an experiential doctrine based upon the Scripture and dependent upon man's faith in and obedience to the Word.

The Question of Normativeness

Traditional Pentecostals believe that speaking with tongues as the Spirit gives the utterance is the initial physical evidence of the baptism in the Holy Spirit. A number of the New Pentecostals teach that speaking with tongues is not necessarily linked with the reception of the baptism. In other words, they do not believe that speaking with other tongues is the normative experience. The argument against speaking with other tongues as the normative experience for those who are baptized in the Holy Spirit is that it should not be classified as a binding doctrine, because it is not categorically stated in the Word of God. In fact, traditional Pentecostals have been accused of making laws for the Holy Spirit by setting forth the pattern in the Book of Acts as the model for receiving the baptism in the Spirit. This traditional Pentecostal approach has been called exegetically untenable and "passage picking." The opponents of this view hold that at best these passages are only "faith texts." However, the cumulative evidence of the scriptural experiences of the baptism in the Holy Spirit corroborates the doctrine of speaking with other tongues as the normative experience.

In three instances out of five, the Scripture definitely states that the recipients spoke with tongues. In the two cases where speaking with tongues is not recorded, there were outward and observable signs of the Spirit-baptism. The two occasions where the Scripture does not record speaking with tongues were the Spirit-baptism of Paul at Damascus and that of the disciples at Samaria. One reads in 1 Corinthians 14:18 that Paul spoke in tongues more than all of the Corinthians. I would submit that this experience had its origin at his Holy Spirit baptism in Damascus.

The terminology used with reference to the Samaritan experience implies that they spoke in tongues. The Scripture leaves no doubt about the fact that there was some physical manifestation accompanying the experience which attracted Simon the Sorcerer. When he saw it, he offered money to purchase it. I would submit that Simon saw what the people of Jerusalem saw on the Day of Pentecost. On that day, the people saw and heard the disciples speak with tongues: " . . . he hath shed forth this, which ye now see and hear" (Acts 2:33, KJV).

In addition to an outward, observable sign in Samaria the terminology of the context suggests an experience like that at the household of Cornelius. The Samaria record states, "(For as yet he was *fallen upon* none of them: only they were baptized in the name of the Lord Jesus.) Then laid they their hands on them, and they received the Holy Ghost" (Acts 8:16f., KJV). At the household of Cornelius it is recorded that: "While Peter yet spake these words, the Holy Ghost *fell on* all them which heard the word" (Acts 10:44, KJV). In recounting this occasion Peter said, " . . . as I began to speak, the Holy Ghost *fell on* them, as on us at the beginning" (Acts 11:15, KJV; italics supplied).

So then we must conclude that if those baptized in the Holy Ghost spoke with tongues when He *fell on* them at the beginning (Pentecost) and when He fell on them at the household of Cornelius, they also spoke with tongues when He *fell on* them at Samaria. Those who criticize the use of these passages to support the argument that speaking with tongues is the normative experience for those who receive the baptism in the Holy Spirit make the charge that Pentecostals tend to absolutize Lucan theology. They make the point that speaking with tongues is not set forth in the Epistles and the Gospels. However, with me this raises another very serious point and that is the inspiration of the Scriptures. Was not the Acts record of Luke inspired by the Holy Ghost and, therefore, infallible? Why would there have to be further supportive Scripture to verify and validate his record? Is the theology of one portion of the Scripture more authentic than another? Is Johannine theology more authentic than Lucan theology?

I would hasten to say that while traditional Pentecostals do hold to the position that speaking with tongues as the Spirit gives the utterance is the initial evidence of the baptism in the Holy Ghost, they also believe that it is by no means the final evidence. The Spirit does not come merely to speak, but His speaking is His announcement that He has come to the believer and will accompany him in performing the task of implementing the Great Commission. This experience is not the apex of Christian service, but the genesis. It is the beginning of a life of full service in Christ Jesus.

The Question of Unity

Many of the New Pentecostals have expressed hope that the common experience will be the rallying point for the unity of all believers. It sounds good to say that we are joined together in a common brotherhood beneath our doctrinal differences. But I am not aware of a historical account where a common experience has brought about unification in the Body. The Spirit is the agent which brings us together. He is the agent which ministers unity. He unifies men around the faith and brings them together in Christ.

Therefore, while the Spirit brings us together, it is the sharing of our precious faith which holds us together. We come together under the banner of the Word and not because of a common experience. While we endeavor to keep the unity of the Spirit in the bond of peace, this unity is posited in one Lord, one faith, and one baptism. There are some who profess an experience of glossolalia but do not subscribe to the tenets of Christianity. In fact, religious movements through the centuries have had their so-called glossolalia or spiritual phenomena, even the Satanists. So I would submit that glossolalia or other spiritual phenomena alone cannot serve to unify. The New Testament church rallied around the faith: ". . . all that believed were together. . ." (Acts 2:44, KJV). ". . . And they spake the word of God with boldness. And the multitude of them that believed were of one heart and of one soul . . ." (Acts 4:31f., KJV). With heart and soul blended together in faith and experience, they focused upon the Word of God.

The charismatic Corinthians, who had a common experience, were urged to be of the same mind and of the same judgment (1 Cor. 1:10), because the apostle knew that those who are at variance ideologically and theologically cannot maintain harmony or travel together in agreement for long. Those who are experience-oriented tend to glorify the experience and call attention to phenomena or signs and not to Christ and His Word. The Spirit does not focus attention upon Himself, but upon Christ: " . . . for [the Spirit] shall not speak of himself; but whatsoever he shall hear, that shall he speak: and he will shew you things to come. He shall glorify me . . . " (John 16:13f., KJV).

In Christian circles there is a general awareness of the need for unity. The answer will not be found in a common experience, however. Neither will it be found in merger, amalgamations, federations, or unions which form a superstructure with no heart or soul—a joining of hands but a division of hearts. Again, I reiterate: unity will be found when we gather around the Word and rediscover the scriptural foundations of New Testament Christianity.

The Question of Life-Style

Another question that has come into focus among the New Pentecostals is life-style. What are the effects of the baptism in the Holy Ghost upon one's life-style? In order to answer this, we must understand the effects of the baptism in one's life. The baptism in the Holy Spirit is not to be identified with cleansing,[3] redemption, and forgiveness of sins—but with power for service. The world (or sinners) cannot receive the baptism in the Holy Spirit, for the Scripture reveals: "Even the Spirit of truth; whom the world cannot receive, because it seeth him not, neither knoweth him: but ye know him; for he dwelleth with you, and shall be in you" (John 14:17, KJV). Therefore, one must have a personal knowledge of Christ and must have experienced the transforming grace of God in his life prior to the experience of the baptism in the Holy Spirit. The rule throughout the Scriptures is that purity precedes power. The apostle Peter, in explaining the Spirit-baptism of the Gentiles, pointed out that their hearts were purified by faith: "And God, which knoweth the hearts, bare them witness, giving them the Holy Ghost, even as he did unto us" (Acts 15:8, KJV). "For God hath not called us unto uncleanness, but unto holiness. He therefore that despiseth, despiseth not man, but God, who hath also given unto us his holy Spirit" (1 Thess. 4:7f., KJV).

---

3. Of course we understand that the Spirit is the agent for all of our experiences. He is also the Sanctifier (Rom. 15:16). But here I am talking about the experience of the baptism in the Holy Spirit.

Some of the New Pentecostals testify that they have been set free from certain habits and sins through the Pentecostal experience. Testimonies are often cited from certain persons who were cured of dope addiction or cleansed from gross iniquity by the baptism in the Holy Spirit. While I do not wish to judge these testimonies, I must test them by the Word of God; and nowhere does the Word of God set forth the forgiveness of sins as a result of the baptism in the Holy Spirit. On the contrary, the Spirit is given unto them that obey Him (Acts 5:32). While we receive the promise of the Spirit through faith, as we do all things which come from God, it is also true that there are requirements for and limitations to the reception of the Spirit.

The Spirit of God is the Spirit of holiness. It follows then that one who is filled with the Spirit will live a life of holiness. Therefore, it is incongruous with the experience of the baptism in the Holy Ghost for one to live a life after the flesh and after the lust of the flesh. A body controlled by lust and evil habits certainly cannot be inhabited by the Holy Ghost. Our bodies are the temples of the Holy Ghost, and it is unthinkable that the Holy Ghost would dwell in a temple that is unholy. "If any man defile the temple of God, him shall God destroy; for the temple of God is holy, which temple ye are" (1 Cor. 3:17, KJV). A valid experience (the key word in this sentence is "valid") of speaking with other tongues as the Spirit gives the utterance is evidence that God has control of one's life and that he is yielded to Him. "It is the nature of the Holy Spirit to form in the believer those graces that manifest the nature of Christ and to forbid the presence of those traits of character that are offensive to the nature of Christ."[4] Therefore, the life-style of one who is filled with the Spirit is conformity to the image of God's Son.

The Question of Relationship to the Church

For one reason or another, the New Pentecostals have formed "renewal communities," "households," or some such group directed by an informal leader outside of the church.

> Christian community is not just getting people together—it isn't just getting people relating and working for a common goal, or even living together, nor does it just happen by letting the Spirit work. Christian community is the response, individually and collectively, of a people to the Word of God, a decision to submit totally to that Word

4. R. Hollis Gause, "Issues in Pentecostalism" (address given at the Pentecostal Fellowship of North American Convention, Jacksonville, Florida, Oct. 29-31, 1973).

together, consciously and explicitly, and to allow the Lord to build a
people, a community.[5]

One wonders why these exclusive gatherings are necessary if the
participants are involved in the life of the church and the church is
allowing them freedom of expression and opportunity for service.
It is not uncommon for a charismatic person to attend his church
on Sunday morning and meet with a prayer group or a renewal community on Sunday night. If one has to go out of his church for Pentecostal fellowship, it raises a question of the effectiveness of that
church. How can one fulfill the ministries of the church and seek to
excel in its edification if he operates separate and apart from it? The
Word of God demands involvement in the church and participation
in the ministries that build up the body. Those who would seek Pentecostal fellowship in a group that is not under the supervision of the
church make themselves liable to error and all manner of spiritual excesses. In most cases they do not have the guidance and leadership of
one who is experienced in the Word. Therefore, some have made ship-
wreck and the name of Christ has been blasphemed.

I have raised five questions, and these are by no means all of the
questions which should be considered. But they are five of the most
important, at least from my viewpoint. These questions are a matter
of concern to the traditional Pentecostals. Let us review them in the
light of some of the specifics of the New Pentecostalism.

1. In relationship to the question of doctrine and commitment, let
us consider the following concerns: the manner and means of the baptism in the Spirit; the use of the charismatic experience to affirm doctrines or to reinforce traditions.

The New Pentecostals use the same terminology as the traditional
Pentecostals, but they do not always mean the same thing. Catholics,
or the sacramentalists, hold that:

> . . . baptism in the Holy Spirit, as we use the term, has been poured
> out in the church since Pentecost Sunday and through every com-
> plete baptismal celebration still today. The church is filled with the
> Holy Spirit; as the Body of Christ, it has already received all the gifts
> and the fruits of the Spirit. What this new pentecostal movement
> seeks to do through faithful prayer, and by trusting in the Word of
> God, is to ask the Lord to actualize in a concrete living way what the
> Christian people have already received. It is an attempt to respond

5. Ralph Martin, *Unless the Lord Build the House* (Notre Dame, IN: Ave Maria Press,
1971), p. 36.

in radical faith to the Spirit who has already been given so that his life, his gifts, and his fruit may be actualized in the lives of the members of Christ's Body.[6]

As I understand it, the Catholic Pentecostals are saying that the baptism in the Holy Spirit is received by every Catholic in a complete baptismal celebration. It is at this point that one has a rebirth and receives the Holy Spirit, whether or not he has an awareness of it. One receives the baptism in the Holy Spirit objectively, when he is sacramentally baptized. But in addition to this hidden communication of the Holy Spirit, there is also a manifest communication that may occur later. This is called the actualization of the experience. Tongues may or may not occur in the actualization. This stance poses a serious problem with traditional Pentecostals as it relates to the experience of salvation, because they do not view it as having a scriptural foundation.

The next area of concern is the use of the charismatic experience to affirm doctrines and reinforce tradition. According to a number of Catholic writers, Catholic Pentecostals tend to go back and cultivate all the avenues of contact with God that they had abandoned—the rosary, the Real Presence, devotion to Mary.[7] Some return to the practice of frequent confession, and daily mass and communion.[8] The whole of the church's sacramental and liturgical life becomes more meaningful. They tend to work out the theology of Pentecostalism in a sacramental and liturgical context.[9] They find themselves more attached to the structural church after receiving the baptism in the Spirit. For some, the actualization of the Spirit comes during the rosary; for others, it comes while singing a hymn at Mass. Still for others, it comes in prayer to the Blessed Virgin.[10]

Since the Holy Spirit is the Spirit of truth, traditional Pentecostals cannot understand how claimants of the Pentecostal experience can continue to subscribe to traditions and doctrines which are not scripturally based. The concern of many traditional Pentecostals is that many sacramentalists have never been brought to an effective personal faith and trust in Jesus Christ as Savior and Lord. As one person

6. Ranaghan, *Catholic Pentecostals*, pp. 141f.

7. Edward D. O'Connor, "A Catholic Pentecostal Movement," *Ave Maria*, 105 (June 3, 1967), 10; Josephine Massyngberde Ford, "A Catholic Pentecostalism: New Testament Christianity or Twentieth-Century Hysteria?" *Jubilee*, 16 (June, 1968), 14.

8. Ranaghan, *Catholic Pentecostals*, pp. 37, 70, 87, 92, 98, 104.

9. Ibid., p. 142.

10. Edward D. O'Connor, *The Pentecostal Movement in the Catholic Church* (Notre Dame, IN: Ave Maria Press, 1971), p. 128.

put it, they have been sacramentalized but not evangelized. Many of the people who desire the baptism in the Holy Ghost are presupposing an evangelization that has never taken place. This is the problem with many who desire the experience but who really need an experience of the new birth, or conversion, which is a prerequisite to the baptism in the Holy Spirit.

2. Now let us consider the question of speaking with tongues as the normative experience for those who receive the baptism in the Holy Spirit. It is at this point that some of the Neo-Pentecostals and the traditional Pentecostals disagree. For example, Catholic Pentecostals almost universally reject the necessary link between the baptism and speaking in tongues.[11] For them, anyone who asks for the baptism receives it, whether or not he speaks with tongues. It is at this point that some have called upon the traditional Pentecostals to compromise their stance.

One of the problems is the failure to distinguish between speaking with other tongues as the Spirit gives the utterance (the initial evidence of the baptism in the Holy Spirit) and the gift of tongues as set forth in 1 Corinthians 12 and 14. A proper understanding at this point would, in all probability, answer some of the questions on the normativeness of speaking with tongues.

3. Let us proceed to the question of unity. At this point, the concern of the traditional Pentecostals is the differences which exist on fundamental and cardinal doctrines. It is a fact that we cannot be unified nor even identified by a common experience. For example, at the charismatic conference on the campus of the University of Notre Dame in 1972, there were non-Catholic charismatics who insisted on water rebaptism; while on the other side, in the closing session of the conference, the "separated brethren" were told that they would not be allowed to partake of the Eucharist. Chaplain Harold Cohen, of New Orleans, said that he hoped "the power of the Word" would bring about healing and the possibility of intercommunion. It was observed in *Christianity Today*, by Edward E. Plowman, that:

> Despite the pentecostal emphasis on unity, it appears that in the nitty-gritty affairs of church distinctives, Catholic and non-Catholic charismatics will, for the foreseeable future, find themselves maintaining their separate identities.[12]

11. Kilian McDonnell, *Catholic Pentecostalism: Problems in Evaluation* (Pecos, NM: Dove Publications, 1970), p. 18.
12. Edward E. Plowman, "Catholic Pentecostals: An Offering of Agony," *Christianity Today*, 16 (June 23, 1972), 35.

At that same conference, Auxiliary Bishop Joseph McKinney, of Grand Rapids, Michigan, expressed that one of the fears of some of the bishops was the belief among charismatics that all faiths are equally valid. He stated further: "Roman Catholicism has a fullness of the Christ tradition found in no other denomination."[13] In the 1973 charismatic conference, Father Cohen received a standing ovation when he asked that Pope Paul give consolation and support to the charismatic movement. He said, "We want your discernment. We are founded on this Rock, and on this Rock we stand."[14] Cardinal Leo Suenens, of Belgium, declared that: "The secret to achieving unity with the Spirit in the best way is our unity with Mary, the mother of God." The Catholics involved in the movement declare that they are not Pentecostals, but that they are Catholics who have had a Pentecostal experience.[15] It is very plainly set forth that the Catholic movement was started by Catholics and that the experience which they have received is to make them better Catholics. The very term "Neo-Pentecostal" or "New Pentecostal" suggests a difference or cleavage in the Pentecostal ranks.

It has been said that this is an era of interpreting, explaining, and reaching toward one another. May God grant it to be so in reality and not in mere word. There is much talk about unity in charismatic circles; but while there is talk of unity, there are also some very divisive elements that are apparent.

4. Possibly, one of the most painful concerns among some traditional Pentecostals is the life-style of those who profess the baptism in the Spirit. Most of the traditional Pentecostals believe in a "separated life," while the life-style of many of the New Pentecostals is not appreciably affected by the experience. One magazine expressed it like this:

> This new movement has leaped over the boundaries that formerly contained its predecessor, the "holiness-tongues movement," and is taking on a character of its own. It now appears to be quite at home among church adherents who feel under no obligation to give serious heed to "holiness" restrictions, for example, on the use of tobacco and alcohol or going to the movies.[16]

13. Ibid., p. 34.
14. Quoted by Mrs. Robert Williamson, "Eutychus and His Kin: Rosary Meditations," *Christianity Today*, 17 (June 22, 1973), 37.
15. Mary Papa, "People Having a Good Time Praying," *The National Catholic Reporter*, 3 (May 17, 1967), 10.
16. Ramond Frame, "Something Unusual," *His*, 24 (Dec., 1963), 18.

Kevin and Dorothy Ranaghan state that:

> We must not confuse the baptism in the Holy Spirit with cultural forms of religious expression common in pentecostal denominations. The righteous life is characterized by clean living; therefore, no smoking, drinking, dancing, make-up, theatre-going, or other amusements. While considerably tempered over the last several decades, the revivalistic culture continues to pervade denominational pentecostalism. It is perhaps the gift box in which the gift comes among those people—but it is not to be confused with the gift itself. In its own cultural setting and development, this religious life-style is quite beautiful, meaningful and relevant. But it is not essential to nor desirable for the baptism in the Holy Spirit, especially among people of far different religious backgrounds.[17]

Traditional Pentecostals believe that holiness is Christlikeness and that holiness is of the heart. They also believe that the transformation will produce a life of nonconformity to the world, which is translated into everyday living. It is true that we must not confuse holiness with cultural mannerisms; but at the same time, Christ must be reflected in our lives, and men must know that we have been with Jesus when they behold our design of living.

The baptism in the Spirit is not merely a matter of correct conceptual thinking, but this experience also has tremendous implications for one's life-style. It is not simply a matter of holding to certain standards because they are traditional, but it is a matter of obeying them because they are scripturally true and because it is the truth that makes the difference in life.

5. Lastly, let us discuss the concern of traditional Pentecostals with regard to those who feel that it is necessary to meet in groups which are not under the auspices of the church. The main concern of the traditional Pentecostals is the error that usually occurs in these groups and the divisiveness that ensues. There is also the concern that such exclusiveness will cultivate a so-called spiritual elite or create a spiritual superiority complex.

One thing that happens frequently among the New Pentecostals who are zealous for others to receive an experience is the attempt to impart the gift. There are instructions such as: "Copy someone who speaks in tongues 'until your gift flows.' " One charismatic gives the advice to "make sounds like baby talk, gibberish," in preparation for confirmation.[18] Certain sounds have been suggested by some who in-

17. Ranaghan, *Catholic Pentecostals*, pp. 154ff.
18. Edward E. Plowman, "Memo from Notre Dame: The Spirit Is Moving," *Christianity Today*, 17 (June 22, 1973), 37.

struct candidates aspiring to the baptism in the Spirit. This results in disillusionment for many who supposedly receive the experience.

There is also the tendency of placing revelations on the same level as the Word, or even above the Word. It must always be pointed out that true revelations are not contrary to the Word, but they are in agreement with the Word. Nor do they supplant the Word.

There are still others who treat speaking with tongues as a psychological release, or catharsis, with which they begin each morning for a personal refreshing. But there is no biblical precedent for this type of human control of speaking in tongues. Tongues are a purposeful gift and are not to be manipulated according to the fancies of men nor to satisfy the curiosity of men. Tongues come not from man, but from God; and man is merely the vehicle for the transmission of the divine message.

Clark H. Pinnock

Clark H. Pinnock holds the B.A. (1960) in ancient Near Eastern studies from the University of Toronto. His Ph.D. in New Testament (1963) was earned at the University of Manchester, England.

Dr. Pinnock has lectured on Christian theological themes at several universities. Among his published articles and books are *Set Forth Your Case* (Chicago: Moody, ²1971) and *Biblical Revelation* (Chicago: Moody, 1971).

After a stint as assistant lecturer at Manchester (1963-65), he became associate professor of theology at New Orleans Baptist Theological Seminary (1965-69). He was associated with Trinity Evangelical Divinity School from 1969 until 1974, when he accepted his current position as associate professor of systematic theology at Regent College in Vancouver.

In this essay, Dr. Pinnock offers irenic proposals for shared inquiry from the standpoint of a sympathetic evangelical observer of the Pentecostal movement.

The New Pentecostalism:
Reflections of an
Evangelical Observer

12

The New Pentecostalism seems to this observer to be a genuine movement of the Spirit of God renewing His church. I speak as an observer who, although standing outside the New Pentecostalism proper, has learned to appreciate it from personal involvement in charismatic groups, both Protestant and Catholic. From these experiences I have emerged a stronger and better Christian. I agree with Karl Barth that there may often be too little of the pneumatic in the church, but never too much.[1] Therefore, it thrills my soul to see multitudes of people allowing the Spirit to operate freely in their midst.

No useful purpose would be served, however, if I limited myself to an uncritical commendation of the movement. Nor would I fairly represent, as I have been asked to do, the actual opinions of those evangelical Christians who stand outside it. For it is a fact that the New Pentecostalism has become the occasion of a division, sometimes quite bitter, within the evangelical community. Therefore, I wish to enter into a discussion with the movement on some of the issues which divide us, so that the New Pentecostal Christians will realize what our

1. Karl Barth, *Church Dogmatics*, IV. 2, trans. G. W. Bromiley (Edinburgh: T. and T. Clark, 1958), 321.

concerns are. It may be that through such discussions we will come to understand each other better and penetrate the mind of God more exactly, so that a more perfect unity and cooperation will result for the good of the church and of all mankind.

Our Gratitude to God

According to Scripture the church *is* a charismatic community. She is the human assembly which has received the eschatological gift of the Spirit. There would be no Christian existence at all were it not for this blessed outpouring. One of the most fundamental things the Bible has to say about the church is that she is the creation of the Holy Spirit.[2] Evangelicals who place the highest value upon a personal relationship with Jesus Christ through the Spirit in the fellowship of His church can hardly fail to praise God for the vivid appreciation of this truth within the New Pentecostalism.

For too much of her history the Christian church has been "binitarian"—concentrating on the Father and the Son. She has neglected theologically and practically the doctrine of the Holy Spirit. If we are honest, we have to express our shame at the worldliness and spiritual ineffectiveness of a large portion of Christendom, both yesterday and today. The church needs nothing more than she needs a supernatural visitation of the Spirit of God.

The New Pentecostalism has arisen to meet this need. Because of this, evangelicals outside the movement can only lay aside their objections and thank the living God who is once again renewing His people. For the emphasis with fresh urgency that believers be filled with the Spirit of God we are deeply grateful. And the fruit of this movement is unmistakable. We find a renewed devotion to Jesus Christ, a new steadfastness in the faith, a new authority in witnessing, an expanded prayer life, and above all a fresh exuberance of joy in walking daily with God.

Evangelical religion in our day has tended to become overly intellectualized and "Apollonian." We have become insecure in the presence of the strange, paralogical powers of the free, dynamic Spirit. And instead of lamenting our deficiency we have sought to restrict the outpouring of the Spirit to the first century so as to direct attention away from our own spiritual poverty. As J. Rodman Williams has observed, we shrink from the unpredictability of the Spirit. We crave blueprints that will map His operations and leave us

2. See Hans Küng, *The Church*, trans. Ray and Rosaleen Ockenden (New York: Sheed and Ward, 1967), pp. 150-203.

at ease. We prefer our quiet lethargy to the explosive situation in which anything might happen.[3] The New Pentecostalism is a well-justified protest against the cold and impersonal form which institutional evangelicalism has often taken. It is paralleled by far less biblical reform proposals which also press for "Dionysian" religion of a more ecstatic kind. But unlike them this movement is likely to have staying power, because it is at root an invitation to recover the authentic doctrine of the Spirit in its full biblical context.[4]

The late Samuel M. Shoemaker captured the meaning of the New Pentecostalism for the rest of Christianity when he wrote:

> God is trying to get through into the Church, staid and stuffy and self-centered as it often is, with a kind of power that will make it radiant and exciting and self-giving. We should seek to understand and be reverent toward this phenomenon, rather than to ignore or scorn it.[5]

I think we can go even further and express our deep gratitude to God for this fresh, gentle blowing of His gracious Spirit.

Theological Questions

Alongside our real appreciation, evangelicals outside the movement also experience some hesitation theologically. For it appears to us as if, despite the best of intentions, there has taken place a degree of doctrinal malformation at certain key points in the New Pentecostal theology. For this reason, a minority of us (this observer not included) have been completely turned off and have sought to discredit the whole movement.

But there is a growing segment of evangelical opinion which would like to see a doctrinal development that would break down the walls that divide us and at the same time represent the biblical concerns of both sides more adequately than has as yet been possible. For it would be little short of catastrophic if there were to develop an ever-widening and unbridgeable rift in the ranks of fellow believers. Only

3. J. Rodman Williams, *Era of the Spirit* (Plainfield, NJ: Logos International, 1971), p. 35. I suspect that the reason why noncharismatic church leaders refuse to allow their people to see the movement as a live option is rooted in the fear that many of their members would find it irresistible and far superior to the relative deadness of their own congregations.

4. Various liberal scholars are calling the church to a Dionysian (ecstatic) religion: Paul Tillich, *Systematic Theology* III (Chicago: University of Chicago Press, 1963), 114-20; Harvey Cox, *The Feast of Fools* (New York: Harper and Row, 1969); Sam Keen, "Manifesto for a Dionysian Theology," *New Theology No. 7*, ed. Martin E. Marty and Dean G. Peerman (New York: Macmillan, 1970), pp. 79-103.

5. Cited in Watson E. Mills, *Understanding Speaking in Tongues* (Grand Rapids: Eerdmans, 1972), p. 61.

Satan could be pleased with such an eventuality. The way to avoid this, it seems to me, is to keep on probing into the central issues—not separately, but cooperatively—in order to find the mind of God, which none has yet exhausted, and if possible achieve a clearer and more accurate articulation of the authentic religious values which grip us all.[6]

The Subsequence of the Baptism in the Holy Spirit

A basic element in the theology of the New Pentecostalism is the teaching that the believer ought to seek a post-conversion baptism in the Spirit, in order to obtain full power for Christian service and to receive the full complement of charismatic gifts. Historically this emphasis on a second work of grace stems from the Methodist-holiness movement, mediated by its vigorous daughter, classical Pentecostalism.

Evangelicals cannot see how such a concept can fail to detract from and demean the initial encounter with the Spirit through saving faith in Jesus. If we wish to speak of *the* baptism in the Spirit, surely we must reserve the expression for the initial saving encounter which is Christian conversion. To be a Christian at all is to be baptized by one Spirit (1 Cor. 12:13) and to receive Him as a gift (Acts 2:38). Through Jesus alone we receive the promise of the Spirit (Gal. 3:14). According to Peter, the baptism of the Spirit was what the disciples and the three thousand received on the Day of Pentecost (Acts 11:15-17). It looks to evangelicals as if the New Pentecostals, like the old, are setting up a two-plateau schema of the Christian life, with faith in Jesus admitting one only to the lower and inferior level. Any doctrine which gives that impression is either unscriptural or, as I think, defectively formulated.[7]

At the same time, "baptism" is a flexible metaphor, not a technical term. Luke seems to regard it as synonymous with "fullness" (Acts 2:4; cf. 11:16). Therefore, so long as we recognize conversion as truly a baptism in the Spirit, there is no reason why we cannot use "baptism" to refer to subsequent fillings of the Spirit as well. This later experience, or experiences, should not be tied in with the tight "second blessing" schema, but should be seen as *actualization* of what we have

6. See my earlier attempt, Clark H. Pinnock and Grant R. Osborne, "A Truce Proposal for the Tongues Controversy," *Christianity Today*, 16 (October 8, 1971), 6-9.

7. The most authoritative statements of this objection are found in James D. G. Dunn, *Baptism in the Holy Spirit, Studies in Biblical Theology*, Series 2, 15 (Naperville, IL: Allenson, 1970), and Frederick D. Bruner, *A Theology of the Holy Spirit. The Pentecostal Experience and the New Testament* (Grand Rapids: Eerdmans, 1970).

already received in the initial charismatic experience, which is conversion. Kevin and Dorothy Ranaghan seem to understand it in this way when they write:

> What this new pentecostal movement seeks to do through faithful prayer, and by trusting in the Word of God, is to ask the Lord to actualize in a concrete living way what the Christian people have already received.[8]

On such an understanding, evangelicals could be united. The weakness of the church, the abnormality of so much contemporary Christian living, would not be seen as the failure to go beyond saving faith and seek something beyond Christ. It would be understood as the failure of Christians to appropriate on a day-by-day basis all that we really have in Jesus (Eph. 1:3). The fullness is in Him, and to Him believers must be urged to go. We are complete in Him (Col. 2:10).[9]

It seems to me that the genuine thrust of the New Pentecostal movement is not one of calling Christians to a second experience of grace, but of calling them to the charismatic fullness of the first. Such a refinement of emphasis, if it is acceptable to the movement, would have a healing and irenical effect upon the Body of Christ in our time.

The Conditions of the Baptism in the Holy Spirit

An unfortunate result of this undue emphasis on the second work of grace has been the teaching of the conditions under which the experience may be received. Inevitably, if we suppose that only some believers enter into it, it must be because they have met the conditions of the baptism and others have not. It might even be suggested that some deserve this blessing while others do not. In short, the movement could very easily degenerate into something for which the least appropriate term would be "full gospel."

Evangelicals find the New Testament very clear in stipulating that the only condition for receiving Christ, and His Spirit, is simple faith. Believing in Jesus releases the fullness of His Spirit (John 7:37-39). Through faith alone this promise of the Father comes to us (Gal. 3:3, 14). The obedience Peter refers to in his answer to the high priest is the

---

8. Kevin and Dorothy Ranaghan, *Catholic Pentecostals* (New York: Paulist Press, 1969), p. 141. Similarly, Larry Christenson, *A Message to the Charismatic Movement* (Minneapolis: Bethany Fellowship, 1972), pp. 62f.

9. The New Pentecostal movement is based experientially in a crisis-type encounter with the Spirit. This results, I believe, from the deficiency of teaching on the work of the Spirit at conversion and subsequently. Therefore, the actualization when it comes is dramatic and sudden. Were the teaching adequate, there is no reason why the actualizing of the Spirit would not be gradual and progressive.

obedience of faith in Jesus the Christ (Acts 5:32). On the Day of Pentecost the Spirit did not fall on some of the disciples who had fulfilled certain conditions, but on all of them. No one was passed over because he failed to meet some condition beyond that of faith. Even their waiting was as unstrenuous as possible.

Yet precisely here the New Pentecostals can teach the broader evangelical community. Faith once and for all in Jesus is not the way to fullness and fruitfulness. There must be an abiding in Christ and a walking in His Spirit, an ongoing trust and openness to all that God has for us. The New Pentecostal movement calls other Christians to give up their virtual unbelief in the power of the Spirit, and to adopt a stance of openness and expectancy—in short the stance of faith, the one condition without which the Spirit is not free to work. On this point both sides must change. New Pentecostals must refrain from any semblance of making the gift of the Spirit dependent upon human achievement, and other evangelicals must begin to appreciate the fullness which God has indeed poured out upon His people.

The Evidence of the Baptism in the Holy Spirit

The New Pentecostals are not agreed on this subject. Some of them insist that the baptism in the Spirit be attested by the physical sign of speaking in tongues. But there are others who remain flexible on the subject. They can envisage the possibility of Spirit baptism apart from glossolalia. But even they usually go on to say that the tongues experience, though not normative, is nonetheless normal and valuable. They seem to believe like the others that everyone touched by the charismatic renewal is meant to speak in tongues. To sum up, for the New Pentecostalism speaking in tongues is either the indispensable evidence or else highly desirable evidence that one has received the coveted baptism in the Spirit.[10]

All evangelicals outside the New Pentecostalism would question the biblical basis for making glossolalia the normative sign of the baptism in the Spirit. A minority (this observer excepted) would go further and seek to argue that all gifts of a supranormal character ceased being given after the close of the apostolic age. This view was first developed by Augustine, and has become influential among present day evangelicals through the writings of B. B. Warfield.[11]

---

10. Ranaghan, *Catholic Pentecostals*, pp. 220ff.; Larry Christenson, *Speaking in Tongues and Its Significance for the Church* (Minneapolis: Bethany Fellowship, 1968), pp. 55f., and *A Message to the Charismatic Movement*, pp. 69f.

11. Benjamin B. Warfield, *Miracles: Yesterday and Today* (Grand Rapids: Eerdmans, 1954), ch. 1.

The New Pentecostal movement, in my judgment, is entirely cor
rect in repudiating this theory. Even if it could be established (which
it cannot) that the supranormal gifts were withdrawn, it would not be
safe to conclude that the Spirit is incapable of bestowing them again
should the need for them arise. We have no right to try to bind God's
hands with a tenuous theological theory which has the effect of denying Him the power to grant spiritual gifts to His church.[12] It is entirely
misleading to distinguish arbitrarily between normal and supranormal gifts, and to assume that the supranormal gifts were marks of the
Body of Christ; and as far as tongues are concerned we can do no
other than to follow Paul's command, "Forbid not!" (1 Cor. 14:39).
We may request legislative controls for speaking in tongues in a
public assembly, but we may not forbid the phenomenon altogether.
It is this closed-mindedness on the part of many evangelicals outside
the New Pentecostal movement which poses the greatest threat to the
unity of our life and witness.

But let us now focus upon the issue in Pentecostal doctrine on
which the evangelicals outside the movement do not disagree,
namely, the normativeness of glossolalia. This teaching is wrong in
two ways.

First, Scripture does not teach that the only sure sign of the baptism
in the Spirit is speaking in tongues. If it did, Luke's silence on this matter in reference to the three thousand saved at Pentecost and to the experience of the Samaritans in Acts 8 is inexplicable. And, surely, the
occurrence of tongues at Caesarea was a sign, not because they were
expected or usual, but precisely because they were unexpected and
unusual. Only the most irrefutable proof would convince bigoted Jewish Christians of what they ought to have accepted without a supernatural sign. Evangelicals outside the New Pentecostalism cannot accept the idea that glossolalia is the normative initial sign of the baptism in the Spirit.

The *second* objection to this notion is that it is theologically mis-
directed. The New Testament epistles have a good deal to say about
the initial evidences of an encounter with Jesus Christ by His Spirit,
and nowhere make supranormal gifts the sign of it. Confessing Christ
as Lord, ascribing deity to Him—this is the test of genuine charismatic
experience (1 Cor. 12:3). The ability to cry "Abba, father" is the
evidence of the Spirit of Christ (Gal. 4:6). It is our experience of the
love of God that assures us of His outpoured Spirit (Rom. 5:5). It is in

12. Donald L. Gelpi, *Pentecostalism. A Theological Viewpoint* (New York: Paulist
Press, 1971), pp. 136-38.

our relationships with our neighbors that the authenticity of our spirituality is tested (Gal. 5:25f.). Is it not Paul's evident concern in writing to the Corinthians that they ought to concentrate on love and gifts that edify the Body rather than promote a sensational, but not very profitable, gift? It is a very common misconception to think of gifts as principally exceptional or miraculous phenomena. Paul would have us concentrate on those everyday duties, which, though they are unobtrusive, build up the church. Self-edification is not a high Christian goal. Prophecy is preferred because of its ability to serve the people of God.

I would like to appeal to the New Pentecostals to correct their one-sided emphasis on tongue-speaking. Many of us outside the movement are quite prepared to grant that glossolalia ranks in the list of bona fide spiritual gifts which God is pouring out on us in these days. Would it be out of the question for its leaders to drop the teaching of the normativeness of tongues, if in return evangelicals freely admitted the full range of gifts and evidences which the Spirit has given? For my part, the New Pentecostal movement has been raised up not to divide the Body on a spurious doctrine of normativeness, but to open our eyes to the diversity of spiritual manifestations of which we have hitherto been unaware.[13]

Words of Caution

In conclusion, I should like to add three words of caution as a theologian observing with great interest and concern the New Pentecostalism.

1. Just as there has been a unitarianism of the Father and of the Son, so there can be a unitarianism of the Spirit, in which everything is subordinated to personal experience and intuition. There is a certain tendency for people within the movement, when pressed on questions like those above, to appeal to personal experience. For these people the exegetical difficulties are outweighed by experiential proofs in their Christian lives. We submit that this is a dangerous procedure. The Spirit who indwells us is the Spirit of Jesus Christ, the Jesus of history and the Christ of Scripture. He is the same Spirit who speaks infallibly in the words of the Bible (Heb. 3:7), and He does not contradict Himself. One of the alarming features of liberal theology today is

---

13. Evangelicals who reject the view that charismata have ceased ought to ask themselves why they behave as if they do in fact accept it. Why is there the absence of so many of the gifts in our churches—prophecy, tongues, healing, deliverance? And why are we uptight when some of them begin to be manifested?

its tendency to reduce the gospel to existential concerns, and to confuse the Word of God with the opinions of men. It would be sad indeed if the New Pentecostalism were for some the door into the theology of human subjectivity.

2. It is easy to equate the presence or absence of the Spirit with our changing human emotions. God's promises concerning the Spirit should not be devalued in this way. He is with us *always*, in *every* situation (Matt. 28:20; John 14:16). Do we need more than His Word for it? The insatiable desire for tongues sometimes seems to stem from the desire to prove God's promise when we ought to just believe it. It is the passion to *know* that one has been baptized in the Spirit which often comes through. Why is not the promise of our Savior and the witness of the Spirit in our hearts crying "Abba!" sufficient for us? Can it be wrong to walk by faith and not by sight?

3. The impression is sometimes given that we ought to engage in two movements of faith, one in Jesus for salvation and one in His Spirit for power. The New Testament, however, contains no command to believe in the Spirit; the simple reason for this is that the Spirit is Christ's and in Christ. Not only does this double faith idea detract from the full sufficiency of Jesus, it also tends in the direction of tritheism. According to my understanding of the trinitarian dogma, we do not have communion *separately* with the three *personae* of the Godhead. Rather we trust in the one triune God, who is eternally a *Thou* to us, and who is not known in one of His modes of existence except as He is known in the others as well. To think of establishing a faith relationship with each of the *personae* of the trinity separately seems to me inescapably tritheistic in its implications.[14]

Let me make a final appeal. Let us not permit Satan to use the occasion of the New Pentecostal revival to drive evangelical believers from one another as he has used eschatology, social practices, and the sovereignty of God in the past. Now that some old wounds have healed, let us not create any new ones. If schism is to be avoided, evangelicals outside the movement must abandon their unscriptural resistance to the truth which is in it, and the New Pentecostals themselves will have to press on to theological formulations which conform better to the biblical standards.

It is commonly charged that the New Pentecostalism breeds division in the church. I would not want to finish this paper without indicating where I think the greatest problem lies in this regard.

14. Claude Welch, *In His Name. The Doctrine of the Trinity in Contemporary Theology* (New York: Scribners, 1952), p. 291.

Undoubtedly some of the blame may be attributed to the movement for failing to show that all its emphases are unequivocally biblical. But the greater problem lies with the non-Pentecostal evangelicals themselves. We have not taken the movement seriously as a work of the Spirit of God. At best we have tolerated New Pentecostals in our churches, at worst driven them out. We have not exercised mature Christian leadership in this matter.

It is high time that evangelical leaders begin to think about how to integrate the charismatic movement into the life of the church, and stop treating its members as spiritual lepers. The Roman Catholic Church and the liberal denominations have far surpassed us in maintaining the unity of the Body.[15]

Having posed some questions to the New Pentecostalism in the name of evangelicals, let me direct one to the evangelicals themselves: How can our professed openness to the fullness of the Spirit be reconciled with our overall negative attitude toward a movement which in its deepest intentions desires nothing but that very openness and gives abundant evidence of possessing a spiritual fullness which we need so desperately in our own midst?

15. Christenson, A Message to the Charismatic Movement, pp. 73-76.

Krister Stendahl

Krister Stendahl is dean of Harvard Divinity School. A distinguished New Testament scholar, he received the Th.D. degree from Uppsala University in Sweden in 1954, after earlier study in Cambridge and Paris. He is a member of the Studiorum Novi Testamenti Societas and was a Guggenheim Fellow in 1959-60 and in 1974-75.

Besides technical articles published in English, German, and Swedish, Dean Stendahl has edited *The Scrolls and the New Testament* (New York: Harper, 1957) and authored *The School of St. Matthew* (Lund: Gleerup, ²1968), *The Bible and the Role of Women* (Philadelphia: Fortress, 1966), and *Paul Among the Jews and Gentiles* (Philadelphia: Fortress, 1976).

Ordained in the Church of Sweden in 1944, Dean Stendahl served in Sweden as a parish minister and university chaplain, coming to Harvard in 1954.

In this address given at the 1972 annual meeting of the society for Pentecostal Studies, Dean Stendahl outlines his impressions of the charismatic movement. The casual features of the original oral form of the address have been retained.

The New Pentecostalism:
Reflections of an
Ecumenical Observer

13

I feel very honored to speak on this topic. I'm not a Pentecostal—old, or new. I have been invited as an ecumenical observer to make some reflections. I am afraid of that term "ecumenical observer" because it could give you the feeling that I think of you as a zoo, which I am coming to visit and look at.

There is something that has happened in the ecumenical world that I consider enormously important. In the World Council of Churches, in our relation to the Roman Catholics (among others), the second act (let's call it *act* and not *phase*) of the ecumenical movement is over and we are going into the third.

The first act consisted of evangelical alliances of various kinds. A kind of evangelical enthusiasm of oneness, the non-sectarianism of the YMCA, for example—various ways to cut through, lifting out of the churches and the traditions individuals who, by one definition or another, were rightly related to the Lord.

And then in the beginning of the twentieth century came the church-oriented ecumenism. And I think rightly so, because you can always find nice guys and rescue them out of their setting. But if you don't also deal with the setting in which you find them, you have not achieved very much. So it was necessary to draw the *churches* into a relationship, and that in a way is what the World Council of Churches stands for. Not even St. Paul could join the World Council of Churches—only *churches* can join the World Council of Churches.

I've been to some of those affairs, to ecumenical dialogues, and I would call them "highly diplomatic." You sit on one side of the table and represent your church or your "tradition" (that cool word of the fifties and sixties, when we didn't have much faith around, but we had "traditions"). We carried out a rather useful work in those meetings, which was to speak for our traditions. The Catholics found out that after all a couple of second thoughts had dawned upon the Protestants since the Council of Trent in the sixteenth century. And to their very enormous surprise the Protestants found out that there had even been a thought or two in the Catholic community since the sixteenth cen-tury! And that was very useful. There was a kind of diplomatic up-dating of what we stood for, what we believed, what we said, where the tradition was.

But after a while that approach also reached the law of diminishing returns. Because there came the moment when partly due to prayer, worship, and concern, the need arose to push a little bit further and not just have everybody play the cool game of diplomatic represen-tatives. We came to the point where we dared to ask one another, "What do *you* think? Where are *you* at? What does the Lord mean to *you*? Let's not hide behind the tradition, but let's come together and speak straight out of our own experience, experience which was nur-tured and enriched by the tradition, thanks be to the Lord, but yet is our own."

And that's roughly where the ecumenical movement is today. The diplomatic coolness has done its useful work and there is a need to be naked in one's faith and fear before the Lord. Or as Fr. Raymond Panikkar, that charismatic Catholic Hindu thinker and theologian, has pointed out so well (regarding relationships both between Chris-tians and between Christianity and other religions): We have no right to be in dialogue with another religious person unless we are open to conversion. We cannot enter the temple of believing men and women in the galoshes that insulate us from the possibility of God striking home to us. Only tourists enter temples in galoshes. If we are going to have a genuine encounter with God, we always must be open to con-version. That's the least respect we can show for our brothers and sisters with whom we differ. And that is also true between stodgy mainline Christians like me and what we broadly call the Pentecostal movement. So, let me not observe, let me not visit, but let us come together, naked under the Lord.

And let us pray: Oh, Holy Spirit, what we are doing here is nonsense and sacrilege without you. Amen.

The Spirit Is Not for Security

I come to you as a Bible-reading Christian. It's partly my job and partly my love. And as I read my Bible, I read it both as a source for standards and, what is perhaps more important, as that which prompts me and pushes me on. There are two kinds of Bible readers. There are those who use the Bible for safety's sake, for assurance. And there are those who use the Bible in order to be sent and pushed. There is a way in which the church has spoken about the Holy Spirit as if the Holy Spirit makes that which is relatively certain even more certain. That's the security model of the Spirit. That's when people speak about biblical inspiration and things of that kind. The job of the Spirit is seen to be making that which is relatively sure super-sure.

But I learned many years ago that the function of the Spirit is not to give a super-assurance when we are relatively sure anyway. It is rather to give the power to seek and ask when we do *not* know, when we are at our wit's end, when we are wobbly and insecure. That's the only time the Spirit comes. The Spirit doesn't give comfort to the comfortable nor security to the secure. But the Spirit comes to him or her who is in need. That's how Paul speaks about the Spirit. And as a Bible-reading Christian who feels and sees that way, I come to you.

I come to you as a theologian reflecting not only on the Scripture and the tradition, but also on what God might be doing among us and in His world at this very time. And as such a theologian, I have to say that there is a new kind of Pentecostalism, a new hunger for spirituality.

In the theological establishment to which I belong with pride and fear, it is certainly true that we are, as I said, coming out of an era in which we cannot answer the questions just by quoting the tradition. The voice, the input, and the insight of religious experience right here and now are of utmost importance. That's one of the reasons why there has been a new release of the Spirit among us. The Spirit has always been here, but has gotten a new chance to register and to be registered.

It's very easy to understand why thoughtful Christians through the ages have been afraid of that Spirit which "bloweth where it listeth." Thoughtful people, responsible people, people with planning instincts and brains, are of course always afraid when they lose control, when they are not on the top of the situation. To be exposed to the Spirit is, I guess, almost as bad as having a student revolution on your hands when you are a dean—you cannot be in control.

The problems about the Spirit are real. For the Spirit is an atomic power, and heaven knows there has been an awful lot of fallout and undesirable effects.

That's true about the Bible, too. There has not been an evil cause in the world that hasn't gotten more evil by being argued on "biblical" grounds. And when racism by God's grace is smoked out of this country, the last racists will be the ones with Bible in hand. Religion is not a harmless thing. The Spirit is not a harmless thing. The easiest way to play it safe is to quench it. And that's what long periods of the Christian tradition have succeeded in doing rather well. But one should not be too snobbish toward them, because there is a problem—a genuine one.

The Wrong Division

There has been a crippling and impoverishing division among the churches regarding the Spirit and the manifestations of the Spirit—glossolalia, healing, etc. Such things were *suppressed* in large parts of Christendom, *cultivated*—and I would say sometimes overcultivated —in other parts of the Christian fellowship. Such a division, my brothers and sisters, is silly, dangerous, and wrong for all of us. I've always believed that if some churches were not suppressing the manifestations of the Spirit, while others were cultivating them, the charismata would become part of the common Christian experience all over the place. But we have either suppressed or overcultivated.

I remember a time when, many years ago, I was preaching in a church back in my native Sweden. In the middle of the sermon a young man way down in the congregation started to speak in tongues. I stopped, and I saw the ushers in this very proper Lutheran church get into action, moving in on this fellow, because there should be order in the house of the Lord and not noise. Now these good ushers had read all the glorious statements in 1 Corinthians 12 and 14. They had read the second chapter of Acts. But they could see no relation whatsoever between that outburst of enthusiasm in the biblical record and this most improper behavior in the royal state church of Sweden.

That's the kind of parodox which has remained in my mind, because such things as glossolalia happen when God wants them to happen—even when they *are* suppressed. And why should that be a reason for dividing up in groups and divisions and denominations and non-denominational denominations, or whatever these groups are that are gathered here? So my basic premise is very simple: if we weren't divided, we would all have such things in common.

Paul and the Charismata

That's roughly what Paul says in 1 Corinthians 12—14. I've very little to add to what the apostle Paul had to say about this matter. He was pretty smart, pretty perceptive. I read his advice and his reflections on this matter to mean roughly that there are *many* gifts of the Spirit. The fact that some of them look a little more impressive than the others, and that some have a certain kind of spectacular quality while others do not, is uninteresting. Paul says that teaching and even administration are just as much the gifts of the Spirit as are healing, speaking with tongues, and prophecy. It is as simple as that.

I like Paul's reference to administration (*kybernēsis*, 1 Cor. 12:28) for a special reason, because there are Christians who have the romantic dream that there could be a kind of non-organized, free, out-of-the-Bible, Spirit-living kind of religious community. But my experience is that such a community is impossible. It is a futile dream. My observation is that when it has been tried, it has usually led to the most worldly type of secularized business organization mixing greedy business attitudes into the promulgation of the gospel—be it through radio stations or other money-making operations. It may be more reasonable to take hold of the fact that stewardship and administration go together, that is to say, how you rake in the money for the Lord and how you spend it. Determining what the Lord wants to spend it for may be the tougher task. Stewardship creates the enormous responsibility of not abusing the willingness of God's people to sacrifice. That's a tough one. That's why administration, my friends, is a gift of the Spirit. And right now I am perhaps more interested in administration as a gift of the Spirit than in speaking with the language of angels.

So Paul teaches us the equality of gifts—spectacular and non-spectacular. And you know it. It's perhaps wrong for me to stress that equality, because those of us who are not in the movement can use it in a way to say, "OK, don't think that you are that great." It's a kind of spiritual sour-grapes approach underlining certain things in 1 Corinthians 12. But I think we understand each other. I hope we do.

Now another point Paul makes is, of course, that the standard for testing spiritual gifts is whether their purpose be the building up of the church.

I have a lecture on Paul, which I give sometimes, called "Love Rather than Integrity." Paul is really way out on this point. He almost sounds like a soap salesman who says, "Whatever builds up the church goes. To the non-Jews, I have become a non-Jew. To the Jews, I have become a Jew that I might gain some." It's like an evangelist who is for Nixon when it fits and for Fr. Berrigan when that makes more friends. It's all for the Lord—and integrity goes down the drain.

Paul really pushes in that direction, when it comes to the gifts of the Spirit: the decisive thing is what builds up the church. But if we look more closely he says rather: The only thing that matters is not whether you feel good, not whether you protect your rights and freedom but whether you are building up your brother. You know how Paul says this in all kinds of ways—remarkable, considering the terrible snob he was! He always had to be great: he was even the greatest of sinners. We know such persons. They always have to be great. This was really Paul's battle. He had integrity galore. He had missionary zeal galore. It is astonishing for him to say, "No, it isn't important that I feel clean and great. What is important is what builds up the church." It is the *oikodomē*, the edification, that counts.

And that attitude is what Paul means by *love* in 1 Corinthians 13: "If I speak in the language of men and of angels, but have not love . . . . If I deliver my body to be burned. . . ." Now that's not a feeling: love is not a feeling. Some people have gotten into the habit of reading this passage at weddings, because it's so beautiful—about love, love, love. I never quite understood what it has to do with weddings. It doesn't deal with love in that sense. The love that Paul speaks about is not a feeling. It is rather the concern for the building up of the community. That's why love is greater than hope and faith.

Or as we have it in Colossians 3:14: "But over all those virtues, put on love as the belt that holds the whole thing together." You can have super-virtues galore; but if those virtues are not held together by love (i.e., the concern for what builds up the community), then you might trip on that flowing robe of your virtues. You might feel good and virtuous, but if you don't build up the community, says Paul, then you don't have love. It's a pretty objective, cool kind of love. It isn't a question of how you feel. The question is whether you build up the community.

The third thing Paul says about the gifts of the Spirit—consistent, I think, with the whole New Testament—is that the more spectacular charismata are useless for missionary purposes and are totally a family affair. Now that's rather strange. I've always been puzzled by Paul saying that if somebody speaks in tongues and an outsider comes into the church, he won't get anything out of it (1 Cor. 14:23f.). The charismata are not for God's P. R.

In the same manner we find that in the synoptic Gospels the healings of Jesus are never called "signs." It is John, who in his way of interpreting the ministry of Jesus, makes sēmeia (signs) out of the healing miracles. But in the synoptics the healings of Jesus are never
thought of as signs. Signs in the synoptic tradition are the signs in the
heavens, the cosmic signs.[1]

Thus charismata are not thought of in the Bible as a witness. They
are not thought of as impressing outsiders. They are certainly not
thought of as proof. They are a family affair. They are the joys around
the family table. They are for the joy and strengthening of the community and the believer. As Paul says himself in 1 Corinthians 14,
there is much strength to be had from speaking to the Lord in tongues,
but that is between you and God. Remember how he says that very,
very clearly (cf. 1 Cor. 14:18f.).

To add a final footnote about Paul and charismata: Paul had a
problem in Corinth. He had many problems in Corinth. I love the
church in Corinth, because they had many faults. But at least the
church in Corinth did not have one fault which my church often has:
it was never dull. He also had a problem with the women at Corinth.
That's why he suppresses the Word of God when he writes to Corinth.
In his pastoral wisdom in Galatians 3:28 he says that in Christ "there
is neither Jew nor Greek, there is neither slave nor free, there is neither
male nor female . . . ." But when he quotes that same thought in 1
Corinthians 12:13, he skips that "male and female" part. And I think
we know why. The Spirit had given special enthusiasm to the women
and liberated them more than Paul was ready to stomach.

There is another passage—many of my exegetical colleagues might
not agree with me—where Paul writes about speaking with tongues, I
think, without any kinds of ifs, buts, or hesitations. That is Romans
8:26, when he says that we do not know what to pray, but the Holy
Spirit intercedes for us with unspeakable groans. I am sure that Paul
here refers to glossolalia, as practiced by him and by many. It
couldn't really be anything else, because he goes on to say, "And he
[God] who searches the hearts of men knows what is the mind of the
Spirit . . . ." And here once again, the Spirit is not the super-gift, but
the Spirit is the gift to the confused, to those who do not even "know
how to pray." So it isn't that we super-pray, and then comes the
Spirit, and then we super-super-pray. No, the Spirit comes to assist us
when we do not know what to pray.

1. This line of argument is exegetically amplified in K. Stendahl, "The New Testament
Evidence," The Charismatic Movement, ed. Michael P. Hamilton (Grand Rapids: Eerdmans, 1975), pp. 49-60.

Imagination and Charismata

And now comes the section in my presentation which addresses itself to what I would call "The Lack of Imagination as to the Gifts of the Spirit." Paul listed a few such gifts, and they are good and perpetual. But there might be more. We have a great Lord.

I remember I was at a Pentecostal meeting in Sweden once and the text was "The Lord will open to you his good treasury, the heavens . . ." (Deut. 28:12). That sounds all right.

But there is a lack of the imagination as to gifts, just as there is to sins: Christians are very unimaginative when it comes to sins. They get so stuck on a few—like smoking and drinking and dancing and card playing; and, in the Anglo-Saxon tradition for some strange reason, gambling (which neither Catholics nor Lutherans have ever thought wrong). But what "sin" is differs from one culture to another. The real history behind "sin" is that the Christian conscience as it faces reality in any one age zeroes in on whatever destroys life. But there is no absoluteness through the ages on that: it's a matter of social consciousness. The Watergate affair, for example, teaches us about the great sins of persons who were flawless as to private and family virtues.

Take the drinking bit, for example. If you read any study of the time when farm workers were paid on holidays, you learn that the only thing they got other than food was liquor. And the church rose up in horror. There are many countries, as in my home country, where the early labor movement and the free-church tradition joined together to fight liquor because it was *the* issue. In some cases it still is, in other situations it is not.

So we have very little imagination as to sin. And the same seems to apply to charismata. What outstanding gifts of the Spirit are there that we usually do not speak about? I came to think about one of them: there is only one specific situation for which the Spirit is promised in the synoptic Gospels. You know what it is? It is when one is brought before the courts. The Gospels say that we should not worry in that situation since the Holy Spirit will give us the words to say (Matt. 10:17-20; Mark 13:11; Luke 12:11f.; cf. Luke 21:12-15).

Actually in the early church it's a mystery—an interesting mystery—how that little group that was really so curved into itself, so groupish, how that little group related to the world. For example, in the First Epistle of John, where the love language reaches its highest intensity, not a single drop of love spills outside of the church: it's totally *groupish*. You love your brother, and your brother loves you.

God loves your brother, and you love God. And there is a whole system of love, love, love—but there is not a single drop that goes outside of the community. And that's all right; praise be to God because He needed to set up this model of love and really get it going, and later it did come to have an enormous impact on the whole world, once that love had been tested in the laboratory of the church.

But how *did* that group relate to the world? I happen to believe that they didn't often stand on the corners and preach. Paul got caught on Mars Hill, and he made a little speech; but that's the only outdoor preaching I know of in the whole Book of Acts. Instead he sneaked into the synagogue and got a few women to sign up, starting a church; and they met in their homes. There was little public activity going on. Pentecost was a special case, concerned with the temple; but once the mission really got going, there was little public activity. People joined because the rumor got around that something was going on in those homes.

So where and how did they confront the world? Not by pamphlets, but in the courts. That's where it happened. And that's why Paul considered it a great honor that he'd have the chance to appear before Caesar (cf. Eph. 3:10-13).

The true church has always been brought before the court. In order to speak to this specific point of the gifts of the Spirit when one is caught, you should rather have invited Philip and Daniel Berrigan. They could tell us something of what it means to trust in the assistance of the Spirit when your Christian witness brings you before the courts. They know that this promise of God is true. This is the most specific case, the most specific gift of the Spirit which the Bible promises. When you appear before the authorities, don't worry: the Holy Spirit will then be with you as never before. And that's worth thinking about.

This may also have something to do with the complicated fact that in the Gospel of John the Spirit is called the *parakletos*. Some people translate the "comforter." The "attorney" is a better translation. This word has a legal connotation; it refers to the showdown in the courts where God defends and vindicates the "little ones," the oppressed, suppressed and repressed.

There is another function of the Spirit over the ages that has fascinated me. In 1 Corinthians 7 Paul speaks about marriage and divorce. At first he starts off with a straight case. He says, "I've a word from the Lord Jesus which says that there should be no divorce." But then he takes up a couple special cases, including the one where one partner is a Christian and the other is a Gentile. He takes up the question of the unmarried, or yet unmarried, and so forth. And in that kind of context he says, "In this case I have no word from the Lord." And I bet you he was the last preacher in Christendom to admit that!

Paul could very well have done what any decent preacher would do—which is of course to take for granted that there *is* a word of the Lord for everything. So you try to interpret, and twist, and you say, "Of course the word of the Lord doesn't quite apply to this matter, but by implication it follows that . . . ." And we can always squeeze *some* meaning out of it.

But Paul says, "Now as to this question of marriage between the Christian and the non-Christian, it seems that Jesus had not thought about that. We have no word from the Lord." But then he—if I may mix the texts—sort of remembers from the Gospel of John (which he certainly had not read) that wonderful passage which says, "I have many things to tell you, and you aren't ready for them yet; but when the Holy Spirit comes, he will spoonfeed you day by day. . . . And from mine will he take and give it to you as the occasion arises" (cf. John 16:12-14). And that's what Paul does. In 1 Corinthians 7 he says: "I have no word from the Lord, but I have prayed about it and I will give you my advice. For I think I sort of have the Spirit of God." And that was *not* because he was a biblical writer, because he didn't know he was. But he trusted the guidance of the Spirit where there was no word from the Lord. And that's the glorious bind and freedom which we have in the Spirit.

Thus there are these two areas, not usually listed among the charismata, which I consider enormously important: the Spirit will help you in court, and the Spirit will help you create a modern "word of the Lord" for specific pastoral needs. And I would pray, and I mean that, I *do* pray that when and if the wind of the Spirit blows over the land these two facets of the gifts of the Spirit not be forgotten: the renewal of the "word of the Lord" and the trust in the Spirit's assistance when you stand up against the authorities.

You are always caught for political reasons—I hope you are aware of that. There is a kind of spiritual wordplay that says, "Berrigan did something *political*; but when one gets caught because of something *spiritual*, then it is different." But that distinction is against the Scriptures. I know of no case in the history of the church where anyone has ever suffered martyrdom for "spiritual" reasons. Jesus was crucified as an insurrectionist. Now *we* say he wasn't. But to Pilate and to the Jewish authorities he sure was. The state, when it gets scared, will always find that when religion has power it is a political force. And don't think that you can wiggle out of that one! From Jesus and

Stephen all the way down to Cardinal Mindszenty and the Berrigans, that's the way it is.

"High Voltage" Religion

Now my final point before the conclusion. What do I *really* think about the New Pentecostal sweep? For I recognize it as a sweep. I recognize it as an upsurge of the Spirit. I think of it as high-voltage religion. And we need high voltage for the breakthrough, and for the overcoming of drugs and other evils. The small voltage of the flashlight Christianity of traditional churches just doesn't have enough power. Now I don't want to press that image too far. But there is much in it. And what we have been blessed with is a new upping of the voltage by God for breakthrough purposes.

The movements and the groups which grow out of this breakthrough face two severe tests. The first is, of course, dealing with the religious experience itself. The ultimate test will be (as we say in the Christian tradition): Will the people fall in love with their experience of God or with God who gave the experience?

It is my firm conviction, on the basis of many observations, that this religious experience is a kind of breakthrough thing. It is also my firm conviction on the basis of counseling students and adults who have been swept up in strong spiritual movements that the "burnt-out case" is a real problem. That living with a breakthrough experience, being unwilling on the one hand to admit that it is a grace and a gift, while trying on the other to help the Almighty and the Spirit a little to keep it going, is one of the greatest dangers to the gifts of the Spirit that the church knows. And yet it happens. And it happens especially with older people, because there is something in the mechanism of the psyche which makes older people experience differently from younger people. There is nothing strange in this.

God, I think, right now, is upping the voltage in the faith in many a place in this land. He knows that this is dangerous, but He knows that it is needed. And that's what we call "the New Pentecostalism."

There is an old way to "explain" the gap between the biblical phenomena and the dearth of charismata in many churches today. It is to say that those phenomena belonged to the founding period of the church, and then they petered out. Now I resent this, because it's too cute. And it just isn't true to experience. But there is a kind of truth to it in another way. The high voltage of religious experience is in most cases and with most people a breakthrough phenomenon—because it is needed. But later comes the question whether one loves the experience of God more than the God who gave the experience.

I think in a certain sense that in that very phrase lies the linkage between Pentecostalism and the church universal, i.e., Christianity in general. One of the very reassuring things to me, which is of a more general sociological nature, is that in this case as in so many other cases we, thanks be to God, live in a situation where everybody doesn't have to start a denomination or a new sect or a new group. Somehow, contemporary movements have learned from Detroit to build-in obsolescence. And while I hate it in Detroit I love it in movements.

This is the challenge to the mainline churches of this land. They need so badly to be open to the infusion of new life, to that raw power of genuine high-voltage Christian experience that is sweeping over the land. If they are not willing and able to, should I say, make room, they are in serious trouble.

Now that's roughly where we stand. My basic view is that the gifts of the Spirit are nobody's. They are from God, and they are given to the whole people of God. And silly little people like you and me have built little huts for the gifts of the Spirit. You know what Peter wanted to do in the moment of the transfiguration when he said, "This is great! Let us immediately build three booths!" Jesus said that that was silly. He appreciated the sentiment, but it was silly. Now what *you* have is mine, and what *I* have is yours. And that *is* the future according to the model of St. Paul.

There are many other things one could speak about, if there were time. One wonders, for example, whether in the mission field the dimension of Pentecostalism is not one of the truly saving and hopeful features. And not only for the reason most of you think, but for another reason. With all their crazy conservative hang-ups some of those Pentecostal missions have in many parts of the world managed better than any other American missions to transcend their American particularism and to absorb indigenous qualities. There are many indications of this in Africa and in Latin America. And it isn't just a question of the Spirit being in this or that. It's just that, in spite of the crazy things that these missionaries say, the Spirit transcends their American culture and fundamentalism. This is a very interesting aspect of the Pentecostal movement in its liberating form.

Still speaking as an ecumenical observer, I have lately fallen in love with the Greek phrase *ti kōluei*, "What hinders?" You remember how Jesus used that phrase when He criticized His disciples' attitude toward children. The King James Version translates: "Suffer little children, and forbid [hinder] them not" (Matt. 19:14). And then it occurs when the eunuch is enlightened. He says, "Here is water: What hinders [ti kōluei] that I be baptized?" (Acts 8:36). And then there is Cornelius on whom the Spirit falls, and Peter says, "If this has happened, what hinders that these be baptized?" (Acts 10:47).

Now why do I find that such an interesting expression? Coming back to where I started, I am an administrator. I know that in administration, in church relations, and in the fears of the believing heart, when someone mentions a precedent, God's will is often not done. I think all of you have been in meetings when suddenly things have come together and the will of the Lord is understood. But there is always someone who says, "But this might set a precedent." And the whole thing falls down.

But there is something in the gambling with the Spirit which lives on the principle, "Why not?" instead of "Why?" That is the liberation that lies in the Spirit: to change the uptight why into a generous why not. That's the stance of the Spirit. So we come back again to the point that the Spirit is not a way to play it safe. Not when we are sure but when we are uncertain, when we quiveringly ask why not? (for example, why not stay together?)—that's when we need the Spirit and dare to count on His coming.

J. Massyngberde Ford

J. Massyngberde Ford is perhaps the leading woman theologian in the charismatic movement. Of British origin, she grew up in the Anglican tradition. While training as a nurse, she converted to the Roman Catholic Church; later she turned to the study of theology.

Dr. Ford holds a B.A. from the University of Nottingham and B.D. from King's College, London. She received her Ph.D. in New Testament from the University of Nottingham. After several years of teaching in East Africa, she was called to the University of Notre Dame where she teaches New Testament.

Dr. Ford's technical articles have appeared in journals such as the *Catholic Biblical Quarterly*, *Journal of Ecclesiastical History*, *Journal of Jewish Studies*, *New Testament Studies*, and *Novum Testamentum*. Besides numerous popular articles, she has also written *The Spirit and the Human Person* (Dayton, OH: Pflaum Press, 1969), *The Pentecostal Experience* (New York: Paulist Press, 1970), *Baptism of the Spirit* (Techny, IL: Divine Work Publications, 1971), and *Ministries and Fruits of the Holy Spirit* (Notre Dame, IN: Catholic Action Office, 1973). She also wrote the Anchor Bible commentary on the New Testament book of *Revelation* (Garden City, NY: Doubleday, 1975).

In this article Dr. Ford describes how she relates her work as a theological scholar with her worship as a charismatic Catholic.

The New Pentecostalism:
Personal Reflections
of a Participating
Roman Catholic Scholar

14

First of all, I should like to inform you that I am restricting my observations to Roman Catholic New Pentecostalism as the entire field of Neo-Pentecostalism research is becoming too vast for one scholar. Secondly, I apologize if this essay appears somewhat egocentric.[1] I wish to relate for you my "pilgrimage" spiritual, academic, and doctrinal with two special points in view: (1) that my New Pentecostalism, far from lessening my love for the Roman Catholic Church, has deepened my understanding of her doctrine and practices and (2) that this spirituality,[2] far from drawing me towards fundamentalism with regard to biblical scholarship, has made me more acutely aware of

1. I shall cite some of my writings, not, I hope, in the spirit of self-advertising, but to show the development of my thought in the light of my Pentecostal experience.
2. I concur with Catholic authorities from Rome who regard Catholic Neo-Pentecostalism as a spirituality which, correctly understood and with proper theological reflection, need in no way be inimical to one's Catholic faith. I differ from Dorothy Ranaghan and others who declare that Pentecostalism is necessary for everyone in the Roman Catholic Church (Ranaghan, A Survey of the Catholic Charismatic Renewal, cassette no. 125 [obtainable from Box 12, Notre Dame, IN 46556]).

the importance of the tools of biblical study and more appreciative of contemporary research especially in the sphere of Jewish-Christian studies of the New Testament. Only when the different persuasions are able to join together in loving, prayerful, professional scholarship on the sacred text will we come to that unity of truth which we ourselves and the Spirit desire.[3]

Autobiographical Sketch

Perhaps it would assist the reader if I give a brief biographical sketch. It will enable him to see that I was not nurtured in a Pentecostal atmosphere and that the Holy Spirit has constantly asked me to face new experiences and responsibilities.

I was brought up in a small village in the Sherwood Forest, England, in a traditional Anglican rural religious atmosphere. It will be interesting for members of non-hierarchical churches to note that our parish (Linby-cum-Papplewick) comprised two churches, one eleventh century (complete with lepers' squint) and one tenth century. The clergyman is rector of the former but the local lay squire, although not performing liturgical functions, is still legally rector of the latter church. He supervises it and has power to choose and depose the incumbent. The parish is a natural, loosely knit community in itself entirely different from anything which I have encountered in America.

My parents were Christians but I would not describe them as "religious." We attended Sunday worship fairly frequently but not each week: I was taught to recite the Our Father before I retired at night. We were not a Bible-reading family.

I had good relationships with, and solid Christian teaching from, the local clergyman; but my strongest religious influence emanated from the Roman Catholic day school which I attended for about four years. It was here that I received my first intense experience of the presence of Jesus. I was deeply edified by the total commitment of the sisters to our Lord and zealously followed their instructions in doctrine and learned Catholic devotions. The sisters, however, were extremely vigilant to see that I did nothing which would disturb my parents and they left me absolutely free as far as attending classes or prayers were concerned. There was no psychological pressure.

---

3. Unfortunately, Pentecostalism has been described as the most fissiparous of all denominations. It seems to me that the Society for Pentecostal Studies may well be one of the chief instruments in providing a solution to the problem of divisiveness.

The Release of the Spirit

My first "release in the Spirit" came from the presence of the risen Lord in the Eucharist. Although at that time I was not eligible to receive holy communion (being a non-Roman Catholic), I was privileged to be in the presence of the sacred host, that is, the consecrated "bread" placed in a special vessel called a monstrance to enable the faithful to adore Jesus present under the species of "bread" more readily.

At this point I should define what I believe to be the essence of the "release" or "baptism" of the Spirit. It is an experiential or experimental sense of the presence of God of such strength that one knows with the deepest sense of certainty that one not only believes in God but "knows" Him—in the Hebrew sense of the word,[4] "know" as experience. In Catholic traditional spirituality this is known as the "presence of God felt" and it is deemed to be a pure gift from God, a gift for which one can dispose oneself but only God Himself, as Sovereign, can dispense. It is not acquired by merely human effort.

I should like to cite two examples, one from a woman doctor of the church, Teresa of Avila, and one from a man. Teresa of Avila says:

> I used to have at times, as I have said, though it used to pass quickly away, certain *commencements* of that which I am now going to describe. . . . and sometimes even when I was reading, *a feeling of the presence of God* would come over me unexpectedly, so that I *could in no wise doubt, either that He was within me,* or that I was wholly absorbed in Him. It was not by way of vision: I believe it was what is called mystical theology. (*Life* X, 1)

Alphonsus Rodriquez describes the experience thus:

> *This feeling of the presence of God* is not obtained by way of imagination; but it is in her [the soul] as a certitude received from on high; she has a *spiritual and experimental* certitude, that God is in the soul and in all places. This presence of God is called an *intellectual presence.* As a rule, it lasts a long time; the farther the soul advances in God's service, the more continuous is it, and the more felt. . . . It has often happened . . . without his even thinking of it, this sovereign Master has placed Himself suddenly before another, with-

---

4. I think that my definition would be consonant with, but not identical to, those given by Edward D. O'Connor, *The Pentecostal Movement in the Catholic Church* (Notre Dame, IN: Ave Maria Press, 1971), pp. 131-36; Simon Tugwell, *Did You Receive the Spirit?* (London: Darton, Longman, and Todd, 1971), pp. 84-93 (this is now available in paperback from Paulist Press in New York); and Susan B. Anthony in her beautiful essay in *As the Spirit Leads Us,* ed. Kevin and Dorothy Ranaghan (New York: Paulist Press, 1971), pp. 91-102.

out this latter being aware of it, etc. (*Vie de St. Alphonse*, from his *Memoires*, no. 40)[5]

This experience does not mean that one is in a state of special holiness (i.e., a contemplative state), but it does mean that the Holy Spirit has invited one to commit oneself to a special pursuit of holiness.[6] In this writer's opinion, the "release" is not a once-for-all occurrence—although the first occasion is naturally perhaps the most memorable. If the Christian walks in the footsteps of Jesus, this "release" recurs, not always in the same modality but in a varying number of modalities, not only throughout his or her life but also in the afterlife. Hence the release is the first fruits of what we will enjoy in heaven.

I can describe the vivid memory of my own first release only in the very simple words, "Jesus looked at me and I at Him; something happened which affected my life." I was about nine or ten at the time. The experience inaugurated a period of intense prayer and spiritual reading, especially Scripture. It was followed by my first "baptism of suffering."[7] This suffering was relatively mild, arising principally from the fact that I changed to a secular school where I missed the religious atmosphere and devotion and felt different from others. Moreover, the two chief desires of my life were denied to me, namely, to give myself entirely to God (there were no convents in our section of the Anglican Church) and to an academic theological career: the seminaries did not admit girls.

I was received into the Roman Catholic Church a few years later while I was engaged in nurses' training. After the completion of this, I entered a convent, the Franciscan Sisters of the Divine Motherhood. We devoted about three or four hours to prayer daily and gave the rest of our time to geriatrics and obstetrics. I was exceedingly happy.

I recall another very dramatic release during that period: I believe that it was on the ninth of November. Again, it was an experience difficult to describe; and again it occurred in connection with the Eucharist, that is, after reception of holy communion. I can only say that I felt lifted above myself and that I lived the entire day in two dimensions, engulfed in an awareness of the supernatural so acute

---

5. The quotations are from A. Poulain, *The Graces of Interior Prayer*, trans. Leonard L. Yorke Smith (St. Louis: B. Herder, 1910; reprint 1950), pp. 73, 76f.

6. For an example of a Catholic work treating progressive sanctification, see Walter Hilton, *The Ladder of Perfection*, trans. L. Sherley-Price (Baltimore: Penguin Classics, 1957).

7. See David Geraets, O.S.B., *Baptism of Suffering* (Pecos, NM: Dove Publications, 1970).

that it permeated the most menial of actions. I was able to continue a normal day's work and I doubt if anyone noticed anything; never have I experienced such transcending joy or jubilation.

Yet, this must have been quite an ordinary experience for a sister. However, in those days no one ever spoke about such experiences, not even to one's confessor. It certainly helped me through my next period, my second baptism of suffering, namely, my leaving the convent with "galloping consumption" (miliary tuberculosis) and my being obliged to continue my spiritual life away from a religious community, outside the ordinary life of the church but with the help of the reception of holy communion about once every fourteen days. I think that some patients were drawn to enquire about Christ when they saw that I was a practicing Christian.

After my tuberculosis I entered the university to prepare for a teaching profession, which seemed more suitable than the physically strenuous life of a nurse. It was during this period that I experienced more frequently and profoundly releases in the Spirit. These usually comprised the experiential presence of the second person of the blessed trinity, curiously enough on my right side.[8] So real was the Presence that I was obliged to take care, especially if I were in company, not to speak vocally to our Lord. The Presence would come and go very frequently (completely beyond my control), always leaving a sense of indescribable peace and joy.

These experiences were to be followed by a third baptism of suffering, arising mainly from the fact that members of the Catholic hierarchy were not prepared to accept lay people with theological training such as I had acquired at the university: to accept a woman was unthinkable. I cannot impute blame to them, but the scorn and ostracism were very intense.

This release called me to an active apostolate, which involved chiefly a lively participation in the University Catholic Society and the Newman Society (for graduate members). There was, as yet, no special ecumenical savor to my spirituality although I developed a deep reverence for the Jewish faith. It was a period of both receiving and giving. After the completion of my academic studies, I served as lecturer in theology at Makerere University College in Kampala, Uganda, in a department which catered for Hindu, Moslem, African traditional, and Protestant and Catholic persuasions. I was exceedingly happy.

---

8. One must emphasize that these experiences are due wholly to the grace of God and not through the merits of the human person.

Once again, however, a baptism of suffering more terrible than the preceding descended upon me: perhaps St. John of the Cross would have called it a "dark night." It was a period of utter dryness in prayer, although I continued to pray as best I could. Some of this is described in the appendix to my book *The Spirit and the Human Person* (Dayton, OH: Pflaum Press, 1969).

It was during this "night" that I came to Notre Dame University and met the New Pentecostal movement during its first weeks there. Before meeting the movement I had received valuable spiritual counsel from Fr. Edward D. O'Connor, who was later to become one of the leading theologians in the Catholic movement. The Pentecostal imposition of hands and prayer restored my ability to pray with joy and ease and increased my affection for my deceased father. Nine months later I received the gifts of tongues (when I was alone in my apartment) and prophecy. But I would say that the two greatest gifts I have received have been (1) further insight into Scripture and (2) friendship with Mary. This release was followed by a fifth baptism of suffering, which, despite my sins, has born immense fruits: it has truly been a growth period.

In summation, I should say that I see the release of the Spirit as a series of experiences of God, experiences more vivid and real than most human experiences, but I see them also intimately and mysteriously interwoven with the theology of the cross. If the release (or awakening) is a "peak experience," then the cross is a "pit" experience: they go hand in hand. I see this as wholly biblical.

Our spiritual development is a silhouette of the life of Christ. Our sacrament of baptism may be compared to the descent of the Holy Spirit upon Mary at the annunciation; the Spirit is present but there may be no outward or dramatic manifestation, or the manifestation may be so refined that the human mind or eye cannot discern it (cf. 1 Cor. 2:14-16). Our sacrament of confirmation is akin to Jesus' becoming *bar miztvah* (cf. Luke 2:41-52). Our release should not be too closely associated with the sacraments of baptism and confirmation. It is more akin to Jesus' baptism[9] for we too are called to public witness. Likewise our release may be followed by a temptation in the desert. Our further releases may be compared to the glorification on Mt. Tabor (or Hermon). This event was preceded by the first two predictions not only of Jesus' own sufferings but also the sufferings of

---

9. See my *The Pentecostal Experience* (New York: Paulist Press, 1970).

those who should take up their cross and follow Him (Mark 8:27—9:50 and parallels).[10]

Academic Pilgrimage

What were the academic results of my releases in the Spirit and especially of my experience of a Pentecostal prayer group? I had not denied the intervention of the supernatural before, and I had no attachment to any particular school of theological thought, e.g., the Bultmannian or post-Bultmannian.[11] However, into my rather ordinary church life came the possibility of the more exotic gifts of the Spirit, such as tongues, prophecy, miracle working, healings, etc., which I had formerly predicated only of the saints. Herein came true the dicta of Leo XIII,[12] namely, that we differ only in degree, not quality from the saints. I could say, "I not only believe, but I have seen."[13] Certain biblical phenomena began to unfold before my eyes and I found myself participating in a koinōnia very closely resembling the one seen in St. Paul's writings to the Corinthians.

Scope of Ministry

However, I must confess that in the early days of my Neo-Pentecostal experience I concentrated almost exclusively on the ministries listed in 1 Corinthians 12:4-11 with an occasional glance at the five-fold ministry in Ephesians 4:11. Our group's emphasis was on "tongues," cultic prophecy,[14] healing and occasional miracle working. We were also frequently and deeply—and perfectly correctly —concerned with dramatic conversions from such perils as drug addiction. Looking back, I see the Corinthian ministries as an ex-

---

10. Arnold Bittlinger, in his essay, "Baptized in Water and in Spirit—Aspects of Christian Initiation," has come to the same conclusion as the Roman Catholics concerning the three stages in an average spiritual life. See Kilian McDonnell, O.S.B., and Arnold Bittlinger, The Baptism in the Holy Spirit as an Ecumenical Problem (Notre Dame, IN: Charismatic Renewal Services, 1972 [obtainable through Box 12, Notre Dame, IN 46556]).

11. One must recognize the contribution that Bultmann has made not only to New Testament scholarship in general but in the charismatic area as well, e.g., his close analysis of the wisdom, prophetic, and apocalyptic sayings of Jesus in The History of The Synoptic Tradition, trans. John Marsh (Oxford: Blackwell, 1963), pp. 69-130.

12. Leo XIII, encyclical on the Holy Spirit (Divinum illud, May 4, 1897).

13. Although we must not attribute more faith to the one who has seen (cf. John 20:29).

14. I should define "cultic" prophecy as the utterances which one hears at prayer meetings. However, more mature manifestation of prophecy is found in those who prayerfully dedicate themselves to social action or concern, e.g., Dr. Martin Luther King.

cellent accompaniment to evangelizing among those who have not known Christ or have deserted Him; and I recognize them as valid in the same way that the early part of Acts countenances miraculous occurrences accompanying evangelization. The later part does not give them so much emphasis. I am coming to the conclusion that these gifts are not so necessary for those who have already been released in the Spirit, whether within or without the formal Pentecostal movement. That is not, however, to doubt that they have some place.

For the post-release stage I have now expanded the scope of ministries and have completed a simple manuscript[15] on the ministries and fruits of the Spirit. For this purpose I have drawn up a preliminary chart of ministries from 1 Thessalonians, Corinthians, Romans, Ephesians, 1 Peter, etc. With the help of a graduate student I am now examining further texts with a view to expansion of my present study. I am tending towards the conclusion that, although all ministries are to be found within the church as a whole (and I speak of all denominations)[16] and although—the Pentecostal spirituality presenting one important and genuine group of ministries—the other ministries are found in considerable profusion in other parts of the church, my eyes had been partly closed to them before. All these ministries must join together in the One Body.[17]

Tentatively I have distinguished (but not made a trichotomy): (1) "evangelizing ministries," e.g., evangelists, miracle workers, healers, speakers in tongues and interpreters; (2) "solidifying ministries," e.g., teachers, prophets,[18] those who exhort, those who share, those who do acts of mercy and (3) "pilot ministries," e.g., apostles, bishops, presbyters (= pilot or administrator in 1 Cor. 12:28), deacons, deaconesses and widows.

The solidifying ministries are often found among those dedicated and prayerful Christians, such as counselors, psychologists, sociologists, and teachers, who combine professional training with a deep spirituality.[19] But all these must be fully committed Christians who have experienced the Lord Jesus.

15. *Ministries and Fruits of the Holy Spirit*, New Perspective Series, 7 (Notre Dame, IN: Catholic Action Office [Box 524, Notre Dame, IN 46556], 1973).

16. One mainline Pentecostal who was engaged in magnificent work among alcoholics remarked to me that his work was that of the "bulldozer"; afterwards the Catholics could come to sow the seed. Both works are equally necessary.

17. This is elaborated in my article "Pentecostal Poise or Docetic Charismatics?" *Spiritual Life*, 19 (Spring 1973), 32-47.

18. It is difficult to know where to place the prophets as their characteristics are so varied.

19. See, e.g., the works of Henri J. Nouwen, *Intimacy: Pastoral Psychological Essays*

I have come to this view of the ministries through a consideration of the fruits of the Spirit (cf. Gal. 5:22f. but also other texts) which I see developed to a very high degree in my Christian friends, men and women, who practice the behavioral sciences for the upbuilding of the community. Indeed, I concur with the answer of Dr. Smiley Blanton, director of the American Foundation of Religion and Psychiatry, when he was asked whether he read the Bible. He replied:

> I not only read it, I study it. It's the greatest textbook on human behavior ever put together. If people would just absorb its message, a lot of us psychiatrists could close our offices and go fishing.[20]

In a similar way it has become increasingly clear to me that the churches are wise to have not only an enthusiastic ministry but also a trained and appointed structural (pilot) ministry. It would seem that we can trace the gradual evolution of a structural ministry *side by side with, but not in place of*, the enthusiastic ministry.

I suggest that the permanent ministries such as bishop/presbyter (perhaps = *kybernēsis* of 1 Cor. 12:28) arose in the pastoral epistles and the primacy text (Matt. 16:18; cf. also Matt. 18) in response not to Gnosticism or any other heresy, but to over-enthusiasts.[21] I would not, however, have seen this unless I had experienced both the beauty and power of the ministries listed in 1 Corinthians, etc., and also the dangers, such as divisions and rivalry among leaders found in 1 and 2 Corinthians. The trained structural ministry serves as an anchor, or rather, a *rudder*,[22] for the enthusiastic.

The World

Contrary to the reaction of some Pentecostals, my own Pentecostal experience has also led me to a greater love or appreciation of the world.[23] This is very biblical, because for the average Hebrew there

(Notre Dame, IN: Fides Press, 1970), *Creative Ministry* (New York: Doubleday, 1971), and *The Wounded Healer: Ministry in Contemporary Society* (New York: Doubleday, 1972); Elisabeth Kübler-Ross, *On Death and Dying* (New York: Macmillan, 1972); Simone de Beauvoir, *The Coming of Age, The Study of the Aging Process* (New York: Putman, 1972).

20. Quoted from Charles R. Hembree, *The Fruits of the Spirit*, Direction Books (Grand Rapids: Baker, 1971), p. 45.

21. I have elaborated this in "A Note on Proto-Montanism in the Pastoral Epistles," *New Testament Studies*, 17 (April, 1971), 338-46, and also in a short commentary on the pastoral epistles in the forthcoming *Universal Bible*.

22. The ship symbol is extremely important with regard to stability of doctrine. See Earle Hilgert, *The Ship and Related Symbols in the New Testament* (Assen: Van Gorcum, 1962).

23. There has been a tendency for some Pentecostals to shun the world.

was no dichotomy between the material and the spiritual: all converged to give glory to the Creator.

Thus, although I would not countenance the substitution of secular religious literature for Scripture in the liturgy, it is becoming increasingly obvious to me that the Holy Spirit speaks through everything which is "true . . . honorable . . . just . . . pure . . . lovely . . . gracious . . . any excellence . . . anything worthy of praise . . ." (Phil. 4:8). We must have an eye to discern the good and to extract it from what may be a hindrance.

Thus I am not inclined towards the screening process which obtains in some Catholic Pentecostal groups which form intense Christian communities.[24] Just as the Yahwist or the compiler of Proverbs "baptized"—or should I say "circumcised"—pagan mythology[25] and secular wisdom and introduced it into the sacred text, so I believe that when the Spirit of Wisdom is with us, we can do the same. Perfect love casts out fear, even fear of being defiled. One is constantly reminded that the exile was perhaps the most creative period in the history of Israel, a period in which there was much enrichment from other cultures. In the same way we Pentecostals can learn from Yoga, Zen, etc., as long as there is nothing contrary to our Christian faith.[26]

Biblical Studies

Whereas in my capacity as a teacher of biblical studies I have felt little inclination towards Bultmannian and post-Bultmannian theology in its more extreme expression, but rather a tremendous urge towards the Rabbinic background of the New Testament, I must submit that I am indebted to my Pentecostal experience for not only strengthening my belief in supernatural intervention but also in the absolute necessity for professional biblical scholarship. Whereas I hold that the Scripture may be profitably used for private prayer and

24. The shunning of the world is exemplified in one of the Roman Catholic covenant groups in South Bend, Indiana. This is named "The True House," and it was under the presidency of James Byrne. In his address to the Community Teaching Units at the 1972 International Catholic Charismatic Conference at Notre Dame, Indiana, he advocated strict screening of persons and literature (cassette recording). In contrast to this type of Roman Catholic groups are the Southern California Charismatic Renewal groups, who held their first conference in June, 1971. Their second took place in June, 1973. They are extremely open to all the good in the world. Information may be obtained from the Southern California Renewal Community, 8419 Lincoln Boulevard, Los Angeles, CA 90045.

25. See, e.g., Peter Ellis, *The Yahwist* (Notre Dame, IN: Fides Press, 1968).

26. Fr. George Malone of Fordham University has pursued research both into Pentecostalism and into Yoga.

guidance for personal actions and that one must listen to the non-specialist, I am more aware than ever that in the expression and development of doctrine per se the Roman Catholic Church must be guided by men and women biblical scholars. Incidentally, only in this way will she be heard by other Christians. The Word of God is our common inheritance and all ecumenical movements must be based upon it.

Modern biblical scholarship avers that the Scripture was formed gradually out of the *experience* of the faith community.[27] It is on this common ground that contemporary New Testament scholars and Neo-Pentecostals can meet. For we Pentecostals assert that our Pentecostal faith is founded upon our experience.

The man or woman of faith can accept the major contributions of literary, form- and redaction-criticism. The faith community under the inspiration of the Holy Spirit was led to elaborate, more deeply interpret, and more vividly recall the teachings of the Master. This is not to say that parables, narratives, or sayings, etc., were newly composed; but rather, through a crisis, a peak or pit experience, a problem or a new insight into the divine plan, the Holy Spirit caused the compilers of the New Testament to recall, albeit not in every detail, what the Master had taught. This is the fulfillment of John 14:25f.:

> These things I have spoken to you, while I am still with you. But the Counselor, the Holy Spirit, whom the Father will send in my name, he will teach you all things, and bring to your remembrance all that I have said to you.

Indeed, redaction can be seen as prophetical reinterpretation of Scripture and/or the words of Christ. For the Pentecostal it does not really matter whether certain teachings came from the second person of the blessed trinity or from the third, for both are God.

But more importantly a study of the development of doctrine within the early Christian community also serves as a model for guidance within our own Pentecostal groups. We shall meet similar problems and the Scripture can tell us how to deal with them. Thus, for instance, the place of speaking in tongues, the position of women,[28] the practice of exclusion,[29] etc., must be dealt with by a prayerful and

27. See my essay "The Spirit in the New Testament," *God, Jesus, and Spirit*, ed. Daniel Callahan (New York: Herder and Herder, 1969), pp. 225-41.
28. See my article "Tongues—Leadership—Women: Further Reflections on the Neo-Pentecostal Movement," *Spiritual Life* 17 (Fall 1971), 186-97.
29. In the essay entitled "Pentecostal Blueprint," *Baptism of the Spirit* (Techny, IL: Divine Word Publications, 1971 [obtainable from Claretian Publications, 221 West Madison St., Chicago, IL 60606]), pp. 31-77, I wrote to mitigate the exclusive element

scholarly examination of the Scripture evidence. Fundamentalism must be answered by a return to the original text and by careful form-critical analysis.

Further, as Pentecostals we are not precluded from entertaining new theories or interpretations and offering them as possible hypotheses. As a Pentecostal my interest in prophecy has been rekindled.

Thus in my research on the Revelation of John, I have been led to see the author as a prophet, not only in the sense of one who forth-tells or foretells but, more pertinently, in a sense similar to the author of Daniel (who interpreted anew the prophecy of Jeremiah) and to the Teacher of Righteous from Qumran (to whom God revealed the meaning of the prophetical message). My thesis, although it may be untenable, can be briefly described as follows: Revelation 4—22 is almost entirely Jewish. Chapters 4—11 do not belong to the circle of John the *Evangelist*, but of John the *Baptist*, and give in essence his revelation concerning the Lamb of God. Chapters 12—22 are later and belong to the disciples of John, such as we find at Ephesus (Acts 19:3f.). The prophecy does not concern the fall of Rome, but the fall of Jerusalem in A.D. 70; and our text is assigned to A.D. 69. Revelation 1—3 and part of chapter 22 are Christian additions.

My next work—*si Deus vult*—will be an examination of (1) the infancy narratives of Luke compared to Revelation; (2) the Gospels of Luke and John as reinterpreting the message of the Apocalypse in the light of the historical Jesus and the experience of the early church. I am merely citing this example from my research to emphasize the point that my Pentecostal experience has given fresh impetus to provocative reinterpretation of Scripture, the reverse of fundamentalism.[30]

Deeper Belief in Catholic Doctrine

Eucharist

My releases in the Spirit have occurred most frequently in association with the Eucharist (the Lord's Supper), which is the totality or climax of the Christian religious experience.[31] Here, just as

arising within Roman Catholic Pentecostalism. I have also prepared a paper on the exclusion texts.

30. The research is published in the Anchor Bible Commentary on *Revelation* (Garden City, NY: Doubleday, 1975).

31. See my *The Pentecostal Experience*, pp. 26-29.

the Holy Spirit came down upon Mary so that she conceived Jesus, true God and true man, so the Holy Spirit descends upon the elements of bread and wine and brings about the presence of the risen Lord.[32] Thus the experience at Emmaus is re-enacted among us (cf. Luke 24:13-35).

I have realized more profoundly that the Lord's Supper, as indicated in 1 Corinthians 11:23ff., must be the chief source of nourishment for the ministries and fruits of the Spirit. Under the guidance of the Holy Spirit, since Vatican Council II the Roman Catholic Church has revised the prayers at the eucharistic celebration. The new prayers of consecration (the anaphora) are very scriptural and contain references to the Holy Spirit and to the covenant.

Further, the eucharistic celebration has become less priest-orientated: lay men and women[33] may read all the lessons except the gospel, which is proclaimed by the priest. In some circles where small groups are gathered for the Eucharist "dialogue sermons"—that is, the celebrant beginning the reflection on Scripture and the worshipers adding their own reflections afterwards—are permitted.

In Pentecostal gatherings the prayer meeting is sometimes the service of the Word, that is, the section of the Eucharist before the consecration of the bread and wine. Spontaneous prayer, prophecy, tongues and interpretation are permitted after the reception of holy communion. The kiss of peace which takes place just before the reception of communion has taken on great significance. Indeed, for fifteen minutes before the rite ended, the bishop celebrating the Eucharist at the First Annual Conference for Charismatic Renewal at Loyola University, Los Angeles, was nearly smothered with embraces and handshaking as the congregation sang "Peace I Leave With You"!

But also of great importance is the new lectionary cycle, that is, serial reading of Scripture which has been used since 1970.[34] Those who attend the Eucharist daily are now nourished with a most wholesome and grace-bearing proclamation of the Word, and it is through these readings that the present writer has frequently heard the Spirit speaking to her in a special way. The prayer meetings outside the Eucharist serve as an opportunity for sharing more deeply our

---

32. Medieval stories about bleeding hosts (that is, blood exuding from the consecrated bread) do not attract me.

33. A very useful exercise permitted in some churches is a brief (about four to five sentences) exposition of introductory material before the reading of the Scripture. Lay theologians are permitted to do this at the discretion of the priest.

34. Two Catholic Pentecostal scholars, Ralph Keifer and I, wrote *We Are Easter People* (New York: Herder and Herder, 1970), a commentary on part of this lectionary cycle.

reflections on these passages.[35] I believe that I am correct in stating that the Episcopalians and the Lutherans are interested in adopting this three-year lectionary. If many more Christians would do this we should then be nourished with the same loaf of the Word of God, and our unity would be enhanced. A joint commentary on the lectionary prepared by men and women scholars would also increase our unity.

Penance

My Pentecostal experience, both the joys and the vicissitudes, has also given me a deeper appreciation of the sacrament of penance, otherwise known as confession. One must admit that this sacrament may have been misused in the past, but my experience of the ban and shunning (based on Matt. 18 and 1 Cor. 5) introduced into some of our groups and used in a rather arbitrary way has opened my eyes to the gentle wise method in which the church has fulfilled the commandments of our Savior.

There must be discipline within the church to uphold both moral and doctrinal precepts. This is seen clearly in Matthew 16 and 18 and 1 Corinthians 5, etc. But this discipline must be practiced with a view to reconciliation of the sinner; nowadays this is more deeply understood by, e.g., our Mennonite brethren.[36] The sacrament of penance preserves both discipline and reconciliation.

The church uses public excommunication only in extreme cases.[37] Catholics who commit lesser faults must abstain from the reception of the holy Eucharist but may attend the service, whereby the church hopes they will repent and return to the fold. The practice is very important because refusal to admit a sinner to the service would deprive him of hearing the powerful proclamation of the Word of God in the assembly of the faithful.

It is the Word which should convict the sinner and bring him or her to repentance. When this repentance occurs, the church requires the sinner to confess the fault in the privacy of the confessional before the priest, who represents the congregation and who has the authority to bind or loose mentioned by Christ. The important factors here are

35. See Fr. John Quinn, *The Holy Spirit and the Sacraments*, cassette no. 152 (obtainable from Box 12, Notre Dame, IN 46556).

36. See, e.g., *Concern: A Pamphlet Series for Questions of Christian Renewal*, no. 14 (Feb., 1967 [order from Business Manager, 721 Walnut Avenue, Scottdale, PA 15638]).

37. The last excommunication of which I am aware was in the fifties on account of public racial discrimination.

that the church keeps the sin entirely confidential[38] and that the sinner as he goes to the sacrament knows that, if he is sincere, reconciliation awaits him. And, further, it is to be hoped that the priest possesses the fruits of the Spirit so that he can serve to awaken the Spirit in the penitent.

The Pentecostal movement within the Catholic Church has brought out very clearly the healing nature of this sacrament,[39] and contemporary theology has stressed the community aspect. Thus nowadays, it is the custom to hold penitential services which include the hearing of Scripture, prayers of repentance, etc., and which give an opportunity for those who wish to go privately to receive the sacrament. Their expression of sorrow and promise of amendment, however, usually take place in the community prayers which conclude the service.

Infallibility

Associated with the authority to bind and loose[40] is my fresh approach to the doctrine of the infallibility of the church, the doctrine against which I struggled the longest before my entry into the Roman Catholic Church. Although I have not been able to articulate my thoughts sufficiently, I feel that there is great room for understanding this doctrine in the light of prophecy and the discernment of spirits. I am in total agreement with Professor Reginald Fuller[41] in seeing the possibility of some research in this area in terms of the covenant relationship of Israel to Yahweh. The subject is especially important in the light of illuminism, which is always a danger in charismatic movements.[42]

Purgatory

Finally, I turn to two subjects which are, perhaps, even more precarious for non-Roman Catholics, namely, the doctrine of purgatory and the place of Mary.

38. Contrast such communities as described in B. Zabloscki, *The Joyful Community* (Baltimore: Penguin Books, 1971).

39. Fr. Michael Scanlon, T.O.R., *The Power of Penance* (Notre Dame, IN: Ave Maria Press, 1972).

40. Gunther Bornkamm sees Matthew 16 pointing to doctrinal authority and Matthew 18 to disciplinary authority. See Bornkamm's article, "The Authority to 'Bind' and 'Loose' in the Church in Matthew's Gospel: The Problem of Sources in Matthew's Gospel," *Jesus and Man's Hope*, ed. David C. Buttrick, "A Perspective Book, I" (Pittsburgh: Pittsburgh Theological Seminary, 1970), pp. 37-50.

41. Prof. Reginald Fuller, in private communication.

42. O'Connor, *The Pentecostal Movement*, pp. 221-25, speaks wisely concerning illuminism.

My Pentecostal experience, both in practice and through the reading which I have done, has caused me to focus more upon salvation and eternal loss. The subject has become of importance to me, because some of my Catholic Pentecostal brothers have confused *salvation*[43] and *sanctification*. As a Roman Catholic I cannot affirm that the release of the Spirit and/or belonging to a Pentecostal (covenant) community is necessary for salvation. Yet, on the other hand, I cannot deny that the release(s) of the Spirit is (are) one important means of sanctification. None of us can even judge our own spiritual state, let alone judge whether others have been released in the Spirit. Yet the essence of the release is an intimate knowledge of the Lord Jesus through the power and love of the Holy Spirit.

It seems to me, *and here I speak with the greatest caution,* that in the loving mercy of God for those who have not come to know Jesus intimately on this earth or have only the baptism of desire[44] there must be a further opportunity for them to be brought to an intimate knowledge of the Lord. Could it be that the light of the Beatific Vision would be too bright for the eyes of those who have an immature knowledge of Christ and that the intermediate state called purgatory in the Roman Catholic Church is, after all, one of the most clement and wise of doctrines? I do not think of flames when I speak of purgatory, but rather I have renamed the state "the Continuing Education Center"! Herein souls not released in the Spirit—and here again I stress that only God can judge who they are—can be released and come to the Beatific Vision.

You will, as good Pentecostals, ask me for a scriptural basis for my thought. I may cite, of course, the usual texts of 2 Maccabees 12:42ff. and 1 Corinthians 3:15,[45] asking you to bear in mind Sundberg's thesis[46] that the deutero-canonical books were accepted by the earlier Christians.

However, perhaps more pertinent are those texts concerning Christ's descent into hell. Hell does not appear to mean the place of the damned but rather the abode of the dead in general (cf. Wisdom 3:1 and Luke 16:23-26: the just occupy a place different from the

---

43. I wish to correct my terminology in *The Pentecostal Experience,* pp. 48f., where I speak of no certainty of salvation. The term "eternal security" would have been better.

44. By "baptism of desire" Catholics refer to those who have lived a good life but for one reason or another have had no opportunity to receive the sacrament of baptism.

45. I do not find a reference to 1 Corinthians 3:15 convincing.

46. Albert C. Sundberg, *The Old Testament of the Early Church; a Study of the Canon,* Harvard Theological Studies, 20 (Cambridge, MA: Harvard University Press, 1964).

wicked). Christ's descent into hell is part of His act of redemption and
is closely related to His death on the cross (Matt. 12:40; Acts 2:24-31;
Rom. 10:7); its connection with the incarnation is shown in Ephesians
4:8ff. (although this is a difficult text) and Philippians 2:5-10. According to 1 Peter 3:18ff. and 4:6, Christ preached to the souls in the
nether world.

I cannot exegete these difficult passages at the moment, but all that
I venture to ask you to consider is that perhaps there is still preaching
and the ministries of the Spirit in the nether world, and that this
present world is not the only decisive sphere with regard to salvation
or loss. I offer this only because of the increasing polarity between the
released and the unreleased. I shall hope to do further work on these
texts.

Yet, hesitatively, I draw once again upon my own experience.
Faced with the imminent death of my mother and in view of a terminal but not imminent diagnosis offered to me by the doctor in
August of 1972, I have asked myself whether we are called to eternal
rest or eternal ministry. My only regret on hearing the diagnosis was
that I might not be able to complete the many interesting tasks in
which I hoped to be engaged for the next few years.

What occurred to me very vividly during prayer and in association
with the sacrament of anointing which was administered to me was
the petition of Teresa of Lisieux, a young nun who died in her early
twenties. She was certainly released in the Spirit. She asked God that
she might spend her heaven doing good on earth. God granted this
request.

After making the same prayer to our Lord the chasm between this
world and the next seemed to disappear. I came to the realization that
we do not reach the fullness of the Spirit upon this earth. Our spiritual
journey must be to walk in the footsteps of Jesus, as I have suggested:
His annunciation, His bar mitzvah, His baptism, His resurrection and
His ascension—it is only with our ascension or leaving this world that
the fullness of the Spirit will be with us. Thus having friendship with
the saints—for canonization only means that the church judges that
these persons have the fullness of the Spirit—is as natural as having
Pentecostal friends on earth.

The Role of Mary

Lastly, I turn to Mary. As an Anglican I had not so much an an-
tipathy towards Mary as merely a lack of interest. When I became a

Roman Catholic I tended to take part in public devotions[47] to Mary, but only rarely to engage in private devotions to her.

However, about two years after my Pentecostal experience I developed a friendship with Mary and felt her presence on several occasions. On this experiential level I do not find her an awe-inspiring figure[48] but a very natural, simple, and extremely kind, cheerful young woman. I speak of "friendship" because I believe "devotion" is a misleading word. Some nowadays would speak of praying *with* rather than *to* Mary. But the church has always made a clear distinction between *latria*, worship given exclusively to God, and veneration given to the saints.[49] In no way must divinity be predicated of Mary; she may be called the "bearer of God" (*theotokos*), because she is the mother of Jesus, God and man. But she should not be addressed with titles such as "Divine Shepherdess."[50] Rather, she is the mother of the Divine Shepherd.

It is these kinds of mistakes made innocently by uneducated Catholics which have given a wrong impression about Mary. Friendships with her should be very natural. If we are bound by divine law to love our mothers, fathers, sisters and brothers, how much more must we love Mary, the mother of Jesus and His friends. As Jesus is truly our brother, she is our "stepmother" (cf. also John 19:26f.).

Mary could be regarded as the first Pentecostal in the New Testament era, because the Holy Spirit first came upon her at the annunciation. She is the mother of Jesus; as such, we owe the respect we should pay to the mother of any noble person. She was privileged to care for Jesus as an infant, to look after Him as a boy and young man, and to join His public ministry with a group of other women. She, unlike the disciples save John, did not fear to assist Him at death.

If we are attracted to contemporary people who walk in the Spirit and have an intimate relationship with the Lord Jesus, why should we hesitate to be friends with Mary—just as John and perhaps Luke were after the ascension of Jesus? Her life is changed, not taken away—we

47. Mary is less prominent in the western church than she is in the eastern. Only one small reference to her occurs in the western Eucharist; the Hail Mary is not said.

48. One must confess, however, that in many parts of the Catholic world (especially among the uneducated) there have been gross exaggerations in devotion to Mary. However, these are not countenanced by the official church.

49. Catholics distinguish between three types of *cultus:* (1) *latria*, which is supreme worship given only to God: if it is rendered to anyone else it is idolatry; (2) *dulia* (veneration), given to saints and angels; and (3) *hyperdulia*, given to Mary owing to her relationship to Christ.

50. The title "Divine Shepherdess" is found in the West Indies, but the translation from the original language may be unfortunate.

can know this because we believe in the resurrection. She is honored because of her place in the plan of salvation and because of the graces of the Holy Spirit poured upon her. However, we must keep our love for her in proportion, just as we must keep in a correct balance our relationship to leaders of prayer groups. Mary seems to be an important person, for I believe that she too is called to eternal ministry, not rest. Her work for Jesus still continues.

But let us turn for a moment to prayer and Mary. The chief prayer is the "Hail Mary":

> Hail, Mary, full of grace, the Lord is with you, blessed are you among women and blessed is the fruit of your womb, Jesus. Holy Mary, Mother of God, pray for us sinners now and at the hour of our death. Amen.

You will note that it comprises verses from Scripture (Luke 1:28 and 42b) and then a simple petition to Mary to pray for us, just as we would turn to any Christian on earth and ask for prayer (cf. Acts 8:24). The Hail Mary is powerful because the very enunciation of the sacred text of Scripture is always grace-bearing and creative.

The second most popular prayer form used in association with Mary is the rosary. This comprises fifteen meditations while one recites one Our Father, ten Hail Marys, and one "Glory be to the Father and to the Son and to the Holy Spirit. As it was in the beginning, it is now and ever shall be, world without end, Amen." The meditations are:

A. *The Joyful Mysteries*
   The Annunciation
   The Visitation (of Mary to Elizabeth)
   The Birth of Jesus
   The Presentation of Jesus in the Temple
   The Finding of the Child Jesus in the Temple
B. *The Sorrowful Mysteries*
   The Agony in the Garden
   The Scourging at the Pillar
   The Crowning with Thorns
   The Carrying of the Cross
   The Crucifixion
C. *The Glorious Mysteries*
   The Resurrection of Jesus
   The Ascension of Jesus
   Pentecost
   The Dormition or Assumption of the Virgin

The Queenship of Our Lady and the Glory of All the
Saints (or in Pentecostal terminology, the
celebration of the Spirit-filled people).

It may be seen that all but two of the meditations are completely biblical. Indeed, the rosary serves to provide illiterate people with biblical meditations. Saying the Our Fathers, Hail Marys, and Glorias as one meditates is rather like praying in tongues while one contemplates heavenly things or like having music as a background to prayer.

The prayers themselves are subordinated to the biblical meditations, i.e., heart takes precedence over head. Both tongues and the Jesus Prayer—that is, repeating "Jesus, Son of the Living God, have mercy on me,"[51] slowly and meditatively—have been compared to the rosary. Several people, non-Roman Catholic and Catholic alike, while praying in tongues have been found to be reciting the Hail Mary either in Latin or Greek.

The third most common prayer is the *Angelus*, which is often recited thrice a day. It comprises three verses of Scripture (concerning the incarnation), each followed by one Hail Mary, and then a prayer addressed to the Father referring to the passion and resurrection of Christ. Thus, again, the prayer is a biblical meditation.

But I know that many of you will be exercised about the assumption and queenship of Mary and also what is known as the immaculate conception.[52] When the Holy Father defined the doctrine of the assumption, he merely affirmed that Our Lady's body did not suffer corruption. This is a belief emanating from the second century;[53] God did for Mary something similar to that which happened to Enoch and Elijah. It is not claimed that Mary did not die or that she alone is "corporally" present in heaven.

To me, the assumption is an excellent affirmation of our belief in the ministry of physical healing. Through the grace of Jesus Christ, who had healed the diseased and raised the dead, the body of Mary did not suffer corruption. The doctrine expresses profound respect for the body which bore the Son of God. The "immaculate conception"

51. See Fr. David Geraets, O.S.B., *Jesus Beads* (Pecos, NM: Dove Publications, 1971).

52. See *The Dogma of the Immaculate Conception: History and Significance*, ed. Edward D. O'Connor, C.S.C. (Notre Dame, IN: University of Notre Dame Press, 1958).

53. A fragment of Hippolytus was found among writings of Theodoret (*Dialogue* 1) comparing Mary to the ark of the covenant made of "incorruptible wood." For the text, see H. Achelis, *Hippolyt's kleinere exegetische und homiletische Schriften. Hippolytus Werke*, vol. 1, part 2 in *Griechische Christliche Schriftsteller*, 1 (Leipzig: J. C. Hinrichs'sche Buchhandlung, 1897), pp. 146/line 20-147/line 6.

(not to be confused with the virginal conception of Jesus) means that Our Lady's soul was free from sin. Personally I see this as the climax of spiritual healing. I see the importance of this doctrine not so much in Mary's freedom from sin as in her fullness of the fruits and gifts of the Spirit (cf. Luke 1:28): Mary was Spirit-filled before birth. The new scriptural lessons for the celebration of that Feast suggest this clearly.[54] However, all this was in virtue of the redemption to be wrought by her Son, not any merit of her own.

Finally, I should speak of Mary and the blood of Jesus. As no man cooperated in the physical conception of Jesus, His precious blood came solely from His mother. A woman's blood, previously regarded as levitically unclean (Lev. 15:19ff.), became the source of the blood of the Lamb. It was when this blood was shed that Jesus bowed His head and gave up the Spirit (John 19:30). Thus Mary's association with the blood and the Spirit makes her worthy of respect and friendship, but she remains a human person and she owes all she has and is to her Son.

54. For further details about Mary see my article in *Marian Studies*, 23 (1972), 79-112. The article is entitled "Our Lady and the Ministry of Women," but it is based on Mary and the ministries and fruits of the Spirit.

PART FIVE
Future Prospects

Morton T. Kelsey

Morton T. Kelsey is a graduate of Washington and Lee University (B.A., 1938) and the Episcopal Theological School (B.D., 1943). He did graduate work at Princeton and Claremont, and he has studied at the C. J. Jung Institute in Zurich, Switzerland.

Having served churches in Syracuse and Phoenix following ordination into the Episcopal ministry in 1943, Fr. Kelsey became Rector of St. Luke's Church in Monrovia, California, where he served from 1950-69. Since then, he has served in the department of education of the graduate school of the University of Notre Dame. He is licensed in California as a marriage, family, and child counselor.

Morton Kelsey's application of the thought of Carl Jung to charismatic experience appeared in his books *Dreams: The Dark Speech of the Spirit* (Garden City, NY: Doubleday, 1960) and *Tongue Speaking* (Garden City, NY: Doubleday, 1964). In his work *Encounter with God* (Minneapolis: Bethany Fellowship, 1972), he provides a philosophic foundation for a charismatic theology. In 1973 appeared his major work on *Healing and Christianity* (New York: Harper and Row). Jungian interests persist in *Myth History, and Faith—The Remythologizing of Christianity* (New York: Paulist Press, 1974), *The Christian and the Supernatural* (Minneapolis: Augsburg, 1976), and *The Other Side of Silence: A Guide to Christian Meditation* (New York: Paulist Press, 1976).

In this essay, Fr. Kelsey proposes experiential theology as an alternative to the rational theology which has marked Christian thought since early Christian times. Then he calls for courage to experience God, saying that a charismatic theology could achieve the Christian unity long but unsuccessfully sought through ecumenical designs.

Courage, Unity
and Theology

15

Modern theology on the whole does not seem to exemplify much courage, except the courage to break with most of traditional Christian thinking. Such theology certainly causes more division than unity among Christians. Yet even today Christian thinking about God need not have that effect. A theology which actually explores Christian experience will bring men together around a God who can be experienced. But this kind of theology, which is based upon men's encounters with God and not just on their human ideas of what is possible or impossible for God, does take courage.

To maintain an experiential theology, in fact, requires all the courage a man can muster because it means denying the prevailing scientism of our modern world and remaining open to an encounter with the living God. There can be no question about its value. An experiential theology, forged out with honesty and courage, can help to bring about unity among the followers of Christ. Those who have encountered God in experience have little difficulty in communicating and relating to one another, and such unity is urgently needed in the world today.

Instead, most of the traditional churches in America are experiencing crisis and chaos. Only decades ago people were flocking to those churches. Membership and attendance were at unprecedented levels; seminaries were filled and turning away applicants. The surveys of public opinion revealed a general confidence in the church's ideals and the effect of religion on the common man. And then this whole trend was suddenly and dramatically reversed. Today the surveys reveal a general fear that religion is failing to influence people's lives. Both in the mainline Protestant denominations and in the Roman Catholic Church, membership, attendance, and financial support are declining at a drastic rate, and many seminaries are in serious difficulty from loss of enrollments and income. The few mainline churches and seminaries that have resisted the decline are those that adhere unquestioningly to a strict and orthodox position.[1]

Neither the growing charismatic movement nor the widely popular Jesus cults have had much effect on the general run of churches. Young people whose religious needs are not being met by a moribund authority and tradition are turning instead to Eastern thought and practice, to drugs, and to the occult. The experience of God which they need and seek does not seem to be provided by the respectable and rationalistic Christianity of the major Christian bodies, and so there is little prospect of anything but continued decline and loss of interest.

What is the trouble? Obviously this is a complex question involving social, political, and other factors, and any effort to provide a simplistic answer will fail to state the whole truth. But I believe that the central problem—which is far from simple—is that of theology. To put it plainly, most modern theology casts doubts upon any belief that God can be known directly through experience. It fails to provide any base that would allow men to believe that such experiences occur—either today, or as they were reported in the New Testament and all through the Bible.

It is my contention that nothing in sophisticated modern thinking necessitates this attitude. On the contrary, there is good support for the view that men do have encounters with God and with a spiritual

---

1. The statistics of this decline are described at length in my *Encounter with God: A Theology of Christian Experience* (Minneapolis: Bethany Fellowship, 1972), ch. I. *Time* magazine for October 9, 1972, gives the data on the seminaries, p. 84.

(nonphysical) world as well as with a physical one. To see what I am proposing, let us consider first the way in which a *rational* theology approaches God and the world. Then let us see how *experiential* theology goes about the same task. I shall then suggest the courage and personal sacrifice an experiential theology requires and outline briefly how Christian experience so understood can undergird a greater Christian unity.

Rational Theology

To start with, there are two essentially different ways of approaching the world around us. The first of them looks upon man's *mind* as the measure of the world, while the second sees man's *experience* as the final determinant—even his experiences that do not fit in with the current patterns of thought. In one case reality is fitted into rational categories. In the other man's reason must be stretched to take in experience as it comes. Let us look carefully at each of these views.

The first view has been widely current in our Western world. It maintains that man's intellect is well equipped to comprehend the world around him. Using the tools of logical reason and the analytical creativity of his mind, man is able to plumb the depths of reality and discover the ultimate nature of the universe. With the same tools, he is then able to put his knowledge into concise, cognitive statements and communicate it clearly. This point of view assumes that there are rational laws governing the universe and that men can dig them out and know with certainty what reality is like. It is also assumed that man's rational capacity is in harmony with nature and gives access to it. Thus reason, relentlessly used, is seen as ultimately infallible. Reason needs only its own processes—carefully examined to know what it requires—in order for men to know not only the nature of thought, but also the nature of the world and of spiritual reality. Reason alone is the source of man's knowledge of himself, and even of God. What is unthinkable about these realities is therefore unreal, or at least unlikely.

This point of view, which was held by a few of the ancient Greek thinkers, was first developed into a consistent system of thought by Aristotle, who thus laid the foundations for all later rationalism. His thesis in the *Metaphysics*—he states that he proves it logically—is that one comes to know the reality of God (the unmoved First Mover) as the necessary beginning of all efficient causality. Elsewhere he rejects the idea of revelation simply being given to men, for instance through dreams, because simple people would then have access to knowledge of the gods as readily as intelligent men. And Aristotle concludes that the gods obviously would not act so irrationally.[2]

His thinking did not become popular, however, until the Middle Ages—until it was adopted as the base for the brilliant Arab civilization and then imported into Europe, where an unrealistic and naive Platonism had taken over. In competition, Aristotle's thought soon won out, and Scholastic thinkers began to recast Christian ideas into the mold of Aristotle. Man was seen as getting knowledge only through sense experience and reason, and getting at reliable knowledge only through reason. Christianity was then seen as a logical structure, which could be discovered or learned through a series of logical questions and answers.

This has been, and still is, the route taken by most of Christian theology since about A.D. 1300. Today the Christian revelation can either be pared down to fit one's intellectual categories, or else it can be kept apart, in solely historical wrappings, and elaborated by reason. The first way is that of German liberal theology in the nineteenth century, and of the present-day existential theologians, notably Bultmann. The second is that of Barth and many conservatives. Even though it may be maintained that a world of *supernatural* reality exists, this is not something man's reason can deal with. As the Scholastics held, this reality is revealed only to the saints by grace, and so the idea that God is present in the world and seeks to break through directly and experientially into human lives has become almost entirely foreign to theology. As John Macquarrie's study, *Twentieth Century Religious Thought* (New York: Harper and Row, 1963) amply demonstrates, God is known to the theologians through inference, not experience.

For a long time following Descartes, the scientific world took the same tack, putting theory before experience. By eliminating all shadowy or unclear experience from consideration, Descartes found that the physical world could be understood as clearly as an algebraic equation. Once Newton had provided the basic mathematical principles, the movement of the heavenly bodies could be understood. So could the process by which the ninety-two "billiard-ball" atoms interacted physically and chemically to produce the earth. With Darwin's theory of the survival of the fittest, the case was complete. Even

---

2. Rather than give detailed references (which would be nearly as long as the text) for this and the following material, I again refer the reader to *Encounter with God*, chs. III-VI, in which these developments are fully documented.

man's development could be explained solely as the result of physical cause and effect. The world was purely physical, organized on causal principles, and that was all the world there was.

Scientific optimism became the rule of nineteenth century men. They believed that it was only a matter of time before the entire universe would be understood; man had the ultimate truths in his hand or within sight. Certainly no spiritual or teleological factors influenced the physical world or man himself. Everything had its explanation without reference to such ideas. If such aspects of reality did exist, they could only be inferred from the natural order. For God does not interfere or play dice with His own lawful and understandable order. As men like Robert Oppenheimer have noted, this world view was almost universally accepted among scientists at the turn of the century. This attitude also had a double effect upon religion. On one hand, it encouraged the basic Scholastic idea of God's being inaccessible to human reason. And on the other, it inhibited the development of any new system of religious thought because religious thinkers, overawed, were intimidated by the successes and the euphoria of the scientific world. And the customary religious ideas were not adequate to stand against the new scientific thought. Most religious thinkers either reacted blindly, clinging to old creeds, or capitulated and spoke of religion as a matter of "feeling" or "authentic living." Is it any wonder that the larger Christian community is a ship at sea without mast or rudder? That society has become a wasteland in which the church exists, no longer the center of men's lives?[3]

A Theology of Experience

Even so, man has unquestionably benefited from having his rationality pushed to its logical conclusion in nineteenth century thought. Man's knowledge of the world was vastly expanded in the process, and even more important, he began to see that his reason did not automatically get to the ultimate root of things. The more that knowledge accumulated, the easier it became to see how much remains to be known; and so men began to change their ideas about the human ability to understand the world. They began to see that experience cannot be fitted rationally into known categories. Instead, reason has to be expanded to make room for new experience. Man will probably never come to any logically certain knowledge of the world.

3. Theodore Roszak, *Where the Wasteland Ends* (Garden City, NY: Doubleday, 1972), describes modern man's separation from spiritual values.

After he does his best to understand, man will find surprises as new experiences open up for him and he discovers which ones are significant and pregnant with meaning.

In ancient times Plato formulated this point of view. In addition to sense experience and reason (which were to be used as carefully and critically as possible), he saw man as open to another kind of knowledge which speaks of a spiritual dimension of reality and gives intuition about the physical world as well. Man's knowledge can never be complete or final since there is always the possibility of divine intuitions breaking through that can change or add to the formulations arrived at by human reason. Thus reason must always be ready to defer to experience, and to grow with experiences of the sensory world and with those experiences which bring divine inspiration and intuitions that are unlimited in number and depth. These latter experiences are given through prophecy, through the experience of healing, through poetry and art, and most significantly through love.

Christian theology was born when this particular Greek way of looking at reality was wedded with Christian experience. And on this foundation the Trinitarian theology of the early church was forged out. While Jesus Himself did not formulate a philosophical system in so many words, the records of His actions and of what He did say make it quite clear that His attitude toward the world was like the Platonic formulation.[4] This was also the world view of Paul and the other apostles. If one examines the writings carefully, it is evident that this Greek philosophy did no violence to Jesus' view of the world. Both the teachings of Jesus and the experiences men had of Him fit easily into this framework.

Faced with the rationalism of those who could not understand how Jesus can be both God and man, the church continued to maintain this view of reality. Its thinkers resisted the efforts of both Docetists and Arians to eliminate one side or the other, and went right on holding to the paradox of its experience, the paradox of having experienced both the historical and the risen Jesus. Through the centuries popular Christianity continued the same attitude toward reality in mystical practice and public devotions, even after that attitude had been practically discarded by the official theology of both Catholic and Protestant churches. But with the Enlightenment it became more and more difficult for the ordinary Christian to believe that God could or would break into the historical process. Those who held to

4. See my article, "Is the World View of Jesus Outmoded?" *The Christian Century*, 86 (Jan. 22, 1969), 112-15.

such ideas were not "with it," and generally they were either ignored or ridiculed. After all, by the nineteenth century intelligent men had come to realize that we live in a purely causal world, created by a God who has better manners than to intrude into His already perfect system.

And then, before that century was over, a change began in the scientific attitude toward the world, a change which was later to explode upon most people with the development of the atomic bomb. Beginning with Max Planck, Becquerel, the Curies, Einstein, Bohr, and Heisenberg, scientists learned that what man had thought was final knowledge about the world of atoms and physics was only partial knowledge, and that scientific "laws" are not ultimate truths at all. Instead they are like road maps, drawn up to help us get around in a reality where many of the actual facts, such as those of quantum mechanics, are rationally inconceivable. Man's confidence in his own ability to comprehend the ultimate nature of things has been profoundly shaken. We humans, it appears, cannot claim to know *all* about anything.

By the same token, there is no longer reason to deny categorically that God and the world of spirit have contact with man and his world, with practical effects upon both. Werner Heisenberg has suggested this in *Physics and Philosophy* (New York: Harper, 1958), holding that words like "God" and "spirit," which belong to man's natural language, may well offer a better description of reality than the carefully defined concepts of science. Other scientists support this view, offering evidence which does not suggest divine interferences, but divine guidance and direction. God, it seems, is present whether called or not, and—Bonhoeffer to the contrary—man has not "come of age" so that he is able to get along without God's help and guidance.

Kurt Gödel, who is probably the most significant living mathematician, has shown that man's reason alone cannot account for the science of mathematics; even the most basic of its propositions cannot be proved logically, but must rest originally upon intuitions which are given. Teilhard de Chardin and others have considered evidence about the development of man, concluding that this process can be fully understood on the basis of meaningful purpose operating in it. Modern psychosomatic medicine has shown the effect of emotion on man's health (even emotions one does not know he has). And as Jerome Frank points out in *Persuasion and Healing* (New York: Schocken Books, 1969), faith in a meaningful universe is a real factor in keeping people well.

Finally, it is Carl Jung, the Zurich psychiatrist, who has expressed this whole point of view most clearly and adequately. His study of the human psyche brought him to the conclusion that man is in touch with both a physical and a nonphysical reality. Men's failure to deal with the nonphysical or spiritual sector of reality, he found, leads to depression, neurosis, and mental illness, as well as to race and class tension and to the mass psychosis of war. Jung's view suggests, in essence, that the function of religion is to provide ways of dealing with this spiritual reality as it touches men in actual experiences (today largely unconsciously and thus negatively). Theology's task is to discover and express the meaning of those experiences.

As Jung has pointed out, the most vital need of our world is for men to become aware of the ways in which this spiritual reality can affect their lives, and this is peculiarly a religious task. To undertake it, theologians are needed (1) who will attempt to understand those experiences which man has with nonphysical reality and how God and the realm in which God exists are revealed in them, and (2) who are able to draw upon the experiences of the past, focusing particularly—where Christians are concerned—on those of the New Testament. A theology is needed which can accept new demands upon it and is willing to open up new expectations.

It is interesting to note that at the same time these changes were developing in science, another movement was beginning which seems to point to similar conclusions about man's experience. This is the Pentecostal movement, which began as the physical and psychological sciences were having second thoughts about the finality of man's knowledge and were looking again at the importance of experience for man's reason. Both this religious movement and the scientific one seem to place the final authority upon experience, and perhaps both express the same essential world spirit. To what demands and what expectations, then, does this emphasis lead?

Courage

Dealing with the living God in experience is no easy task. It is far easier to deal with ideas about God than with God Himself. Ideas about God rarely overwhelm the thinker, nor do they generally make demands upon him (beyond the expected intellectual ones); nor do they open one to the destructive aspects of his own being, or to any of the demonic elements that come from beyond oneself. On the other hand, an actual experience of God, a genuine religious experience, does have such results. When a man does encounter God in experience, it is not God who is put under the microscope and examined with reason, but man who finds himself under scrutiny. Among those who have never encountered God there is a fear that God will dissolve under man's penetrating, critical gaze. This idea would be funny if it were not so widely held.

The forms of modern thought do not encourage opening oneself to God in the belief that He might be there. But I suggest that this is not the only reason for the reluctance of present-day theologians to base their thinking on experience. The fact is that experience is demanding and painful; it costs too much. Thus a lack of nerve, of courage, may well be as prime a reason as cultural conditioning for the theological avoidance of experience. In contrast, Aquinas had almost finished his magnificent intellectual treatise about God when he had a vision such as no Scholastic should ever have. Laying aside his writing from then on, he acknowledged that all his closely reasoned propositions were as straw compared with the value of this experience. Few intellectual theologians would have the courage to make such a confession. But then Aquinas was a saint, an experiential Christian.

Once one encounters the living God, he cannot drop Him. One is hooked for life, and there is no backing out except at the risk of disaster. Growth and development are required—and then more growth, and increased consciousness. One dies and is born again, over and over, as the ego tries to resist growth and bring things back to a stationary point. At times only the courage to go on brings the way into focus. I can blame no one for bypassing this way—except the theologian. He needs to know what he is writing about. To write theology without having had any experience of God is like practicing medicine without ever serving one's internship or working with a sick person. Not many of us would want to put our trust in such a physician. One can become this kind of theologian, of course, and discuss endless thoughts about "knowing" God. But a man can come to theology from the standpoint of actual knowledge of God, and thus become an *experiential* theologian, only as he has surrendered his life to the reality of encounter and all that this means in continual transformation. The early Christians who faced persecution had already made their decision that the experience of the risen Lord was more important than life itself, and so a theology of experience was easy for them. For comfortable modern man, the starting point—the encounter—is not much easier than facing persecution. The dying is done inwardly—where not even the courage really shows—rather than outwardly. Encounter with God means losing one's life to find it. And this is what an experiential theology is all about. It is no wonder men stray off into ideas about God rather than dealing with the real thing.

The encounter also involves something else. When one is open to God, then one is also open to the totality of nonphysical reality, evil as well as good. One of the most damaging ideas of modern rationality is the idea that, because a principle of evil operating in God's universe is incomprehensible, evil is therefore unreal. Aristotle was one of the first to articulate this. For him evil was only the absence of good, the accidental lack of perfection. On the other hand, when Tertullian remarked with his characteristic exaggeration that "the devil is fully known only to Christians," he was simply stating the Christian view in condensed form. And this view at least tallies with human experience. Man does know the powers of evil.

Still, those powers do not put out their best efforts to corrupt those who are already fairly well within the camp. The man who is most likely to experience the attention of his Satanic majesty is the one who has become really open to God, who has discovered the creative life of the risen Christ and is beginning to respond. He is worth an all-out attack, an experience of which Pentecostal fellowships are well aware. Of course, through the power of Christ this can be resisted, but unfortunately few of us, even theologians, live that close to God. The encounter with what Jesus calls the Evil One—which goes along with encountering God—means continual spiritual combat. And again, once one has become open to that level of reality through an experience of God or the Holy Spirit, there is no closing it off. The contact is for keeps, and one must keep asking for the Spirit and for courage to handle the conflict.

At the same time, there are outer demands. If one has encountered the God of Jesus Christ, then he will find that he is expected to treat other human beings with the same love and concern that God has shown for him. The experience of God is seldom if ever given as a reward for merits, but rather as a sheer gift of grace, and God seems to expect us to use it in the same way. The God who gives of Himself expects us to give freely of ourselves to saint and sinner, derelict and doubter, rational theologian and schismatic, to mother-in-law and betraying friend, to unfaithful husband and wayward child. This, too, means dying daily, and one has to turn again and again for the courage that is found only at the source. Living in this way, one experiences more and more of this unreasonably loving and demanding God. How else, but with the courage to seek, can one come to an experiential theology, to an actual knowledge of God from which some immediate results are to be expected?

Unity

One of the great scandals in the church is the disunity among Christians. I suggest that today's rational—rather than experiential—theology may be among the principal causes of this disunity. When one deals from his pack of ideas about God, his own shortsightedness and bias can influence his attitude and warp it. Our supposedly complete rationality is not immune to selfishness and egotism. The more insecure we feel about our ideas the more dramatically and pompously we are likely to maintain them, and the less we listen to others.

When knowledge comes from experience, on the other hand, there are facts which are known, facts that can be communicated and compared. It is what is out there, beyond *me*, which is real. I do not argue about it; I point to it. If that reality means a great deal to me, I will want to know more about it and to share what I do know. And the more secure I am about the reality that is beyond me, the less defensive I will be, the more willing to share rather than to force ideas on others. One of the most interesting aspects of the scientific community is its desire to share its ideas. The physicist or chemist who is really determined to find out about his subject is nearly always open to the experiences and ideas of other seekers.

Why should not the same thing be true in relation to our experience of the risen Christ? As one parochial school student whom I know asked his chemistry teacher (who also taught the class in religion), Why can't religion be taught—or communicated—as convincingly as the science of chemistry? If we are as interested in experiencing God as Father, Son, and Holy Spirit as the scientist is in experiencing atoms as protons, electrons, and neutrons, then we shall be open and seeking out others who are seeking in the same way. The reality will be more important than our ideas about that reality, the experience more important than our formulations of it. A theology in which experience has pre-eminence will be a theology that draws Christians together instead of separating them.

Within the greater charismatic fellowship it is heartening to see this unity take place as Christians of every background, Catholic or Protestant, Lutheran, Evangelical, or Holiness, find that they have shared transforming experience which draws them together. They do in fact experience one Spirit and this gives a common life and direction.

Equally important, as this same Spirit is manifested more and more in our loving concern for others, thoughts of disunity become more repugnant, and we are mutually open to one another and drawn to one another. We are also aware of the courage that is required, and of the demands—both inner and outer—on each individual, so that sympathy, respect and love for each other as individuals are enhanced. Thus the experience of God provides a base for common sharing and at the same time the impetus, even the demand, for it.

A theology of experience demands much of men. It prepares men to open themselves increasingly to the ever-present reality of the Holy Spirit. In so doing, it can help along our personal transformation, and also the transformation of the churches into one fellowship of followers each with its own understanding and emphasis. Together we can become better witnesses to the reality of the Lord we confess. As we work courageously together within a common experiential framework, the world will be impressed, and once more it will be said of Christians: Look, How they love one another!

Kilian McDonnell, O.S.B.

Fr. Kilian McDonnell, a Roman Catholic priest of the Benedictine order, is widely recognized as a leading authority on international Pentecostalism in all its varieties. His participation in ecumenical affairs was foreshadowed by studies in Protestant theology at German universities. He was granted his doctoral degree by the theological faculty at Trier (West Germany). He also has studied at the universities of Heidelberg, Münster, and Tübingen (in Germany) as well as Catholic University, Notre Dame University, and St. John's University (in the United States).

He is co-chairman (with David du Plessis representing the classical Pentecostals) of the International Pentecostal/Catholic dialogue, sponsored on the Catholic side by the Vatican Secretariat for Promoting Christian Unity. He has participated in similar dialogues between Roman Catholics and Lutherans, Presbyterians, and Southern Baptists. He was a guest of the World Council of Churches at the Fourth Assembly in Uppsala, Sweden (1968).

Besides frequent and continuing journal articles, he has published several books, including *John Calvin, the Church, and the Eucharist* (Princeton, NJ: Princeton University Press, 1967). Fr. McDonnell edited *The Holy Spirit and Power: The Catholic Charismatic Renewal* (Garden City, NY: Doubleday, 1975) and provided a significant assessment in *Charismatic Renewal and the Churches* (New York: Seabury, 1976). At present he is president of the Institute for Ecumenical and Cultural Research in Collegeville, Minnesota, and professor of theology at St. John's University in the same city.

In this article, Fr. McDonnell focuses on a review of the Pentecostal/Roman Catholic dialogue from a perspective early in the scheduled five-year (1972-76) series.

Classical Pentecostal/Roman Catholic Dialogue: Hopes and Possibilities

16

At Zurich-Horgen, Switzerland, June 20-24, 1972, was held the first meeting of the international dialogue between the Secretariat for Promoting Christian Unity of the Roman Catholic Church and some members of Pentecostal churches as well as participants in charismatic movements within Protestant and Orthodox churches. The present essay for the most part limits itself to remarks on the classical Pentecostal and Roman Catholic participation in the international dialogue. The concern is not to detail the meaning of this particular meeting but to elaborate the broader issues which might emerge when two such historically divergent traditions come together in this rather formal context.

The Death of Mythologies

One of the more obvious results of this kind of formal dialogue is the death of mythologies. Many Roman Catholics, if they know anything about either classical Pentecostalism or the Protestant charismatic movement, have bits of carefully preserved misinformation. Classical Pentecostalism, for instance, is thought to represent a kind of pneumatological monism, that is, a highly exaggerated, overblown doctrine of the Holy Spirit, to the point where the centrality of the Holy Spirit displaces the centrality of Christ. Though there have been cases of a one-sided doctrine of the Holy Spirit in classical Pentecostalism and in the Protestant charismatic movement, neither is typified by such an imbalance.[1] It has been one of the major contributions of David du Plessis that he has insisted on the role of Christ in the baptism of the Holy Spirit: "Jesus is the baptizer in the Holy Spirit."[2]

Indeed one of the strengths of Pentecostalism at its best is the mutuality of Jesus Christ and the Holy Spirit. That is, Jesus Christ sends the Spirit, gives the Spirit. On the other hand, it is the specific function of the Holy Spirit to lead to the confession that Jesus is Lord. The lordship of Jesus here is not understood as a theological statement on the quality of His divinity. Rather it is the language of praise, adoration, and love which places Jesus Christ at the center of religious meaning and existence. Jesus is the Alpha and the Omega, the Beginning and the End. There is no Lord other than Jesus.

---

1. Frederick Dale Bruner, *A Theology of the Holy Spirit* (Grand Rapids: Eerdmans, 1970), p. 73. The Dutch Hervormde Kerk noted that there were dangers of exaggeration in classical Pentecostalism; cf. *Herderlijk Schrijven van de Generale Synode der Nederlandse Hervormde Kerk* ('s-Gravenhage: Boekencentrum N.V., 1960), p. 35. The classical Pentecostals answered that when the Pentecostals restored the doctrine of the Holy Spirit to its rightful place at the beginning of the movement it is possible that distortions crept in. That is what happens when a forgotten truth is rediscovered. The Pentecostals do, however, recognize them as distortions; cf. *De Pinkster Gemeente en de Kerk* (Rotterdam: Stichting Volle Evangelie Lectuur, 1962), p. 10. This exchange between an historic church and a group of Pentecostal churches is a model of theological exchange. Cf. also Oswald Eggenberger, "Die Geistestaufe in der gegenwärtigen Pfingstbewegung," *Theologische Zeitschrift*, 4 (1955), 288. Eggenberger contends that in the areas of preaching and personal evangelism it cannot be said that the Pentecostals place more stress on the Holy Spirit than on Christ.

In the matter of the relationship of Christology to pneumatology, Pentecostal practice is a better source than Pentecostal doctrine. Cf. Abdalizis de Moura, "Importancia das Igrejas Pentecostais para a Igreja Catolica" (multilithed manuscript), p. 23, and "O Pentecostalismo como fenômeno religioso popular no Brasil," *Revista Eclesiástica Brasileira*, 31 (March, 1971), 82.

2. "The baptism into the Holy Spirit is not an encounter with the Spirit but with Christ, the baptizer. This means total surrender and absolute commitment to Jesus. Without this He cannot baptize you in the Spirit" (David J. du Plessis, *The Spirit Bade Me Go* [published by the author, 3742 Linwood Avenue, Oakland, CA 94602, n.d.], p. 71). Cf. also George Jeffreys, "Jesus Christ the Baptizer," *The Miraculous Foursquare Gospel*, vol. 1, *Doctrinal* (London: Elim Publishing Co., 1929), pp. 43-52.

Quite the contrary of representing a dethroning of Jesus in favor of the Spirit, much of classical Pentecostalism and also the Protestant charismatic movement represents a decided Jesus-cult.[3] If the classical movement fails at all, it is because it does not give sufficient place to the role of the Father. Except for the "Jesus-Only" Pentecostals, which is a species of Pentecostal unitarianism (and constitutes about one-fourth of American classical Pentecostals[4]), Pentecostals are generally trinitarian. However, the early Pentecostals took over the trinitarian doctrine and formulation from historic Protestantism without really understanding them.[5] The international dialogue will be an instrument by virtue of which Roman Catholics can be disabused of this particular myth.

One hopes that the death of mythologies will also mean the death in classical Pentecostalism and in the Protestant charismatic movement of the supposition that the highly structured character of Catholic ministry and liturgy means the death of the Spirit. In early Pentecostalism all structures, liturgical and organizational, were suspect. W. F. Carothers reflected the feelings of many of the early Pentecostals when he said: "We don't need rulers, all we need to do is to walk in the Spirit."[6] The pioneers saw the necessity of some manner of organization so as to avoid religious chaos, but they were clearly unhappy about this necessity.[7] After the First General Council of the Assemblies of God, one Pentecostal wrote: "This is neither the general church of the first born nor is it the local church. It is simply a voluntary and Scriptural council to stand for God between the saints. . . ."[8]

Many Pentecostal groups have long ago given up the principle of nonorganization. In fact, there are complaints that classical Pen-

3. Nils Bloch-Hoell, The Pentecostal Movement (Copenhagen: Universitetsforlaget, 1964), p. 109.

4. Harold Vinson Synan, "The Pentecostal Movement in the United States" (Ph.D. dissertation, University of Georgia, 1967), p. 205. This is omitted in the published form of the dissertation: The Holiness-Pentecostal Movement (Grand Rapids: Eerdmans, 1971).

5. Walter J. Hollenweger, The Pentecostals: The Charismatic Movement in the Churches (Minneapolis: Augsburg Publishing House, 1972), p. 311.

6. Quoted in Irvine John Harrison, "A History of the Assemblies of God" (unpublished Th.D. dissertation, Berkeley Baptist Divinity School, 1954), p. 96. Cf. also Charles W. Conn, Like a Mighty Army Moves the Church of God (Cleveland, TN: Church of God Publishing House, 1955), p. 51.

7. W. Hollenweger, Black Pentecostal Concept: Interpretations and Variations, "Papers from the Department on Studies in Evangelism, Special Issue no. 30" (Geneva: World Council of Churches, June, 1970), pp. 46f.; J. R. Flower, "History of the Assemblies of God" (multilith manuscript, n.d.), p. 19.

8. The Word and Witness (April 20, 1914), p. 4.

tecostal churches are excessively centralized in structural terms.[9] Other newer Pentecostal groups have emerged which accuse the established Pentecostal denominations of that of which the early Pentecostals had accused the historic churches, that is, of too much organization.[10] This accusation is not uniformly true. In France the opposition to organization has continued.[11]

In view of the amazing growth of independent churches in Africa it is not surprising to hear Nicholas Bhengu, the fiery black from Zululand, South Africa, saying: "That is the purpose of Pentecost. To preach Jesus. Jesus will solve all the problems. But organized Christianity—do you know what it does? It glorifies man. It uplifts dogmas. It divides the church of God. But Jesus Christ—do you know what he does? He saves!"[12] In many parts of black Africa the opposition to organization remains.

Roman Catholicism has its own pathological suppositions. But one of the pathological suppositions of Pentecostalism is that the Holy Spirit is reduced to impotence when He is faced with any structures above the local or national level, that in fact international structures are probably demonic.[13] The Holy Spirit is all-powerful and He blows where He wills. But classical Pentecostals suggest that He cannot and will not blow at the level of international structures. That is something the Spirit cannot do. This view is not uncommon among classical Pentecostals, but is especially strong among the Swedish Pentecostals.[14]

9. Donald Gee, "Contact Is Not Compromise," *Pentecost*, 53 (Sept.-Nov., 1960), 17.

10. W. Hollenweger, *Handbuch der Pfingstbewegung* (multilithed Th.D. dissertation, University of Zurich, 1965), 00.02.002.

11. H. Ch. Chery, *L'Offensive des sectes* (Paris: du Cerf, 1959), pp. 335f.

12. *Pentecostal World Conference Messages*, ed. Donald Gee (Toronto: Testimony Press, 1958), p. 92.

13. Harrison, "A History of the Assemblies of God," pp. 278-83.

14. "We wish to understand the difficulties of all brethren in different countries. All of us in Scandinavia are very much opposed to organizational ties; that is [to] strong organization. We are against it because when organization is formed, it becomes a binding element to the work in the field. Our experience is that the independent individual church is better and it is a pity to be tied. We have to respect each other's business in the Swedish Assemblies. . . . Whilst discussing this great question, we would like to say that we desire a deep spiritual unity with all the Pentecostal people" (Alvar Lindskog of Sweden, "Minutes of the Second Pentecostal World Conference, Paris, May 21-29, 1949" [published by David du Plessis, P.O. Box 328, Cleveland, TN], p. 7).

Speaking of the relationship of the Pentecostals to the World Council of Churches, Donald Gee wrote: "The Pentecostal churches are committed to the concept of the true Church being a spiritual entity composed of all who are truly in Christ by virtue of the new birth, apart from membership in an outward organization. Even among themselves they regard ecclesiastical organization with profound suspicion. . . . Only after much

I would predict that Pentecostalism will overcome its profound suspicion of all international structures. Pentecostals will undoubtedly arrive, in their own way and in their own time, at a more positive evaluation of international instruments through the same experiential perception which brought them to recognize the presence and gifts of the Spirit beyond the local congregation, that is, in national structures.

Classical Pentecostals can find justification for this move in their own early history. Many of the early Pentecostal pastors had been pastors in established denominations before they affiliated with the Pentecostal movement. What these men sought was not a purely enthusiastic community of the faithful, a church without an organizational institution. A study of four hundred biographies has shown that what they sought was a church which is prepared to set aside structural elements which have ceased to perform a function.[15] In a word, they wanted a flexible, serviceable church structure.

At the national level many Pentecostals have set aside their distrust of organizational forms because they have experienced the presence of the Spirit there where they least expected it. If classical Pentecostals come to accept some measure of international Pentecostal life it will be for the same reason: they experience the Spirit present there where they were sure He would not be found. In no sense will this mean the erection of an international Pentecostal hierarchy, or a centralized authority at the world level. Whatever form it will take will have to be thoroughly Pentecostal in character. This form will undoubtedly be quite different from the structural forms found in the World Council of Churches.

If and when the classical Pentecostals do adopt some form of international life, it would be well for them not to forget to remind themselves and Roman Catholics of the valid insight of their pioneers. Both Pentecostals and Roman Catholics need to be reminded that when the structure becomes turned in on itself, when the scaffolding of organization becomes the core of the gospel and the mechanics of

---

disputing was it found possible to establish the triennial World Pentecostal Conferences, when any attempt thereby to form a world Pentecostal organization was formally repudiated. The triennial conferences are quite open, and their only formal business is the appointment of an advisory committee to arrange for the next one. Therefore, they hold that a movement confessedly aiming at ultimately arriving at a visible world Church embracing all denominations is wrong in concept and pursuing a mistaken policy" ("The Pentecostal Churches and the World Council of Churches," *Pentecost*, 67 [March-May, 1964], 16f.).

15. W. Hollenweger, *The Pentecostals*, p. 480.

clerical existence become the reason for the church's mission, then structures and organization do become "flesh." In such circumstances Rome *does* become Antichrist, the great whore of Babylon. And so does Springfield, Missouri; Franklin Springs, Georgia; Cleveland, Tennessee; and Joplin, Missouri. Any theological instrumentality which becomes an end in itself *is* Antichrist. This insight of the early Pentecostals should not be lost in a more ecumenical era.

Reassessing Christian Initiation

Another result of the international dialogue will be a re-examination on the part of Roman Catholic theologians of the rite of initiation. My personal conviction is that the history of the rite of initiation—which in its early form included what is now baptism, confirmation, and the Eucharist—will show that the basic Pentecostal realities to which classical Pentecostalism and the rest of the charismatic movement witness are already present there in the theological core.[16] This will make it much easier for Roman Catholicism at the international level to accommodate itself to Pentecostalism. Roman Catholics have only to recognize the full reality which is already part of their heritage.

The only thing Roman Catholics have to borrow from classical Pentecostalism, and it is a borrowing of great importance, is the willingness to let the Spirit come to visibility in the full spectrum of His gifts. Of course, this is not to say that the Holy Spirit and His gifts have been absent from Roman Catholicism. Not even classical Pentecostals, at least those who know us well, will tolerate such a position.[17] It does mean that there are certain gifts of the Spirit which, in terms of Roman Catholic expectancy, awareness, and openness, were not really possibilities.

16. In a preliminary way this has been done from a Roman Catholic and Lutheran perspective in Kilian McDonnell and Arnold Bittlinger, *The Baptism in the Holy Spirit as an Ecumenical Problem* (Notre Dame, IN: Charismatic Renewal Services, 1972).

17. The attitude of classical Pentecostals to Roman Catholics needs some nuancing. In Chile and parts of Mexico one can find classical Pentecostals who do not consider Catholics to be Christian. For Chile see Christian Lalive d'Epinay, *Haven of the Masses* (New York: Friendship Press, 1969), p. 179. In Brazil a well educated Pentecostal felt that the role of the World Council of Churches was to lead the Protestants back to Rome. In Italy the classical Pentecostals, with the notable exception of Dr. John Mc-Ternan, president (until his untimely death in 1975) of the Chiesa Evangelica Internazionale, have a difficult time forgetting the years when they were persecuted. Especially do they remember the years when the Roman Church enlisted the aid of the Fascists against the Pentecostals. This has been written up by a Roman Catholic lawyer, Ciacomo Rosapepe, *Inquisizione Addomesticata* (Bari: Editori Laterza, 1960). The

Except for certain sovereign acts of God when He crushes one's defenses, God acts in accordance with a person's awareness, expectations, and openness. If in terms of giving visibility to the Spirit the expectation of a Christian extends from A to P, then that is all he will experience. God respects the Christian and takes him as he is. The specific contribution of classical Pentecostals to Roman Catholics is to help them expand their spiritual awareness, expectations, and openness so that they do not extend from A to P but from A to Z. With expanded expectations Roman Catholics can then let the Holy Spirit come to visibility along the whole range of His gifts.[18] The expanded awareness is not the bestowing of the Holy Spirit, for He has been present from the time of initiation.

The contribution therefore of classical Pentecostals to Roman Catholics is not to lead them to locate the baptism in the Holy Spirit in some extrasacramental moment, but to lead Roman Catholics (and all those who belong to the liturgical churches) to an expanded expectation.

presence of Dr. McTernan in Rome gave reason to hope that the classical Pentecostals would forgive the Roman Church the real injuries they suffered.

My research trip to parts of Africa showed that classical Pentecostals are adopting new attitudes. W. C. Cornelius, a Canadian Pentecostal doing missionary work in Nairobi, Kenya, once doubted that Roman Catholics could "receive the baptism in the Holy Spirit" while remaining members of the Roman Church. "If they have not been saved how could they receive the baptism?" Now he is convinced that Roman Catholics can be "saved" even while remaining within the Roman Church. The author's visit to Pretoria, South Africa, August 7, 1970, was the occasion for the largest gathering ever of pastors from the Apostolic Faith Mission and Full Gospel Church of God of Southern Africa. Though there were some expressions of the traditional polemic the meeting was typified by openness. I was also received with great friendliness by a regional meeting of the Assemblées de Dieu in Burgundy, France, in October of 1971. The classical Pentecostals showed a more ecumenical spirit than did the local pastors of the Roman Church. In Spain the situation of Pentecostals seems to have changed. Classical Pentecostals mixed with Roman Catholics with great freedom at a meeting in Salamanca in 1970; cf. Mauric Villain, "Semaine Oecumenique à l'Université de Salamanque," *Figaro*, Sept. 8; 1970. There were classical Pentecostals present at Salamanca who were so aggressive in their witnessing that it was interpreted as proselytizing. With tongue in cheek the London *Tablet* reported: "Some practised faith healing in Plaza Mayor—a dangerous procedure, for Spanish law forbids non-Catholics to perform miracles in public" ("Pentecostals in Salamanca," *The Tablet*, Sept. 12, 1970, p. 895). I also lectured at a national meeting of classical Pentecostals and charismatics in Nijmegen, Holland, in October, 1971. There was little evidence of old antagonisms. The history of Pentecostal-Roman Catholic contacts in Holland goes further back than in most countries. This in part is due to the ecumenical nature of the magazine *Vuur*, in which Roman Catholic authors regularly appeared. Cf. also J. Zeegers, "Het Volle Evangelie in de R. K. Kerk," *De Pinksterboodschap*, 3 (April, 1962), 13.

18. This aspect is treated more fully in my essay in *The Baptism in the Holy Spirit as an Ecumenical Problem* (Notre Dame, IN: Charismatic Renewal Services, 1972), 41-51.

To expand their consciousness will be a major step for Roman Catholics, and not without its peculiar kind of pain. Most of us Roman Catholics think that there is nothing wrong with our present expectations. However, classical Pentecostals will be called to suffer their own particular kind of ecumenical pain. Without compromising their own doctrine of the baptism in the Holy Spirit they will be asked to recognize that the Spirit can really blow where He wills. This is to say that the reality of the baptism in the Holy Spirit can be found in a highly structured sacramental liturgical context. Further they will be asked to recognize that one who has been baptized as an infant may come into the fullness of the Spirit only later in life when as an adult he says an unambiguous "yes" to what happened in his infant baptism. In no sense does this mean that classical Pentecostals will have to adopt infant baptism, or consider it an absolute ideal. Rather it means that they will have to recognize that for Roman Catholics, this is a valid, authentic way of meeting God.

The Expansion of Faith

Personal Dimensions, for Roman Catholics

A further effect of the international dialogue will be a re-evaluation on the part of Roman Catholics of the personal dimensions of faith. Roman Catholics have to rediscover what it means to say that the act of faith finds its termination not in a truth but in a person: "Everyone who believes assents to someone's words; and thus, in any form of belief, it seems that it is the person to whose words the assent is given who is of principal importance and, as it were, the end; while the individual truths through which one assents to that person are secondary."[19] To terminate in a person means to terminate in the personal life of God, in His self-giving.

The personal dimensions of faith would demand that for an adult Christian, and necessarily for an adult Roman Catholic, there is no commitment by proxy. As an adult one cannot be a Christian on the basis of a commitment made by one's father or mother. This is not a rejection of infant baptism. However, when one who was baptized as an infant becomes an adult he must say his own "yes." As an adult, one cannot live off the commitment made for one as an infant. As an adult one cannot be a Christian by proxy.

19. St. Thomas, *Summa Theologica*, II, II, q. 11, a. 1. Cf. Jean Claude Mouroux, *The Meaning of Man* (New York: Sheed and Ward, 1958), and *I Believe: The Personal Structure of Faith* (New York: Sheed and Ward, 1959).

Social Dimensions, for Pentecostals

One would hope that just as Catholics re-evaluate the personal dimensions of faith, classical Pentecostals would re-evaluate the social dimensions. Could not classical and Protestant charismatics follow the example of Manoel de Mello and re-examine what the gospel has to say about subsistence living, inadequate housing, race relations and war? De Mello asks:

> What is the use of converting a person only to send him back to the rotten Brazilian society . . . ? While we convert a million, the devil de-converts ten millions through hunger, misery, militarism, dictatorship—and the churches remain complacent. Atheism is on the increase due to the conditions of injustice and misery in which the people are living. Preachers are preaching about a far distant future and forget the fact that Jesus valued and gave close attention to the time in which people lived. . . . The Church has arrived at the point where, in the present situation, it has nothing more to offer. It brings people together, sings a hymn, prays, delivers a sermon and then lets people go their own way. That is to say, the people are not challenged to undertake a serious task within the structures of society. . . . Actually I do not see a single preacher who is proclaiming the Gospel in all its fulness and purity, because the Gospel has a revolutionary content that is violently opposed to injustice.[20]

Manoel de Mello brought his church, "Brasil para Cristo," into the World Council of Churches, not because the WCC had much to teach the classical Pentecostals from the specifically religious and spiritual point of view. Indeed in this area, said de Mello, the classical Pentecostals "are in the jet age," while the WCC "is riding a bicycle."[21] The reason why de Mello sought membership was that he thought that the Pentecostals had much to gain from the social programs of the WCC. The WCC "is doing tremendous work such as we are not able to do with all our religiosity: a gigantic work of social action."[22] To show that he was willing to go beyond words he accepted two suggestions made to him by the University of Chicago: "Why not set up agricultural schools in some of the uncultivated areas of Brazil? Why not transform the hundreds of church buildings into schools during week days, and even into trade unions and associations in order to train the people?"[23] It should be remembered that de Mello represents an important and fast-growing Pentecostal church in

---

20. "Participation Is Everything: Evangelism from the Point of View of a Brazilian Pentecostal," *International Review of Missions*, 60 (April, 1971), 247f.

21. Ibid., p. 247.

22. Ibid.

23. Ibid., p. 248.

Brazil, and he therefore speaks with some authority within South American Pentecostalism.

In asking the classical Pentecostals to re-evaluate the social dimensions of the gospel the impression should not be given that Pentecostal history is devoid of social concern. One could mention social action programs which classical Pentecostals have initiated in Brazil, Chile, Russia, Sweden, Indonesia.[24] In the United States there is the Teen Challenge movement with its rather impressive record of drug rehabilitation.[25]

But there is a kind of intramural, "churchy" quality about much of the Pentecostal social action programs, especially in the English-speaking countries. Donald Gee was expressing his impatience with a view of evangelization which was too narrowly revivalistic when he wrote:

> The pietistic principle that the only purpose of evangelism is to pluck individual souls as brands from the burning and gather them into separated little congregations out of the world will not satisfy the outlook of a new generation of Pentecostal leadership. There has been some strong criticism that our big conferences usually have no pronouncement to make upon the burning issues of the day, such as war, race, sex, youth, atheism, want, etc. It is easier to live in a ghetto, but is it the will of God? Are we to be called "Pentecostal" and yet have little impact upon human affairs? It is not enough to be always condemnatory. It is time to be constructive.[26]

24. W. Hollenweger, *The Pentecostals*, pp. 79-81; 90f.; 107f.; 133-36; 467-72. Cf. also Katesa Schlosser, *Eingeborenenkirchen in Süd- und Südwest-Afrika: Ihre Geschichte und Sozialstruktur* (Kiel: Kommissionsverlag Walter G. Mühlau, 1958), pp. 25-58; d'Epinay, *Haven of the Masses*, pp. 125-27; Synan, *The Holiness-Pentecostal Movement*, p. 204.

25. Kilian McDonnell, "Pentecostals and Drug Addiction," *America*, 118 (March 30, 1968), 402-06. An unbiased judgment can be found in Angela Kitzinger and Patricia J. Hill, *Drug Abuse: A Source Book and Guide for Teachers* (Sacramento: California State Department of Education, 1967), p. 71: "Teen Challenge, a group that exists in California as well as elsewhere in the country, stems from the work of Rev. David Wilkerson with teen-age addicts in New York. Teen Challenge has a religious basis and has been eminently successful in developing within youthful addicts a constructive view of their individual potential. Houses have been established by the group for the rehabilitation of youthful addicts in areas where the incidence of narcotic use is high.

"The President's Advisory Commission (appointed by President Kennedy in 1962) mentions the need for scientific evaluation of the work of these and other private groups. Some of them appear to be achieving good results, and their activities should be encouraged."

There are now fifty-five "official" Teen Challenge Centers. There are some problems trying to harmonize interdenominational financial support with their status of being a recognized ministry of the Assemblies of God. Cf. "A Time of Reflection," *The Pentecostal Evangel*, 3057 (Dec. 10, 1972), 22f.

26. "Remote or Realistic?" *Pentecost*, 68 (June-Aug., 1964), 17.

Heribert Mühlen has suggested that the role of the Spirit in the Old Testament was the unity of Israel, while the role of the Spirit in the New Testament is the unity of the whole of mankind.

If the classical Pentecostals would embrace the social dimension not as a strategic maneuver but because it belongs to the full gospel, then classical Pentecostalism would be a force far beyond its now not inconsiderable effectiveness. The historic churches would not write off classical Pentecostalism as a return to a gospel of undiluted inwardness and interiority but would see in classical Pentecostalism the justice of the claim that it is preaching the full gospel.

Sanctification: Growth or Crisis?

The international dialogue will force the Roman Catholic Church and the classical Pentecostals as well as the Protestant charismatics to examine typologies of sanctification other than their own. The classical Pentecostal doctrine of sanctification is typified by *crisis* categories. Though the concept of growth in the Spirit is by no means foreign to Pentecostals, they think more typically in the category of peak experience than in the category of development. God breaks into the life of the true seeker, and this invasion from above is experiential in nature. It can be dated as to the year, month, day, hour, and located as to the room where it all happened. The presupposition for such a doctrine of sanctification is frequently a two-level world view. God and the supernatural are up there and the natural, which is sometimes identified with the flesh, is down here. God makes sorties into history and into the souls of those who are open to Him.

Indeed this perceptible, experienced presence is one of the major threads which run through the whole of classical Pentecostalism and bind the movement together. More than any other doctrinal tenet this sense of presence forms the basis of Pentecostal unity.

The nature of this presence is not the same as found in Roman Catholic devotional literature or in manuals of meditation.[27] One finds in such sources a recommendation to practice the presence of God. Various methods are suggested. What is called "corporal presence" is effected by looking at some sensible object (the stars, a flower, a fountain, the sea, a light) and using the object as a means of projecting the mind to God, who is present in the object by His power and essence. Or there is "imaginative presence," an exercise in which one sum-

---

27. Adolphe Tanquerey, *The Spiritual Life: A Treatise on Ascetical and Mystical Theology* (Tournai: Desclee, 1930), pp. 219-21; Gustav Thils, *Christian Holiness: A Précis of Ascetical Theology* (Tielt, Belgium: Lannoo Publishers, 1961), p. 617.

mons up an imaginative picture or looks at a holy picture, making believe that it is not a mere representation but that God is really present. "Intellectual presence" uses reason and faith to focus on God present by reason of His immensity and by grace. Finally, there is "affective presence," which elicits some act (love, adoration, trust) toward God as the Present One, and thus enters into communication with Him.[28] As can be seen, the practice of the presence of God in this sense has to do with an act of the will, a focusing of attention.

The sense of presence in the Pentecostal typology of sanctification also has to do with acts of the will and focusing of attention, but it is far more a "givenness" which is experienced. The presence of God is not only perceived by the intellect to be real and made an object of desire by the will, but it is experienced with some immediacy.

Even though somewhat lengthy, two accounts of baptism in the Holy Spirit will be given here. The first, which occurred in 1912, is not untypical of the older Pentecostal experience with its more pronounced motor manifestations. I do not call into radical doubt the authenticity of the experience but suggest that there is much cultural conditioning in these manifestations, and in the manner of speaking about them. Today the pronounced motor manifestations would arouse in many classical Pentecostals the same suspicions they arouse in other Christians. In this regard uneducated Pentecostals not infrequently have an unexpected sophistication and are not taken in by the drama of external manifestations:

> On January twenty-eight at half-past ten, Jesus fulfilled his promise and baptized me with the Holy Ghost. This is the greatest experience of my life. . . . I could feel how my shoulder jerked; at the same time something like an electrical current entered into my body and flowed through my whole being. I understood that the Holy Ghost had approached me. I felt how the lower part of my body trembled, and I felt how involuntary movements and extraordinary power flowed through my body. Through this power the trembling increased, and so also the awe of my prayers. . . . My speech melted in my mouth and the silent prayer became louder and louder and was transformed into a foreign language. I felt dizzy. My hands, which were folded for prayer, were thrown against the head of the bed. I was not myself anymore. In spite of this I was not unaware of what was happening. My tongue jerked so strongly that I feared that it would be torn out of my mouth. But I could not open my mouth with my own power. All of a sudden I felt how my mouth was opened and words in a foreign language streamed out. In the beginning quietly,

28. Joseph de Guibert, *The Theology of the Spiritual Life* (New York: Sheed and Ward, 1953), p. 251.

but then with increasing volume, my voice poured forth words like a stream from my lips. The voice became louder and still louder. At the beginning it was beautiful, but then it was changed into a terrible lamentation and I felt myself weeping. I was like a horn into which one was blowing. Before me there was a great opening. I cried into it and I understood the meaning of the words which I spoke. This speaking and singing lasted about ten minutes, according to the reports of persons in an adjoining room. When it was finished it was very quiet and an almost noiseless prayer in a foreign language followed. . . . After this my soul was filled with an unspeakable feeling of happiness and bliss. I could not do otherwise than give thanks aloud. The feeling of the nearness of God was as wonderful as if heaven had come to earth, and heaven was in my soul.[29]

The second account is from the Second World War. Here the socio-cultural matrix is quite different. Pentecostalism in the United States had itself undergone a marked change. It was during the Second World War that classical Pentecostalism in the United States moved up from the lower socio-economic groups into middle-class America. The experience of the presence is much the same and the motor manifestations are also present, but more controlled. This testimony was given by a sailor who had been attracted by the fervent faith of a group of sailors on his carrier:

I had to lay aside my own ideas in order to receive the infilling of the Holy Spirit. I had to accept it on God's terms. And God's terms for me were that I go back there with that group of loud-praying Christians. I had to humble myself and let them pray for me.

I didn't know much about the Holy Spirit. I had heard one of my buddies tell of one of the boys who was slain under the power of God and he had fallen to the deck under the power of the Spirit. I knew how hard that flight deck was, so when I finally went back to the prayer meeting that night I said, "Lord you won't have to knock me down; I am going to lie down on the deck to start with!" And I did. It may seem humorous now, but I was completely serious. In my hunger for God I did the simple act of lying down on the deck and lifting my heart and hands to the Lord Jesus.

I wasn't there long until a boy whom I had won to Christ a few months before but who had received the Baptism before I did, he came over and put his hands on me. The Lord began to pour forth His Spirit in great torrents of blessing. If I had the vocabulary of Webster it would be insufficient to explain the joy, the blessing, the new dimension of praise in worship, the new comprehension of divine truth, the new appreciation of the Cross, the increased devotion to the Christ who died for my salvation which came as a result of my infilling.

29. Wolfgang Schmidt, *Die Pfingstbewegung in Finnland*, "Finska Kyrkohistoriska Samfundets, Handlingar XXVII" (Helsingfors: Centraltryckeriet, 1935), pp. 114-17.

Hour after hour, it was as if a waterfall was falling on me in Spirit; it was as if liquid love penetrated me all the way through as I praised in the Spirit. I worshipped Him in a language I never learned. I felt this great liberty to praise Jesus as I'd always wanted to but never could. I felt the Holy Spirit flow through me in a divine electricity, or a divine energy current—current after current until I didn't feel like I could stand any more and yet there was no desire at all that it would stop. It was a glorious meeting—a glorious revelation that he did to my heart until about two o'clock in the morning. That was the beginning of the Spirit walk.

When we receive the Baptism, we don't jump from a buck private to a four star general overnight, but we do become officer material. The Baptism of the Spirit isn't a goal, it's only a gateway. If we walk in obedience to the captain of our salvation, He will lead us into the deep things of God.[30]

In these two accounts God is not only perceived as real: He is experienced as effectively real. He is not only understood as being present, but He is experienced as effectively present. He is experienced as the God who acts now. The great sense of the immediacy of God in personal terms gives rise to two other elements in the Pentecostal typology of sanctification: prayer and praise.

If the sense of presence is the one element which binds together the whole of the classical Pentecostal world, more so than any doctrinal tenet, then one must say that the most typical act of the Pentecostal is a response to presence in the form of prayer. The invasion from above becomes the fountain of living water springing up from within, and thus becomes internalized, and is manifested by a great love of prayer.

Further, because presence is personal and focused on the lordship of Jesus the prayers are vocalized in proclamation of that lordship. In this the Holy Spirit is more than an external facilitator, one who inspires from without or who aids the prayer by a series of graces. Rather as the fountain of living water which is within, the Holy Spirit from within leads the believer to the recognition of the lordship of Jesus. This lordship is also an interior quality and not simply an external rule and dominion. The lordship of Jesus is a modality of the presence. It is a rule and reign from within. This mutuality of Jesus and the Holy Spirit is a model for the intimate relationship between Pentecostal Christology and pneumatology.

The response to presence in the form of prayer takes the specific form of the prayer of praise. The wonder of a God who is so im-

---

30. Quoted from Luther P. Gerlach and Virginia H. Hine, *People, Power, Change: Movement of Social Transformation* (Indianapolis: Bobbs-Merrill, 1970), pp. 120f.

mediately real and accessible finds its appropriate response in praise. Not a formal kind of praise, but a deeply personal prayer of praise. This is attached to the recognition that God cares and loves. Praise is the answer to the wonder of that realization. But beyond this kind of internalized praise, there is an objective element to Pentecostal prayer. God is praised and glorified not just in relation to needs. The prayer of praise is focused on the glory of God's personal existence. This more objective side of Pentecostal piety is frequently forgotten. The piety is not infrequently presented in purely subjective, ego-centered terms.

It is obvious that the practice of the presence of God in this Pentecostal sense is not the same as the Roman Catholic devotional practice of the presence of God with its methods of focusing on sensible objects, summoning up an imaginative picture, considering by faith that God dwells in us, and eliciting an affective act toward God as present. The Pentecostal sense of presence is much more a "givenness," and in this sense the presence can be found in the Roman mystical tradition in the higher states of transforming union and mystical marriage, where it is a "givenness" in the sense of a gift strictly infused.[31]

But the Pentecostal sense of presence is not a rare gift, reserved for those few who have been raised to the highest states of prayer. Quite the contrary. The classical Pentecostals warn against thinking that something extraordinary has happened. "It is simply a common Christian experience, something that belongs to the first principles and first stages of a Christian life."[32]

This also seems to have been the way the New Testament looked upon the experience of God as the Present One.[33] The Pentecostal experience of the outpouring of the Spirit was what made a man a Christian (Rom. 5:5). This was not something one could have and be unaware of it.[34]

Both the Spirit and the gifts of the Spirit were facts of experience in the lives of the earliest Christians. This is so obvious from the biblical text that it need not be labored.[35] Within the Catholic charismatic

31. de Guibert, *The Theology of the Spiritual Life*, p. 249.

32. Levi Pethrus, *The Wind Bloweth Where It Listeth* (Minneapolis: Bethany Fellowship, 1968), p. 19.

33. James D. G. Dunn, *Baptism in the Holy Spirit, Studies in Biblical Theology*, Series 2, 15 (Naperville, IL: Aleç Allenson, 1970), pp. 51, 52, 58, 105, 113, 121, 124, 132, 133, 138, 149, 172, 225.

34. Ibid., p. 133.

35. John 3:8; 4:14; 7:38f.; 16:7; Acts 2:4; 4:31; 9:31; 10:44-46; 13:52; 19:6; Rom. 5:5;

movement there is a recognition of the essentially initiatory quality of this experience, that is, that it is not a matter of an exceptional grace. But one also finds that the prayer gifts which the experience brings, though of a lower order, are not unlike what is given in infused contemplation. It is possible that the door which the experience opens is entered and, indeed, gone beyond so that, as Fr. O'Connor contends, some receive graces of infused contemplation.[36]

The crisis categories of the classical Pentecostal doctrine of sanctification make it difficult for non-Pentecostals to appreciate the profundity of the classical Pentecostal insight. Moreover, historical Protestantism and Roman Catholicism remember the excesses of the revivalist tradition which dominated much of American Protestantism in the last century.[37] What many within the historic Protestant and Roman churches do not know is that within classical Pentecostalism there were from the very beginning those within the movement who, recognizing the excesses, lamented and denounced them. Not untypical in English-speaking and other European countries is the position of David du Plessis:

> Let me say right here that I consider it heresy to speak of shaking, trembling, falling, dancing, clapping, shouting, and such actions as manifestations of the Holy Spirit. These are purely human reactions to the power of the Holy Spirit and frequently hinder more than help to bring forth genuine manifestations. There are far too many Christians who are satisfied with such emotional reactions and thus do not seek to grow in grace and become channels through whom

8:1-16; 1 Cor. 12:7, 13; 2 Cor. 3:6; 5:5; Gal. 4:6; 5:16-18, 25; 1 Thess. 1:5f.; Titus 3:5f. Cf. summary statement of Dunn, *Baptism in the Holy Spirit*, p. 225.

36. "I am convinced that some grace of infused contemplation has been given to quite a number of these people. This is what explains the joy with which they pray, and the fact that, with little or no previous training in mental prayer, many of them suddenly find themselves able to pray for extended periods of time simply by placing themselves in the presence of God and abiding there quietly, wordlessly, lovingly . . . " (Edward D. O'Connor, *The Pentecostal Movement in the Catholic Church* [Notre Dame, IN: Ave Maria Press, 1971], p. 153). "Moreover, speaking in tongues is a form of prayer (cf. 1 Cor. 14:13f.). Paul says in Romans 8:26-27 that the Spirit helps us in our weakness, for we know not how to pray as we ought, so the Spirit himself intercedes for us. This is not unlike a kind of infused contemplation" (Matthew Killian, "Speaking in Tongues," *The Priest*, 25 [Nov. 1969], 611).

37. Sidney E. Mead, "Denominationalism: The Shape of Protestantism in America," *Church History*, 23 (1954), 306-11; Winfred E. Garrison, *The March of Faith* (Westport, CT: Greenwood Press, 1933), pp. 73-82, and "Characteristics of American Organized Religion," *The Annals of the American Academy of Political and Social Science*, 256 (March, 1948), 20; Bernard A. Weisberger, *They Gathered at the River* (Chicago: Quadrangle Books, 1958), pp. 20-50.

the Holy Spirit may manifest His gift for the edification of the church.[38]

The revivalist tradition, however, is historically linked to classical Pentecostalism through its ties with the Holiness movement.[39] Historic Protestantism will not easily forget the excesses of that tradition and the churches are sure, whatever other doubts they have, that they do not want to go down that road again. Catholics, especially through the writings of John of the Cross and Teresa of Avila, have inherited a tradition which is systematically suspicious of any religious experience.[40] Neither historic Protestantism nor Roman Catholicism is much disposed to give a fair hearing to any religious system which incorporates the experiential dimension.[41]

The experiential is admittedly open to deception and self-delusion and where one finds religious experience a measure of scepticism is always in place, but the antidote to dangers arising from religious ex-

---

38. *The Spirit Bade Me Go*, p. 93. Cf. also "Die Hamburger Dezember-Konferenz," *Pfingstgrüsse*, 1 (Feb., 1909), 7; "Wie Schützen wir uns vor falschen Weissagungen?" *Pfingstgrüsse*, 2 (July 10, 1910), 137; F. Boerwinkel, "De Pinkstergroepen," *Oekumenische Leergang*, no. 5 (no date), 11; Melvin Hodges, *Spiritual Gifts* (Springfield, MO: Gospel Publishing House, 1964), p. 8; Donald Gee, "The Pentecostal Churches and the World Council of Churches," *Pentecost*, 67 (March-May, 1964), inside front page.

39. It is a special concern of Vinson Synan, *The Holiness-Pentecostal Movement*, to show that relationship.

40. Kilian McDonnell, "Catholic Pentecostalism: Problems in Evaluation," *Dialog*, 9 (Winter, 1970), 37, 38. This evaluation, originally written for the Bishops' Commission on Ecumenical and Inter-religious Affairs for distribution to the American Roman Catholic bishops, was later issued as a pamphlet by Dove Publications, Pecos, NM 87552.

41. Though classical Pentecostals have tended to adopt more formal modes of worship, though they even have ministers' manuals in which are to be found suggested forms for burial and marriage services, yet there remains a distrust of formal liturgy. Thomas Johnstone, past General Superintendent of the Assemblies of God of Canada, in a speech given at the Ninth Pentecostal World Conference, November 5, 1970, said that when a church becomes lukewarm the first thing it turns to is ceremonies and man-made traditions.

Within the Roman tradition the ideal liturgical celebration would be one in which there is both form and freedom. But the form in fact became not only dominant but exclusive.

There is a certain justification for classical Pentecostals esteeming their free worship tradition so highly. Already in 1929 H. Richard Niebuhr had said that the reason for the continued growth of the Pentecostal movement was to be found in its rejection of the intellectual, fixed and frozen worship services of the traditional churches in favor of the spontaneous, and sometimes primitive piety. See *The Social Sources of Denominationalism* (New York: World Publishing Co., 1929), p. 30. In places like Canada, the United States, South Africa, the social situation of Pentecostals is now quite different from what it was in 1929 and therefore the more primitive, spontaneous forms will have to be modified.

perience can hardly be the a priori exclusion of the whole experiential aspect of Christianity. Such an exclusion may act as a safeguard against emotionalism, subjectivism, and the "privatization" of religion, but it also brings with it a species of religious rationalism with its concomitant poverty. What, for instance, would Roman Catholicism do with the whole mystical tradition if such an a priori exclusion were taken seriously? Could the full history of Roman Catholicism be told were the experiential simply excised from that history? The answer is obviously "no." But because of the radical rejection of revivalism and pietism by historic Protestantism and because of the suspicion of religious experience on the part of the Roman Catholic Church, both traditions have found it very difficult to hear what their brothers in the classical Pentecostal churches and in the Protestant charismatic movements have been saying.

These suspicions have made it very difficult for many Protestants and Roman Catholics to take seriously the crisis categories of Pentecostal sanctification. The tendency has been to dismiss the peak experiences, the sense of presence, and the joy in the prayer of praise as instant contemplation and emotional excesses. Classical Pentecostals have made it easy for other Protestants and for Roman Catholics to take this attitude because they have classified historic Protestantism as dead formalism and Roman Catholicism as ritual magic.[42] In this polemic atmosphere non-Pentecostals have not been able to judge Pentecostalism dispassionately. It does however seem both unrealistic and wanting in theological discernment for the non-Pentecostal world to write off the deep commitment, profound prayer life, and exceptional growth of classical Pentecostalism, which represents, to speak only of the classical Pentecostals, from fifteen to thirty-five million people. Hopefully, the international dialogue will be instrumental in bringing Roman Catholics to recognize that crisis sanctification is an authentic way to meet and walk with God.

Classical Pentecostals have parallel problems with the Roman Catholic doctrine of sanctification, which is cast in growth categories. Though the growth dimension is not entirely absent from most classical Pentecostal doctrines of sanctification, the large emphasis in Catholicism on gradual unfolding and an ongoing process of sanctification seems to Pentecostals to lack both the eminently personal moment of commitment and a real personal meeting with Christ.

The sacramental objectivism of Catholicism, especially as seen in

---

42. Such a belief is not peculiar to classical Pentecostals but is found among other evangelical groups.

the practice of infant baptism, seems to classical Pentecostals to be a sign of a cultural Catholicism where the formalities of objective rites, liturgical formulas and hierarchical ministries have precedence over personal appropriation and personal witness. The absence of the crisis experience suggests to them that possibly Roman Catholics "do not know the Lord."[43] Since Catholic initiation occurs at infant baptism instead of at the moment of personal conscious commitment, Pentecostals wonder what there is to develop and grow. The species of objectivism found in Roman Catholic baptismal practice is so foreign to the personal, experiential modes of Pentecostal thought that Pentecostals often wonder how it is possible to become Christian within this framework. When classical Pentecostals come to know Roman Catholics personally, they sometimes come to the realization that Catholics do "know the Lord" though they still deplore the lack of the more experiential meeting.

Classical Pentecostals are more accustomed to validating religious realities by spiritual discernment, that is, experientially. Though they will have major problems accepting as valid even for Roman Catholics the practice of infant baptism, they will very likely have fewer problems accepting Roman Catholic growth categories than Roman Catholics will have accepting crisis categories. The reason for this comparative ease is their ability to authenticate experientially. The international dialogue may possibly help them to move from the experiential level to the theological level in this matter. Were this to take place, they might recognize that the objectivities of Roman Catholicism constitute an authentic, though not exclusive, way of meeting God.

Rethinking Ecumenical Notions

Finally, it is possible that formal dialogue will help both Roman Catholics and classical Pentecostals to rethink their ecumenical presuppositions. Roman Catholics have quite generally given up the vocabulary of "return." They no longer say that the ultimate will of God for His church is that the Protestants return to the Roman Catholic fold. Rather, they speak of the coming together of churches. However, though the *vocabulary* is not that of return, the *mentality* often is. Mere semantic changes are not helpful, and indeed, are damaging to the cause when they falsely represent the reality to which they point. Roman Catholics have some rethinking to do in this area.

43. In many places, Roman Catholics are not considered to be Christians. Cf. "Aggressive Evangelism," *Elim Evangel*, 44 (March 16, 1963), 167.

At the Assemblies of God Council on Spiritual Life held in Minneapolis, August 14, 1972, there was given a charismatic study report by the Executive Presbytery on the growth of the charismatic movement in other churches, especially in the Roman Church. After enumerating what it considered to be the marks of the genuine moving of the Holy Spirit,[44] the study report continued:

> The Assemblies of God wishes to identify with what God is doing in the world today. We recognize that no existing organization fully represents the body of Christ. Neither do we believe that for all true Christians—whether Pentecostal in doctrine and practice or not—to align themselves with an existing organization or a new one, will bring the unity of the Spirit. We do believe in the institution of the Church. We trust the Holy Spirit to bring the members of Christ's body into a true unity of the Spirit. If there is yet a truth to be revealed to the Church, it is the essential unity of the Body of Christ, which transcends but does not destroy existing organizational bounds.[45]

One could agree that the scaffolding of organizational life will not of itself bring unity in the Spirit. Both classical Pentecostals and Roman Catholics agree that the primary locus of unity is an interior reality, not an external structure. Unity of faith and life in the Spirit is the essential basis of all unity. But does not visibility play some role in unity? Classical Pentecostals urge Roman Catholics to let come to visibility the life of the Spirit and the full range of the gifts of the Spirit. So in principle they accept visibility as an authentic manifestation of the Spirit. Cannot organizational structures, however secondary, *also* be visible expressions of that unity in faith and in the Spirit which Christians might come to have?

Further, could not some very loose association of churches, which would not be the church, be a secondary instrument in bringing about mutual understanding and ultimately unity in faith and the Spirit? This is the function of the World Council of Churches, which, it repeats somewhat wearily, is not a church. The suspicion of organizational structures in an ecumenical context is deep in the classical Pentecostal ethos,[46] though some have overcome it and en-

---

44. "Emphasis on worship in spirit and in truth of almighty God; recognition of the person of Christ—His deity, His incarnation and His redemptive work; recognition of the authority of the hunger for the Word of God; emphasis on the person and work of the Holy Spirit; emphasis on the Second Coming of Christ; emphasis on prayer for the sick; emphasis on sharing Christ in witnessing and evangelism."

45. *Minutes of the Thirty-Fifth General Council of the Assemblies of God* (Miami Beach, Florida, Aug. 16-21, 1973), p. 80.

46. K. Van Balen, "De Plaats van de Goddelijke Genezing in de Gemeente von Christus," *De Pinkster Boodschap*, 3 (June-July, 1962), 4. Justus de Plessis of South

tered the WCC. If the tightly structured institutional unity of the Assemblies of God was seen by some American classical Pentecostals to be an instrument for the mission of the church, would not loose organizational relationships possibly be a means to a gathering of all into one flock and one Shepherd? Further, when all are of the same Spirit, having essentially the same faith, would not some kind of visibility be proper? Should not oneness of faith have a visible expression as an effective tool of evangelization and witness? This is not "mere" organization. It is the community life in the Spirit coming to visibility. Visibility is also of the Spirit.

Here I see that the classical Pentecostals too have a semantic problem. Many have come to accept organizational life at the national level as a tool of the Spirit, yet they talk as though ecumenical organizational unity were of the flesh. They also turn their suspicion of ecumenical structures of organization into a principle, namely, that even if Christians attained unity in the Spirit and unity of faith, visible organizational unity would still not be desirable. This is asserted so often one might suppose it stood at the core of the gospel.

It is at this point that I think that the Roman Church has adopted an attitude which is basically more charismatic and more pneumatological. At the end of the *Decree on Ecumenism* are found these words: "This most sacred Synod urgently desires that the initiatives of the sons of the Catholic Church, joined with those of the separated brethren, go forward without obstructing the ways of divine Providence and without prejudging the future inspiration of the Holy Spirit."[47]

The Roman Church is saying that she does not know the ultimate shape of the unity all are seeking, and that we should not lay down preconditions which obstruct the ways of Providence. The Roman Church, which is rarely unsure of what God wills for His people, says that in the future the Holy Spirit will lead us in ways we cannot now foresee. Those future inspirations should not be prejudged by laying

---

Africa represents the classical position: "Ecumenicity is not promoted by the formation of church unions humanly engineered. Organizational or institutional unity is no guarantee for true unity of the Church" ("The Contribution of the Apostolic Faith Mission to True Ecumenism," *Supplement—Christian Recorder* [South Africa], June 1968, unpaged).

47. Art. 24. "Haec Sacrosancta Synodus instanter exoptat ut filiorum Ecclesiae catholicae incepta cum inceptis fratrum seiunctorum coniuncta progrediantur, quin Providentiae viis ullum ponetur obstaculum et quin futuris Spiritus Sancti impulsionibus praeiudicetur" (*Acta Apostolicae Sedis*, 57 [1965], 107).

down conditions. Of the ultimate shape of the unity we seek, we do know this much: Nothing which is of the gospel will be excluded from it.

Both Roman Catholics and classical Pentecostals have much to gain from the international dialogue. For many it will be the first contact, formal or otherwise, with representatives of the other tradition. Though the traditions are vastly different there are points of great similarity. The concept of the wondrous is at home in both traditions in a way which is not true of many other ecclesiastical groups. This would seem to indicate that what can be called "the Pentecostal metaphysics" and the Catholic ethos are not as alien as their separate histories might indicate. The rapid growth of the Roman Catholic charismatic movement is an indication that this is true.[48]

---

48. In most years since 1968, the national conventions have tripled in size. In 1968, there were 100 in attendance and in the subsequent two years the number grew from 500 to 1,300. In 1971 there were over 5,000, and in 1972 about 12,000. Above 20,000 came in 1973, with over 30,000 in 1974. At the beginning of January each year there is a national leaders' meeting in Ann Arbor, Michigan, where one of the major problems is keeping people away. For new emphasis within the Catholic movement cf. Kilian McDonnell, "Catholic Charismatics," *Commonweal*, 96 (May 5, 1972), 207-11.